Writing and Logic

Gerald Levin

The University of Akron

Harcourt Brace Jovanovich, Inc.

New York • San Diego • Chicago • San Francisco • Atlanta
London • Sydney • Toronto

ISBN: 0-15-597788-1
Library of Congress Catalog Card Number: 81-85552
Printed in the United States of America

Copyright and Acknowledgements

AKRON BEACON JOURNAL   for an editorial appearing under the headline "Original Reasons Valid for 55-mph Speed Limit" in the *Akron Beacon Journal*, Mar. 1, 1977. Copyright 1977, Akron Beacon Journal. Reprinted by permission.

AMERICAN JUDICATURE SOCIETY   for "Thou Shalt Not Kill," reprinted from *Judicature*, vol. 52, no. 6, Jan. 1969. Copyright 1969 by the American Judicature Society. Reprinted by permission of the publisher.

THE AMERICAN SCHOLAR   for the excerpt from "In Favor of Capital Punishment" by Jacques Barzun, reprinted from *The American Scholar*, vol. 31, no. 2, Spring, 1962. Copyright © 1962 by the United Chapters of Phi Beta Kappa. Reprinted by permission of the publishers.

THE CHRISTIAN SCIENCE PUBLISHING SOCIETY   for "In Search of a Clear View" by Kristin Knutson, reprinted from *The Christian Science Monitor*, Jan. 4, 1979, © 1979, The Christian Science Publishing Society. All rights reserved. Reprinted by permission of the publisher.

HARPER & ROW, PUBLISHERS, INC.   for excerpt from *Why We Can't Wait* by Martin Luther King, Jr. Copyright © 1963 by Martin Luther King, Jr. Reprinted by permission of Harper & Row, Publishers, Inc.

NATIONAL COUNCIL OF TEACHERS OF ENGLISH   for excerpt from "Discovery Through Questioning" by Richard L. Larson, reprinted from *College English*, vol. 30, Nov. 1968, © copyright 1968, NCTE. Reprinted by permission of the publisher and author.

NEWSWEEK, INC.   for "Our Youth Should Serve" by Steven Muller, reprinted from *Newsweek*, July 10, 1978. Copyright 1978 by Newsweek, Inc. All rights reserved. Reprinted by permission.

THE NEW YORK TIMES COMPANY   for "Gossip" by Ralph L. Rosnow, reprinted from the *New York Times*, June 23, 1976, © 1976 by The New York Times Company. For "For Compulsory Voting" by Alan Wertheimer, reprinted from the *New York Times*, Aug. 23, 1976, © 1976 by the New York Times Company. For "Who Is Right?" by Vadim Golovanov, reprinted from the *New York*

Copyrights and Acknowledgments continue on page 271, which is regarded as part of the copyright page.

Preface

Logic, the study of rational thinking, is an integral part of most writing. We try to organize our ideas and the expression of them rationally, for we wish to have our thoughts follow clearly from one another so that they can be understood and accepted by our readers. To achieve this goal, we need a method that will enable us to judge what we have written. Logic, joined with rhetoric, is that method.

The combination of logic and writing is not as unusual as it might at first appear. In classical times, the study of rhetoric included logic. Later, during the Renaissance, these subjects were separated, and logic was neglected in composition courses or was given only cursory attention. Today, we once again recognize that writing and logic need to be considered together.

This book presents logic and writing in a unified way. Many important topics of logic are discussed and throughout the book are related to the ways writings are organized and fitted to particular audiences. The exercises and writing assignments interspersed throughout each chapter give students practice in the important forms of exposition and argument and connect logical thinking to writing.

A special feature of the book is the series of detailed suggestions on prewriting and organizing the essay. The first two chapters provide a summary of basic ideas—topic sentence, thesis, paragraph development, writing and organizing expository and argumentative essays. The next three chapters consider matters of logic and audience. The sixth chapter focuses on language, especially as used in expository and argumentative essays; the seventh chapter considers informal fallacies. The final chapter examines the methods of research and documentation, concentrating on a single subject to show how a topic may be studied in depth. Students are led gradually to a consideration of these research methods by first dealing with source materials in various writing assignments and exercises; these sources include advertisements, editorials, newspaper stories, and other material with which we can expect students to be familiar.

Writing and Logic also contains a large number of short illustrative excerpts. These are drawn from many areas—law, medicine, urban life, ecology, and education—to name a few. Twenty longer works are included as well, all of them models of the kinds of writing that are discussed. Most of the short excerpts and longer works show the way logic can be used in discursive writing; several of the essays are analyzed paragraph by paragraph in terms of their rhetorical and logical structures.

The three chapters devoted primarily to logic do not go beyond the elementary principles of correct reasoning. Indeed, advanced topics normally taken up in formal or symbolic logic have been avoided. The focus is rather on the syllogism and what the premises commit the writer to in deductive arguments, and on the uses and types of evidence that are acceptable in inductive ones. Here too several essays exemplify the processes of induction and deduction. How these kinds of reasoning are joined in particular writings is taken up in Chapter 5 on argument and audience.

Important recent developments in rhetoric and logic are reflected in the discussion of argument. Chapter 5 examines the methods advanced by Kenneth Burke and Carl Rogers for reaching agreement with an audience in persuasive discourse. Chaim Perelman's distinction between demonstration and argumentation, which has parallels in the logic of Stephen E. Toulmin, is maintained throughout. Though attention is given in Chapter 4 to contexts and warrants as developed by Toulmin and other logicians, the discussion of logic holds to the traditional distinction between deductive and inductive arguments.

This book has been conceived as a composition text and as a companion to a reader or handbook. Individual sections can be assigned as aids to the writing and revision of essays. Chapter 6 on language and Chapter 8 on the documented paper can be assigned earlier in the course if the instructor prefers. The Instructor's Manual includes discussions of the exercises, writing processes, and teaching suggestions for the subject of each chapter.

This, in brief, is the purpose and plan of the book. I hope that, instead of introducing logic as an occasional and independent consideration, composition teachers will be able to deal with the subject in some depth from the writer's perspective.

I want to thank my students and colleagues at the University of Akron who over many years have taught me much about writing. William Francis, Bruce Holland, Robert Holland, and Alice MacDonald helped me clarify my ideas on the teaching of writing and logic. I owe special thanks to Alan Hart and James C. Anderson, who discussed logic with me and gave me invaluable advice on several of the chapters. Louise Forsch, Bierce Library, University of Akron, was as indispensable as always. I also owe a special debt to Richard Fulkerson of East Texas State University and Bill Connelly of Middle Tennessee University, both of whom commented extensively on earlier drafts. Needless to say, the responsibility of the book is entirely mine.

Eben W. Ludlow, of Harcourt Brace Jovanovich, gave me the strongest possible encouragement and excellent advice at each stage of the planning and writing of the book. Those who have worked with him know his exceptional qualities of imagination and judgment. My editor, Sidney Zimmerman, improved the content and style of every page, and I am grateful for his patience and hard work. I thank finally my wife, Lillian Levin, to whom my debt is always great.

Gerald Levin

Contents

Chapter Two

Exposition and Argument   26

Chapter Three

The Inductive Essay   46

C h a p t e r F o u r

The Deductive Essay   88

Chapter Five

Argument and Audience   127

The Uses of Argument   127

Ways of Organizing the Argumentative Essay   141

Additional Supporting Arguments   150

Ways of Reaching Agreement   155

Prewriting

C h a p t e r S i x

The Uses of Language   175

C h a p t e r S e v e n

Fallacies   195

Chapter Eight

The Documented Paper   232

Defining a Problem for Research   232

Chapter One

Introduction: Writing Methods

Why we write

Writing is not the only way we communicate, but it is an important and common one. We write in answer to letters we receive. We write answers to exam questions. We write to explain our ideas or to communicate knowledge. We write to reason out a decision, and sometimes to persuade someone that our reasons are good ones.

Writing situations involve different purposes and circumstances, and these determine how we prepare for them. Sometimes we choose the occasion, as when we decide to justify a decision concerning college and persuade our parents to accept both the decision and our reasons for it. And sometimes others choose the occasion for us, as in a letter from a school official asking for information needed to renew a loan or scholarship. How much preparation we make—and what kind—depends on whether we choose to write or others ask us to.

When we choose to write, there is time to sort out thoughts and feelings and decide on an approach or strategy: deciding the best way of making our ideas clear, holding the attention of those we want to reach, and getting them to accept our viewpoint and reasons. At other times, as in examinations, we must gather our facts quickly. Usually, or ideally, answers to essay questions are short and to the point, but these too require organization and focus. For the most part, we write with a reader in mind, whether parent, school official, or some stranger who needs convincing, such as a possible employer.

1

The audiences we write for

Considering the audience for whom we write is crucial, although we probably give this matter little attention as a rule. In almost all circumstances we are concerned with our audience—with what it knows or believes, with what we want it to think or do.

Let us imagine an instance when a writer must consider an audience. An official of a chemical company, in writing to a newspaper, explains how a lake near the plant was polluted in an accident. This explanation probably will be less technical than another given in a letter to government officials responsible for monitoring chemical spills. Although readers of the news account will need a definition of terms and perhaps a description of the process that caused the spill, the writer will make a careful selection of details to avoid confusion. By contrast, government officials will probably not require either the definition of terms or the description, but they will need details on procedures and events leading to the spill—details that may require numerous pages of analysis and even diagrams. How much detail is included depends, then, on the view taken of the audience.

How we organize facts and ideas depends also on the audience. We may organize our ideas in several ways, proceeding from familiar and less controversial ideas to unfamiliar, more controversial ones. For a general audience of newspaper readers, we usually proceed from simple facts to complex ones. But for the special audience of government officials, we may decide to go from procedures of least concern to ones of greatest concern, to those that are in dispute. There are varying principles of order that we may use in organizing the discussion: we may proceed from the less interesting to the more interesting, or from the less to the more familiar. The organization will be determined by what the audience knows about the subject and what order of ideas will best convince them.

In organizing essays, we need to anticipate questions the audience will want answered. These help the writer to discover the facts and reasons that are needed to defend ideas. Here are a few that might be asked of the company official:

1. What was the nature of the chemical spill, and how did it resemble and differ from past spills?
2. What procedures are routinely followed to prevent spills?
3. Were these in effect at the time of the spill?
4. If not, what circumstances explain why they were not?
5. What other circumstances contributed to the accident?
6. Was the plant in compliance with federal standards and regulations? What are these standards and regulations?

7. What danger does the spill pose to people in the area and to the immediate environment?

8. What liability should the company accept for possible damage?

9. What new procedures or safeguards should be instituted to prevent future spills?

10. Are present standards, regulations, and procedures adequate?

The more a writer is able to include answers to these questions in writing, the more persuasive it will be. Readers will know that their interests and concerns are important to the writer.

Exercises

1. Answer the following questions about the advertisement on the opposite page. Cite evidence from the ad in support of your answer:
   a. How technical is the definition of terms and the description of procedures or processes?
   b. Is this definition and description designed for a general or a special audience? Is it directed to people in a particular region of the country?
   c. What is the purpose of the ad? Is it concerned with a longstanding problem or a new and recent one? Does the ad *state* a purpose?

2. Examine a recent issue of a newspaper or magazine, and distinguish at least six pieces of writing (editorials, advertisements, letters to the editor, etc.) that inform, persuade, or amuse, or do some or all of these. Write down the evidence you find in each piece for the intention of the writer.

Writing Assignment

Choose a topic for a piece of writing of your own, and write brief answers to the following questions:

a. What audience do I want to reach? Is it a general or a special one?

b. What is my purpose in writing—to give information merely, or to give information that will change the thinking of the reader?

c. What kind of organization will best serve my purpose?

Then write a short essay, fitting your organization to your audience and your purpose in writing.

Managing Chemical Wastes

What the chemical industry is doing to improve waste-disposal methods

America's chemical companies have already invested hundreds of millions of dollars in safer, better waste-disposal methods. We'll spend over *$2 billion* more on waste-disposal facilities in the next two years. Here's how we're advancing the "state of the art":

1. Eliminating wasteful processes

We're redesigning manufacturing processes and improving efficiency. We're adding on-line treatment systems to neutralize, reduce in volume or change the nature of waste by-products. We're also using recovery techniques that let us recycle wastes back into the production process. One company, for example, is salvaging phenol, used to manufacture plastics, pharmaceuticals and other useful products.

2. Building secure landfills

Secure landfills have a barrier that keeps wastes from seeping out into groundwater and keeps groundwater from migrating through the landfill. Other features may include facilities for recycling liquids or a wastewater treatment unit to clean up liquids for safe disposal. Landfills—if *properly* designed, operated and monitored—are one of the best ways to dispose of many kinds of solid wastes.

3. Continuing industry commitment

We were finding ways to manage solid wastes long before the nation recognized the need for better waste-disposal methods. In fact, we already had much of the required waste-disposal technology and remedial strategies in place—or being developed—when Congress passed the Resource Conservation and Recovery Act of 1976, which sets forth strict waste-disposal guidelines.

4. Sharing knowledge and new technology

As we develop new waste-disposal techniques, we share our knowledge with industry, government and the public. In 1979, we began conducting a series of regional seminars that presented current techniques for solid-waste disposal. Individual companies may use videotapes, visual aids or other techniques to train personnel in waste-disposal methods.

5. Encouraging solid-waste exchanges

Sometimes one chemical company's wastes can become another company's raw material. Fluoride wastes from a phosphoric acid plant, for example, can be used by a company producing aluminum. So the chemical industry has encouraged the development of waste-exchange organizations, which develop and distribute lists of available wastes.

For a booklet that tells more about what we're doing to protect the environment, write to: Chemical Manufacturers Association, Dept. HW-12, Box 363, Beltsville, MD 20705.

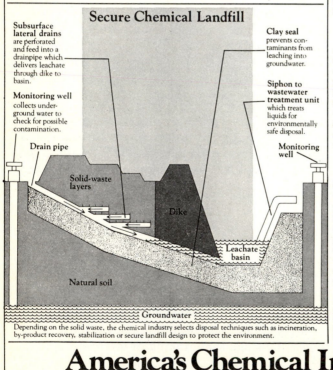

Secure Chemical Landfill

Subsurface lateral drains are perforated and feed into a drainpipe which delivers leachate through dike to basin.

Monitoring well collects underground water to check for possible contamination.

Drain pipe

Clay seal prevents contaminants from leaching into groundwater.

Siphon to wastewater treatment unit which treats liquids for environmentally safe disposal.

Monitoring well

Solid-waste layers

Dike

Leachate basin

Natural soil

Groundwater

Depending on the solid waste, the chemical industry selects disposal techniques such as incineration, by-product recovery, stabilization or secure landfill design to protect the environment.

America's Chemical Industry

The member companies of the Chemical Manufacturers Association

The methods of writing

Once we have decided on the audience and what we have to say to it, we can decide on the most appropriate method of writing for those readers. This book will discuss the methods we can use to explain ideas or events and to organize arguments in effective ways. In this section we will quickly review the four chief modes of discourse: exposition, narration, description, and argumentation.

An exposition is an account of an idea or an event, an explanation of how something works, a laying out or exposing to view of anything. It is the most common form of writing and is used for almost every situation: to give directions for cooking a meal or traveling to someone's home, to explain the cellular structure of a plant or the mechanism of a steam engine, to portray historical events or political decision making, to demonstrate a new theory in science or a new interpretation in philosophy. As we can see from these examples, some pieces of expository writing can be very short and simple, like a recipe, and some can be very long and as complicated as a difficult book on ethics. Yet, all these instances share one essential characteristic: they increase our understanding by explaining something we are interested in, whether it is the method for making chocolate cake or the principles of social justice.

Exposition often includes narration and description, for we need details on the sequence of events, the people involved, the setting, the background, and the objects covered by our account. When we wish to explain how to make chocolate cake, for example, we call for a number of ingredients that must be prepared in a specific order. Our recipe for the cake is, in a sense, a narrative, for narration presents events in the order they occur. Of course recipes are relatively short, but histories of a nation or period are not, yet they too are narratives, for like the recipe they present events that take place in time. It is exactly the representation of events in time that is the essential feature of narration, whether it is a short paragraph on the movements of a piston in a combustion engine or a long novel portraying the adventures of a roustabout.

While narrative deals with time, description deals with space. A descriptive passage or essay presents people or objects as our eyes see them. When description occurs in expository writing it is usually for the purpose of conveying information and as a rule it is emotionally neutral. It is almost exactly the opposite in a work of literature, such as a poem, a novel, or an imaginative essay. When description is used in a literary work its purpose is to evoke an image that will produce an emotional response. Not all of the details may be supplied. They are not in this description of the sycamore tree:

> Sycamores are among the last trees to go into leaf; in the fall, they are the first to shed. They make sweet food in green broadleaves for a while—leaves wide as plates—and then go wild and wave their long arms.
>
> Annie Dilliard, *Pilgrim at Tinker Creek*

Compare this evocative description with the following description of the sycamore in a dictionary:

> A very large spreading tree (*Platanus occidentalis*) of eastern and central North America with 3-to-5 lobed broadly ovate leaves.
>
> *Webster's Seventh New Collegiate Dictionary*

Although the differences between these two descriptions are obvious, there is also an essential similarity between them. They are both based on observation, if not by these writers themselves, at least by some others who have seen the tree and written about it.

We have just said that narration and description are often included in exposition; we should also note that they are sometimes included in argumentation as well. Often we think of an argument as a verbal conflict between two or more people, a kind of shouting match. But this is not the only sense in which this word is used. An argument can also mean giving reasons for or against believing something or acting in a particular way. It is the chief form of persuasion, and as such includes many devices to achieve its goal, among them being narration and description.

When we argue we present evidence in favor of or in opposition to an idea. This evidence may take the form of sense data that are described, historical events that may be narrated, or supporting ideas that are considered highly probable or true. Whatever kinds of evidence are used, however, they all serve as reasons for agreeing with the main idea or thesis. In an argument, the thesis must be proved and the evidence serves as this proof or support. An argument differs from an exposition precisely in that an exposition lays something out or exposes it to view, whereas an argument offers grounds for accepting an idea, claim, or thesis. For example, we engage in exposition when we describe various methods of waste disposal, but engage in argument when we give evidence in support of regulations governing chemical waste disposal.

Exposition and argument, however, often work together. The ad on page 4 gives an exposition of what the chemical industry is doing to improve waste-disposal methods, and uses this exposition to argue the thesis that the chemical industry was concerned with environmental safety long before the government and general public were:

> We were finding ways to manage solid wastes long before the nation recognized the need for better waste-disposal methods. In fact, we already had much of the required waste-disposal technology and remedial strategies in place—or being developed—when Congress passed the Resource Conservation and Recovery Act of 1976, which sets forth strict waste-disposal guidelines.

In reading ads of this sort and similar kinds of writing, it is important to know what the writer wants to accomplish. As readers our response will be different if we think we are being given just an explanation of waste-disposal methods rather than an argument for accepting existing methods or for changing them.

As writers we need to be clear in our minds about what we want to accomplish, and for what audience. We write to someone—to ourselves when we keep a diary or make notes about things to do, but more often to other people. What may be clear to one audience will not be clear to another. To be effective, we must consider the interests and concerns of each audience, whether it be a general or a special one, the general readership of a newspaper or a group of government officials. Though a piece of writing may be correct in its grammar and spelling, it will not be effective unless the audience understands it, pays attention, and reacts. Our concern in this book will be with how to make our writing clear and effective.

Logic has an important role to play in learning how to write well. As the study of correct reasoning, logic teaches us how to be consistent in our thinking and writing, as well as how to recognize and deal with inconsistency in other people. It can also teach us how to see the implications in statements we or others make, and how to test the relevance of arguments and evidence to a central idea. Relevance and consistency are important characteristics of all good writing.

In this book we will be concerned with the methods of informal logic only, not with the symbolic techniques and philosophical problems that are customarily studied in logic courses. Before we turn to logic, however, we will consider some important elements of the essay—paragraph development, transitions, and the like—and the way in which two of the forms of discourse, exposition and argument, work together.

Organizing the paragraph

Organizing effective paragraphs is much like organizing effective essays. The topic sentence of a paragraph usually serves the same purpose as the thesis of an essay. Transitions that connect ideas in a paragraph serve an identical purpose in the essay, too. By discussing matters of organization in a paragraph we will anticipate our discussion of similar matters later in this book.

Let us consider briefly the characteristics of effective paragraphs. Whether it develops one idea or two or more related ones, an effective paragraph is unified, coherent, and adequate in its development. Unity is achieved by dealing with one idea in as much detail as necessary and not straying to irrelevant considerations, and if the paragraph deals with several related ideas, by not jumping from one to another haphazardly. A useful phrase to keep in mind, in trying to keep paragraphs unified, is "one idea at a time."

Coherence is achieved by clearly connecting one idea (or example) to the next. If a series of examples develop the central idea, the reader should immediately see their relationship to the idea and their consistency. If the paragraph develops a series of ideas, the reader should see how these are related, why they occur in the order they do, and how they are relevant to the central idea. A good paragraph exhibits a clear order of ideas and examples or supporting details.

It is easier to say when a paragraph is inadequate in its development than to state a measure of adequacy. An effective paragraph gives as much explanation of the idea and supporting detail as the reader needs to understand it. It does not ramble on, developing examples and accumulating details for their own sake.

Let us consider first how the topic sentence can help achieve these aims.

Topic sentence

The topic sentence is the name sometimes given to the statement of *subject* in a paragraph and sometimes given to the *central idea*. If it is used to state the subject, the topic sentence comes at the beginning, as in the following paragraph where the subject is stated in the form of a question:

> *Why do we read fiction?* The answer is simple. We read it because we like it. And we like it because fiction, as an image of life, stimulates and gratifies our interest in life. But whatever interests may be appealed to by fiction, the special and immediate interest that takes us to fiction is always our interest in a story.
>
> Robert Penn Warren, *"Why Do We Read Fiction?"*

If the topic sentence is used to state the central idea, it may appear anywhere in the paragraph, but it often occurs at the beginning:

> *The most frequent reason for addict admission was abscess formation.* Anyone who uses the needle often enough is bound, at one time or another, to infect himself, and some addicts were on the needle two or three times a day. The infection couldn't be avoided indefinitely, no matter how careful they were to clean the skin and sterilize the needle. The heroin, which was what most addicts were on, was almost always adulterated with some other substance, frequently aspirin. Consequently, the addicts were partially dependent for protection on the peddlers, or pushers, who weren't the neatest people in the world. Sooner or later they would push some contaminated or infected drugs.
>
> William A. Nolen, *The Making of a Surgeon*

If the paragraph builds to the topic sentence, the opening sentence may be transitional:

Let us pause to take stock. . . .
And here is something more basic. . . .

Or it may begin with an idea that will be a component of the central idea:

Reconciliation—that is what we all, in some depth of being, want. All religion, all philosophy, all psychiatry, all ethics involve this human fact [lead-in-ideas]. And so does fiction [transition to central idea]. If fiction begins in daydream, if it springs from the cramp of the world, if it relieves us from the burden of being ourselves, it ends, if it is good fiction and we are good readers, by returning us to the world and to ourselves [topic sentence: statement of central idea]. It reconciles us with reality [restatement of central idea].

Warren, "Why Do We Read Fiction?"

When the paragraph contains several important ideas of the same weight, the topic sentence may take the form of a statement of subject or general summary. In the following example, sentences are indented to show the relative weight of ideas:

Here are a couple of generalizations about England that would be accepted by almost all observers [topic sentence].
One is that the English are not gifted artistically [first main idea].
They are not as musical as the Germans or Italians, painting and sculpture have never flourished in England as they have in France.
Another is that, as Europeans go, the English are not intellectual [second main idea].
They have a horror of abstract thought, they feel no need for any philosophy or systematic "world view."
Nor is this because they are "practical," as they are so fond of claiming for themselves [third main idea].
One has only to look at their methods of town-planning and water-supply, their obstinate clinging to everything that is out of date and a nuisance, a spelling system that defies analysis and a system of weights and measures that is intelligible only to the compilers of arithmetic books, to see how little they care about mere efficiency.
But they have a certain power of acting without taking thought [fourth main idea].
Their world-famed hypocrisy—their double-faced attitude toward the Empire, for instance—is bound up with this.
Also, in moments of supreme crisis the whole nation can suddenly draw together and act upon a species of instinct, really a code of conduct which is understood by almost everyone, though never formulated [fifth main idea].

The phrase that Hitler coined for the Germans, "a sleep-walking people," would have been better applied to the English [*concluding main idea*].
   Not that there is anything to be proud of in being a sleep-walker.

George Orwell, "*England Your England*"

Occasionally a paragraph that continues a discussion begun in the previous paragraph will not contain a topic sentence. And occasionally a paragraph will not have an explicit one: a series of details or statements will imply the topic idea.

Writing the paragraph with a topic sentence in mind allows the writer to focus on one idea, or a series of related ones. These ideas, and the details that develop them, will hold together for the reader if their relationship is clear. The topic sentence is thus like a road sign that announces the destination or gives warning of what the driver may find on the way to it.

Exercises

1. Write a paragraph of your own that begins with the central idea. Write another in which you build to the same idea instead of beginning with it.

2. Examine the first ten paragraphs of a chapter in one of your textbooks, and determine the function of each of the opening sentences. Remember that the sentence may be:
   transitional, connecting paragraphs;
   the statement of the subject of the paragraph;
   the statement of the central idea;
   a lead-in idea to the central idea later in the paragraph;
   a statement of facts pertinent to the topic.

Transitions

Transitional words and phrases show the reader the relationship of ideas within paragraphs or between them. Here are a few in Ralph L. Rosnow's essay "Gossip" (see p. 27):

Indeed, there is a close parallel between the "rules" of gossiping and the principles of economic exchange. [amplification]

Thus the value of news increases in direct proportion to its scarcity. [explanation]

For example, someone agrees publicly to divulge information about certain backstairs happenings in return for a fat fee and instantaneous notoriety. [illustration]

Transitions can also express qualification (*however, although*), concession (*admittedly, granted*), addition (*moreover, in addition, also*), reiteration (*to repeat*), comparison (*similarly, likewise*), and summary (*finally, to sum up*). Complete sentences can also be transitional, as in this sentence from paragraph 7 of Rosnow:

> This variety calls to mind early definitions of the term.

The less transitions call attention to themselves, the better. Opening every sentence with transitions can make them stand out—which is why many writers, to avoid making them prominent, tuck them into the middle of the sentence. The greater the emphasis we want them to have, the closer to the beginning of the sentence they should go. If the sequence of ideas is clear without transitions, they may be left out; but usually paragraphs do require connectives to show how ideas are related.

The choice of transitions depends also on the organization of the paragraph or essay. The larger divisions may call for broader transitions of the kind illustrated by the complete sentence above.

Exercises

1. In the chapter of the textbook you examined in the preceding exercise, identify all formal transitions like *indeed, thus, for example,* and *however.* Then read these paragraphs, omitting them. Do these paragraphs hold together without them? What other transitions might be substituted?

2. Here are some relationships that transitions can express. Record as many examples of each as you can find in an issue of a newspaper or magazine:
   amplification
   explanation
   illustration
   qualification
   concession
   addition
   reiteration
   comparison
   summary

Developing paragraphs

The paragraphs we have been looking at develop one or more ideas, and they do so coherently. As we noted earlier, coherence means that the paragraph holds together its ideas and details in such a way that all develop the topic or question announced at the beginning. More than this, we see how each idea and detail is connected to the topic as we read the paragraph. We do not lose our way.

As we have seen, a paragraph may begin with a general truth, then may restate and illustrate this truth, from which it may draw conclusions at the end. Or the paragraph may open with a series of details that lead to and support a general truth. Conversely, a paragraph may begin with the statement of a problem and then go on to develop a solution.

There are additional ways of developing paragraphs. The following list indicates methods that may be used singly or jointly to develop a whole paragraph or part of it.

definition
division and classification
process
analysis
comparison and contrast
analogy
example
cause and effect

To see how some of these can be used together, let us return to an earlier example, Assume that as the representative for a chemical company you want to explain, in a letter to a newspaper, how a disastrous spill occurred. Each paragraph of your letter provides different information about the spill.

First, you may wish to define words essential to understanding what happened—perhaps the kinds of chemicals that played a part in the spill and the processes involved in their manufacture. Then chemical spills may be classified according to their effects on the environment and general population. In explaining these effects, you will want to give examples. Following this general discussion, you will want to analyze the process of manufacturing most important to an understanding of how the spill at your company occurred. You may also decide to analyze a piece of machinery involved in this process. Finally, you will state the causes of the spill at your plant, discuss its possible effects, and compare these with the effects of earlier and well-publicized spills.

Let us look at each of these methods of paragraph development in detail.

Definition

A lexical definition gives us the current meaning of a word, or a series of current meanings. Such dictionary definitions usually place an object in a general class of objects (the *genus*) and distinguish it from all other members of the class (*specific difference*):

plumb line: A cord [genus] by which a weight is suspended [one *specific difference*] to test the perpendicularity or depth of something [*a second specific difference*].

Standard College Dictionary

Or the definition of a piece of writing may simply describe the object and what it does, without classifying it. The writer of the following passage is describing how he explains a surveying instrument to schoolchildren.

> Most of the children will not have seen the plumb bob before. We might well have some conversation like this: "What is it used for?" It is used in surveying, and in building, to get a vertical line. "What does vertical mean?" It means what you get when you hang a weight, like a plumb bob, on a string—a line, going straight up and straight down. Pointing toward the center of the earth, or actually the center of gravity of the earth.

John Holt, *What Do I Do Monday?*

Holt's purpose is apparent from the discussion: he is showing how children can be taught through experience to think about measurement. Accordingly, he gives as much information about the weight or plumb bob as the child needs to understand its use. He does not distinguish the bob or the line from all other objects that can be used for the same purpose: that information is irrelevant to his goal.

Later in the same discussion Holt gives an etymological definition to explain the current meaning of plumb bob, and he also introduces a related word to clarify the meaning further:

> It is called a *plumb* bob because these bobs were once made of lead, which is *plomb* in French. Hence our word *plumber*—a man who works with lead.

Such a definition supplies the original meaning of the word—its etymology—a meaning that the word may not now possess. The purpose of etymological definition is to clarify current meanings, not to indicate the meaning the word ought to have.

We will return to these kinds of definition in a later chapter, and look also at other kinds and uses.

Division and classification

Recall that one kind of definition places a thing in a general class, then differentiates it from other members of the class. A plumb bob is one member of the class of weights, and it differs from all other weights in a number of specific ways—size, substance, use, for example.

The first part of this process—placing a thing in a general class—is what we mean by classification. Here is how classification might serve in an analysis of criminal justice. Various offenses—shoplifting, jaywalking, manslaughter, murder, treason—might be classified as felonies or misdemeanors to clarify the basic difference between them.

Division begins with a class—for example, weights—and breaks it into subclasses or subdivisions according to a principle of analysis. Thus, we can divide the class *weights* according to their size or their substance or their use. Sometimes the division can be exhaustive if all the constituents or subclasses are known. But usually it can only be as exhausting as experience or nature allows. In physics, the division of subatomic particles is being revised from year to year, even month to month. In medicine, new discoveries about viruses are leading to new definitions and classifications.

Like classification, division is an essential method of development in exposition and argument. Here is an example of its use in a discussion of the living environment:

> There is little argument about the three basic subdivisions of the biosphere: the seas, the land and fresh water. The conditions of life are quite different in each of these environments; by and large, each has its characteristic inhabitants, each is in turn divisible into an endless series of living communities differing in details yet with basic similarities.
>
> Marston Bates, *The Forest and the Sea*

Bates states the subdivisions, indicating that the method of division is complete. Then he identifies the principle or basis of the division: the conditions prevailing in each environment. Later, he qualifies his original division:

> But when we approach the boundaries, the differences between even these basic subdivisions of the living world become blurred. The sea margin everywhere illustrates the blending of the marine and terrestrial environments: mangrove swamps, tidal flats, sandy beaches, all such habitats include a mixture of inhabitants from the land and the sea.

More than one kind of classification or division may be used in a particular exposition or argument. But each kind must be independent and consistent. In dividing weights, we should not divide by size and substance as a single method: large weights, small weights, lead weights, wooden weights. We should instead divide by size, then by use, noting that weights of different sizes may serve the same purpose.

Analysis

When we want to describe the parts of a structure and their relationship, we develop the paragraph by analysis. A chemistry text will analyze the atom by stating its parts and explaining their relationship. Organic chemistry is concerned with the structure of molecules, many of enormous complexity. Literary works may be analyzed through their structure—the structure of a Greek tragedy, or a Scottish ballad. How-to-books depend on analysis to explain how to assemble or repair a piece of machinery. We need to know how the machine is constructed—the names of the parts and how they are connected—before we can follow the process of repair or assembly.

Here is an example of analysis in an essay concerned with home building. The writer is here analyzing the problem of where to put windows, not giving directions for their placement:

> Until you actually begin planning, windows seem to be the most natural part of a house. But they just don't fall into place. They let light in, they ventilate the house, they determine the view, and they decorate the exterior. As if that isn't enough, energy considerations bring the compass into play. Ideally, there should be no windows north or west, a few to the east if needed, and plenty to the south. No question about it, window placement is an armload. It's quite easy to saturate the south side with glass, both patio door units and windows. Putting the garage on the west cancels out that side, and judiciously placing a few windows on the east seems to fit in OK. But if the north side is to be barren of all windows, will it also be dark inside, unattractive outside, and create a pocket of dead, stale air?
>
> Roy Jason, "Diary of a Home Builder," Handyman, April, 1981

Ideas can be analyzed, too. To understand how nuclear energy is different from another kind, we may be given an analysis of the general theory underlying each. We may, for example, be given an analysis of Einstein's famous equation—$E = mc^2$—before the process of nuclear fission is described.

Process analysis

A process consists of steps that sometimes must occur in a fixed order, and sometimes can be varied. A recipe may contain fixed steps, and also some that may be omitted or performed in a different order. When the process is a natural one, like the circulation of the blood, the stages will be invariable. The essential characteristic of a process is that it is repeatable. Thus a scientist will describe how a discovery was made by tracing the steps taken; we can repeat the steps of the process if we want to verify the discovery.

In some pieces of writing the process may be described merely to inform us about its main features. Thus a textbook discussion of stained-glass windows in Gothic churches of the middle ages gives us a general description of their manufacture:

> The great variety of jewellike color was achieved chemically by the addition of certain minerals to the glass while it was in a molten state. When cool, the

sheets were cut into smaller sections, and the designer fitted them into his previously prepared outline. Pieces of various sizes next were joined together by lead strips. Details, such as the features in the faces, were then applied in the form of metal oxides and made permanent by firing in a kiln. Finally, the individual panels making up the pattern of the whole window were fastened to the iron bars already imbedded in the masonry.

William Fleming, Arts and Ideas

We could not perform any of these steps without more specific information. By contrast, the following analysis is specific enough for the reader to perform an action exactly as described. The writer is giving instructions to bicyclists on where to ride in a wide lane:

> If the lane is wide enough for you to share with cars side by side, then you keep just a comfortable distance to the right of where the cars go—about three feet. This may be near the edge of the road, or farther in, depending on the lane width.
>
> Do *not* pull farther to the right than necessary to let the cars overtake you, even if the lane becomes very wide. Keep the same position, just to the right of the cars. Then motorists will see you sooner from the side streets ahead of you and from behind. Motorists from behind will be less likely to cut across in front of you to make right turns. But if one does, you'll be able to avoid an accident by turning with the car. If you were way to the right, you couldn't. The car would already be crossing your path at a sharp angle by the time you could see it.
>
> Don't duck to the right into spaces between parked cars, or when crossing intersections. If you duck behind a parked car, you may be hidden. You could become an unpleasant surprise for a driver behind you when you reappear. Keep a straight line in your lane.

John S. Allen, "Where to Ride on the Road," Bicycling, June, 1981

Notice how analysis of the problems faced by bicyclists is joined to the solution—the process of bicycling safely in hazardous conditions.

Cause and effect

Perhaps the commonest form of causal analysis in ordinary exposition is a plain statement of effects, as in the following introduction to a scientific analysis of fog:

> Fog, once little more than a nuisance except at sea, has become an important hazard to modern man. Its effects on travel are intensified by the speed of the airplane and the automobile. Dense fogs close airports in the U.S. for an average of 115 hours per year, and in 1967 they cost the nation's airlines an estimated $75 million in disrupted schedules as well as inestimable inconvenience to passengers. On present-day turnpikes fog can be disastrous; a single

pileup on a fog-shrouded freeway in Los Angeles involved more than 100 vehicles. Above all, fog in combination with air pollution now increasingly afflicts large cities. Its potential was suggested alarmingly by the London smog of December, 1952.

Joel N. Myers, "Fog"

Myers is dealing here with immediate effects, and he states also the immediate cause, the fog, and less immediate (or remote) ones, the speed of the airplane and automobile and the volume of traffic.

The analysis of cause can be technical and complex, as this later paragraph of Myers shows:

> The principal source of toxicity in most pathological smogs appears to be sulfur dioxide from the smokestacks. The sulfur dioxide is oxidized in the air to sulfur trioxide, which in turn combines with fog droplets to form sulfuric acid. One therefore inhales sulfuric acid with each breath, with resulting acute irritation of the throat and lungs. This seems to have been the chief cause of injury and death in the London smog and in the 1948 smog in Donora, Pennsylvania, which killed 20 victims and sickened nearly half of the 14,000 inhabitants.

How technical the analysis is depends again on our audience as well as on our purpose in writing. In explaining why new highway design is called for in fog-ridden areas, we need only review the effects, and perhaps the general causes of fog. In arguing for a tightening of emission control standards, a general review of causes will undoubtedly be insufficient.

We will return to the uses of causal analysis in argument later in this book.

Comparison and contrast

This method of development traces similarities and differences, usually to arrive at a relative estimate of the things being compared. Both things are of equal concern, and more than this, we discover the qualities of one through those of the other. Such a relative estimate is reached in this comparison of Abraham Lincoln and Mark Twain:

> There are striking affinities between Lincoln and Mark Twain. Both spent their boyhoods in a society that was still essentially frontier; both were rivermen. Both absorbed the midcontinental heritage: fiercely equalitarian democracy, hatred of injustice and oppression, the man-to-man individualism of an expanding society. Both were deeply acquainted with melancholy and despair; both were fatalists. On the other hand, both were instinct with the humor of the common life and from their earliest years made fables of it. As humorists, both felt the basic gravity of humor; with both it was an adaptation of the mind, a reflex of the struggle to be sane; both knew, and Mark Twain

said, that there is no humor in heaven. It was of such resemblances that William Dean Howells was thinking when he called Mark Twain "the Lincoln of our literature."

Bernard De Voto, "Mark Twain"

The comparison or contrast may be less developed, focusing on a few related similarities or differences; and similarities and differences may be used together. De Voto might have followed his comparison with a contrast of differences between the two men. In addition, comparison and contrast can be point by point, as in the paragraph above, or the various qualities of one item can be stated first, followed by those of the second in the same order.

Analogy

Analogy is a special kind of comparison in which a familiar object is compared to an unfamiliar one for the purpose of explanation, not to arrive at a relative estimate. The points of similarity are central to the analogy, but these make their effect only if the differences between the two objects are striking. Here is a highly effective analogy used in the definition of the ideal teacher:

> The mountain guide, like the true teacher, has a quiet authority. He or she engenders trust and confidence so that one is willing to join the endeavor. The guide accepts his leadership role, yet recognizes that success (measured by the heights that are scaled) depends upon the close cooperation and active participation of each member of the group. He has crossed the terrain before and is familiar with the landmarks, but each trip is new and generates its own anxiety and excitement. Essential skills must be mastered; if they are lacking, disaster looms. The situation demands keen focus and rapt attention; slackness, misjudgment, or laziness can abort the venture.

Nancy K. Hill, "Scaling the Heights: the Teacher as Mountaineer"

Sometimes the analogy is developed exhaustively, and sometimes only partially. Hill develops hers in more detail in later paragraphs. Where the differences are striking enough to qualify the analogy, the writer may point out that the analogy is a limited one, and may note significant dissimilarities. Thus Hill also compares the teacher to the actor, the preacher, the shepherd, and the salesman, but rejects these comparisons as finally inadequate. None of these or other analogies suggests "the essential magic and majesty of the learning experience," and none suggest "the self-eradicating feature" in teaching whereby the successful student no longer has need of the teacher:

> The teacher is not a pleader, not a performer, not a huckster, but a confident, exuberant guide on expeditions of shared responsibility into the most exciting and least-understood terrain on earth—the mind itself.

Later in this book we will discuss analogy as a form of inductive argument.

Example

Many ideas are unclear until the observations that produced them are given to us. This is why in conversation or in our writing we are asked for examples. The example is, in this sense of the word, a *test* of the idea. Usually, an example is a typical instance of the generalization we are making. The writer of the following paragraph from an essay on human error gives us several:

> The lower animals do not have this splendid freedom. They are limited, most of them, to absolute infallibility. Cats, for all their good side, never make mistakes. I have never seen a maladroit, clumsy, or blundering cat. Dogs are sometimes fallible, occasionally able to make charming minor mistakes, but they get this way by trying to mimic their masters. Fish are flawless in everything they do. Individual cells in a tissue are mindless machines, perfect in their performance, as absolutely inhuman as bees.
>
> Lewis Thomas, "To Err Is Human"

In another essay on what makes us human, Thomas develops one example at length:

> Sometimes people argue this point of view seriously and with deep thought. Be individuals, solitary and selfish, is the message. Altruism, a jargon word for what used to be called love, is worse than weakness, it is sin, a violation of nature. Be separate. Do not be a social animal. But this is a hard argument to make convincingly when you have to depend on language to make it. You have to print up leaflets or publish books and get them bought and sent around, you have to turn up on television and catch the attention of millions of other human beings all at once, all collected and paying attention: be solitary; do not depend on each other. You can't do this and keep a straight face.
>
> "The Tucson Zoo"

The number and kind of examples we provide depends partly on our opinion of how much our readers know about the subject. We will have to illustrate a difficult idea in physics for the general reader; we may not do so if we are writing to an audience of physicists.

Exercises

1. Consult the dictionary definitions of *plumb bob* and *plumb line*. What kind of information is given about each? How much of the information given by Holt is stated, and what has been left out? What is the purpose of the dictionary definition, in comparison

to Holt's? Write your own definition of a similar object: compass, pliers, for example.

2. What common objects found in the kitchen or the garage can be analyzed into their parts? Write a paragraph analyzing one of these objects.

3. Write a paragraph describing a process essential to a game like football or ice hockey. Be careful to present the steps in their chronological order. If you depart from this order, tell your reader that you are doing so.

4. Find in one of your textbooks a description of a natural historical process. Determine whether the description is strictly chronological. If it is not, be ready to explain why it is not.

5. Compare and contrast the construction and uses of two similar objects, for example a fountain pen and a pencil, or a bicycle and motor scooter. Deal with similarities first, then with differences, or describe the features of the bicycle first, then the features of the scooter, keeping the same order of details.

6. Think of an analogy that will explain a difficult concept you are studying in one of your courses. Write out both the similarities and the differences, then write a paragraph discussing the similarities. Point to significant differences only if these seriously affect the analogy.

7. Divide *cameras* into two subclasses, as, for example, their use or their cost. State a purpose for your division, then write a paragraph describing the distinction you have made. Be sure your division serves the purpose you have in mind.

8. Find paragraphs in one of your textbooks that illustrate each of the methods of development discussed in this section.

9. Write a paragraph that uses two or more of the methods of paragraph development. Let your topic sentence state the subject of the paragraph, and perhaps indicate what methods will be used to develop the idea. Be sure to connect the various ideas with transitions.

10. Write a description of a process you know well for a how-to-book to be used by people who have performed a similar process in the past—for example, automobile mechanics who have repaired older carburetors or ignition systems and need instruction on new kinds. Then rewrite the description for people who have had no experience with the equipment to be used or the process. Include in this second description analysis of one piece of equipment.

Review

In conclusion, let us review briefly some characteristics of effective paragraphs.

First, we want as writers to tell our readers all they need to know to understand the topic. How much information we provide depends, as we have said, on the audience. What would be too much for a special audience might be too little for a general one. In paragraphs and in the whole essay, making our ideas clear is a primary concern: that is why definition is likely to precede other kinds of analysis.

Second, the paragraph has a movement or direction that our readers can follow: this is the purpose of transitions—to show where the paragraph is going, to point the way. Readers should not get lost in a maze of ideas, details, and examples; they should be able to follow the line of thought as they read, not discover it only when they have finished the paragraph.

And last, the paragraph should be unified. The details and subordinate ideas should connect to the topic idea and to one another. There should be no sense of stray details or unfinished thoughts. The paragraph will lack momentum if readers lose their way or stumble over words that are not clear in their context.

Prewriting

Richard L. Larson has given us a complete list of questions that can be used in analyzing the subject of an essay before we begin writing. The advantage of such a list is that it allows the writer to anticipate questions readers might ask, and in this way decide what details to include and leave out. Of course, not all of the questions will be answered in the essay; those included must be pertinent to the subject and the purpose of the essay. But, in giving attention to these questions before writing the essay, we are likely to discover aspects of the subject and views of it that may go unnoticed without such a preliminary inspection.

TOPICS FOR WRITING
by Richard L. Larson

I. "Topics" that Invite Comment
  A. *Writing about Single Items* (*in present existence*)
     What are its precise physical characteristics (shape, dimensions, composition, etc.)?
     How does it differ from things that resemble it?

What is its "range of variation" (how much can we change it and still
   identify it as the thing we started with)?
Does it call to mind other objects we have observed earlier in our
   lives? why? in what respects?
From what points of view can it be examined?
What sort of structure does it have?
How do the parts of it work together?
How are the parts put together?
How are the parts proportioned in relation to each other?
To what structure (class or sequence of items) does it belong?
Who or what produced it in this form? Why?
Who needs it?
Who uses it? for what?
What purposes might it serve?
   How can it be evaluated, for these purposes?

B. *Writing about Single Completed Events, or Parts of an Ongoing Process* (*These questions can apply to scenes and pictures, as well as to works of fiction and drama.*)
   Exactly what happened? (Tell the precise sequence: who? what?
      when? how? why? Who did what to whom? why? What did what to
      what? how?)
   What were the circumstances in which the event occurred? What did
      they contribute to its happening?
   How was the event like or unlike similar events?
   What were its causes?
   What were its consequences?
   What does its occurrence imply? What action (if any) is called for?
   What was affected (indirectly) by it?
   What, if anything, does it reveal or emphasize about some general
      condition?
   To what group or class might it be assigned?
   Is it (in general) good or bad? by what standard? How do we arrive at
      the standard?
   How do we know about it? What is the authority for our information?
      How reliable is the authority? How do we know it to be reliable? (or
      unreliable?)
   How might the event have been changed or avoided?
   To what other events was it connected? how?
   To what kinds of structure (if any) can it be assigned? On what basis?

C. *Writing about Abstract Concepts (e.g., "religion," "socialism")*
   To what specific items, groups of items, events, or groups of events,
      does the word or words connect, in your experience or imagina-
      tion?
   What characteristics must an item or event have before the name of
      the concept can apply to it?
   How do the referents of that concept differ from the things we name
      with similar concepts (e.g., "democracy" and "socialism")?
   How has the term been used by writers whom you have read? How
      have they implicitly defined it?

Does the word have "persuasive" value? Does the use of it in connection with another concept seem to praise or condemn the other concept?

Are you favorably disposed to all things included in the concept? Why or why not?

D. *Writing about Collections of Items* (*in present existence*) [These questions are in addition to the questions about single items, which can presumably be asked of each item in the group.]

What, exactly, do the items have in common?

If they have features in common, how do they differ?

How are the items related to each other, if not by common characteristics? What is revealed about them by the possibility of grouping them in this way?

How may the group be divided? What bases for division can be found?

What correlations, if any, may be found among the various possible subgroups? Is anything disclosed by the study of these correlations?

Into what class, if any, can the group as a whole be put?

E. *Writing about Groups of Completed Events, Including Processes* [These questions are in addition to questions about single completed events; such questions are applicable to each event in the group. These questions also apply to literary works, principally fiction and drama.]

What have the events in common?

If they have features in common, how do they differ?

How are the events related to each other (if they are not part of a chronological sequence)? What is revealed by the possibility of grouping them in this way (these ways)?

What is revealed by the events when taken as a group?

How can the group be divided? On what bases?

What possible correlations can be found among the several subgroups?

Into what class, if any, can the events taken as a group fit?

Does the group belong to any other structures than simply a larger group of similar events? (Is it part of a more inclusive chronological sequence? one more piece of evidence that may point toward a conclusion about history? and so on)

To what antecedents does the group of events look back? Where can they be found?

What implications, if any, does the group of events have? Does the group point to a need for some sort of action?

II. "Topics" with "Comments" Already Attached

A. *Writing about Propositions* (*statements set forth to be proved or disproved*)

What must be established for the reader before he will believe it?

Into what sub-propositions, if any, can it be broken down? (What smaller assertions does it contain?)

What are the meanings of key words in it?

To what line of reasoning is it apparently a conclusion?

How can we contrast it with other, similar, propositions? (How can we change it, if at all, and still have roughly the same proposition?)

To what class (or classes) of propositions does it belong?

How inclusive (or how limited) is it?

What is at issue, if one tries to prove the proposition?

How can it be illustrated?

How can it be proven (by what kinds of evidence)?

What will or can be said in opposition to it?

Is it true or false? How do we know? (direct observation, authority, deduction, statistics, other sources?)

Why might someone disbelieve it?

What does it assume? (What other propositions does it take for granted?)

What does it imply? (What follows from it?) Does it follow from the proposition that action of some sort must be taken?

What does it reveal (signify, if true)?

If it is a prediction, how probable is it? On what observations of past experience is it based?

If it is a call to action, what are the possibilities that action can be taken? (Is what is called for feasible?) What are the probabilities that the action, if taken, will do what it is supposed to do? (Will the action called for work?)

B. *Writing about Questions* (*interrogative sentences*)

Does the question refer to past, present, or future time?

What does the question assume (take for granted)?

In what data might answers be sought?

Why does the question arise?

What, fundamentally, is in doubt? How can it be tested? evaluated?

What propositions might be advanced in answer to it?

    Is each proposition true?

    If it is true:

        What will happen in the future? What follows from it?

        Which of these predictions are possible? probable?

        What action should be taken (avoided) in consequence?

    [Most of the other questions listed under "Propositions" also apply.]

Exercises

1. Decide which group of questions in Larson may best be applied to four of the following:

   a. high school math courses

   b. a bicycle

   c. high school dropouts

   d. the opening paragraph of the Declaration of Independence

   e. traffic signs

   f. Shakespeare's *Hamlet*

   g. American musical comedies

   h. the Golden Rule

   i. Vietnam War

   j. capital punishment

   k. Ford *Mustang*

2. Write down some ways that analysis of two of the above would be different, given two different audiences and purposes in writing. For each indicate what questions of Larson would be included and would be omitted, and why.

3. Choose an audience and purpose of your own, and write several paragraphs analyzing an item, a collection of items, an event, or an idea, according to Larson.

4. Rewrite these paragraphs for a different audience and perhaps for a different purpose. Notice that you will be answering some of the same questions and introducing others. Be ready to discuss the changes you made, and the reasons for them.

Chapter Two

Exposition and Argument

Exposition as part of argument

We have seen that exposition presents and explains facts and ideas, whereas argument uses these as evidence for conclusions. The newspaper account of a chemical spill is an exposition, the editorial that draws a conclusion from this account is an argument. A recipe or set of directions is expository; it does not draw a conclusion from the facts it presents. The Declaration of Independence is argumentative; it does draw conclusions from the rights and wrongs it defends and describes.

It is clear, then, that exposition has an important part to play in argument. For we must know the facts or ideas that the conclusion is based upon. Sometimes this exposition or presentation is quite brief, and sometimes it is lengthy, as when the Declaration of Independence gives an extended account of what George III of England had done to deserve the name of tyrant. Here is one sentence from the indictment:

> He has plundered our seas, ravaged our coasts, burnt our towns, and destroyed the lives of our people.

From such acts the following conclusion is drawn:

> A prince, whose character is thus marked by every act which may define a tyrant, is unfit to be the ruler of a free people.

Conversely, an exposition such as the first sentence quoted from the Declaration of Independence may imply or even state a conclusion. In other words, the presentation of facts alone makes the point that George III has behaved like a tyrant. We can see from this example that exposition can be used for different purposes—to inform us of the facts of the case, or to persuade us to draw a conclusion from these facts and change our thinking on the issue. A recipe tells us how to perform an action or process; it presents the steps of the process without asking us to draw any conclusion about them. Another kind of exposition, the statement of facts in a murder trial, does ask us to draw a conclusion.

To see how expositions and arguments are constructed, we will look first at an essay on gossip by Ralph L. Rosnow that is mainly expository. In it Rosnow is concerned with explaining what gossip is, but he uses his explanation to develop the thesis that gossip is not idle talk as many think, but rather has a social purpose. In drawing this conclusion, he has used his extended exposition to argue a thesis. In the margin to the left, we have identified both the thesis and the methods of development—definition, division, example, comparison, analogy, process and causal analysis—that we considered in the previous chapter. Following the essay, we shall consider in more detail some features of development in essays of this kind.

GOSSIP

by Ralph L. Rosnow

Introduction
Thesis
Definition

1   Gossip is not just "idle chatter" (the common definition) but "talk" with social purpose. In psychological and economic terms, gossiping is an instrumental transaction in which people trade small talk for status, power, fun, money, information, or any resource with the capacity to fulfill preconditioned needs, wishes and expectations.

Examples

2   It is because gossip serves myriad functions that it is a valued commodity in the marketplace of social exchange. Benjamin Franklin took advantage of this when, in 1730, he introduced the gossip column to the Colonies in his Pennsylvania Gazette. His lineal descendants in the press have included Mark Twain, Franklin P. Adams, Eugene Field, Walter Winchell, Hedda Hopper, Louella Parsons, and Drew Pearson.

Analogy (Comparison)
Points of Similarity

3   Indeed, there is a close parallel between the "rules" of gossiping and the principles of economic exchange. Thus the value of news increases in direct proportion to its scarcity. When the market for news expands, the amount of gossip in circulation will proliferate. Consumers of gossip have their own brand loyalties—columnists, tabloids, magazines.

Division

4   One primary psychological objective of gossiping is status or esteem. Such gossiping conforms to a pattern of

exchange in which the value placed upon a commodity results from bargaining for economic or psychological advantage.

Example

5   For example, someone agrees publicly to divulge information about certain backstairs happenings in return for a fat fee and instantaneous notoriety. The short-lived ABC-TV afternoon game show, "The Neighbors," provided an intriguing variation on this theme. The target of gossip was confronted by the gossipers and both were rewarded if she could detect which of her neighbors was in fact the specific source of the story told. Stories of a vindictive nature can provide additional salve for the gossiper's ego. Classical anthropological studies of To'ambaita and Busama of Melanesia observed that gossip given in a public confessional had a double value, since it enhanced the gossiper's self-image while inflicting vengeance on his transgressors by publicly humiliating them.

Division (cont.), **Definition Etymological Definition**

6   Another objective of gossiping is mutual entertainment. Here the guiding principle is usually one of reciprocity, or even-handed interaction. The gossiping may ultimately operate to the disadvantage of a third party, but the defining characteristic is that it mutually benefits the interacting parties. This variety calls to mind early definitions of the term. Derived from the Old English godsibb, for God-parent, it came to mean the women friends of the child's mother who were present at the birth and passed the long hours of waiting in small talk. This origin may also explain the sexist stereotype that brands gossiping as a feminine pastime.

Division (cont.) **Process Analogy**

7   Gossiping also maps out the social environment. It constitutes the dramaturgical format of certain of our art forms—theater, the novel, television soap operas—which simultaneously reflect and articulate the role expectations that guide our everyday behavior. The two-step flow of "non-essential news" from the news media to intermediary opinion leaders who redistribute it to the public at large is another way in which gossip delineating the social environment is distributed. This can be compared to the economic trading pattern in which resources are brought to a central operation and from there dispersed.

Conclusion Comparison Cause and Effect

8   All three varieties of gossip are prominently featured by the mass media, which compete with one another to be first with the most juicy story. The reporter acts as a gatekeeper who channels the flow of information, in return for which the rewards are money, recognition and power. As a result, successful gatekeepers become celebrities in their own right and find themselves subjects of gossip. The hazard, in terms of the economics of social exchange, is that a marketplace surfeited on gossip may produce a society

increasingly negativistic about all news sources and cynical to the point of nihilism.

Exposition and audience

As we noted in the previous chapter, the methods used to develop ideas depend both on the audience and the ideas themselves. A topic calling for an explanation of terms is developed through definition. But how we develop the definition depends on the audience. Similarly, the kind and number of examples depends on how much readers know about the subject.

What kind of audience does Rosnow have in mind? He is obviously writing to educated general readers who know little if anything about the history of gossip as he presents it, but probably know the names of columnists of the 1940s and 1950s like Walter Winchell and Louella Parsons. Rosnow is not writing primarily to the specialist—for example, the psychologist or sociologist, for whom a technical discussion of psychological, social, or economic processes would have been inappropriate.

Like paragraphs, expository essays occasionally are developed by one method throughout—by definition, for example, or comparison and contrast. But like paragraphs, they can be developed in several ways at the same time and usually are. As our analysis of Rosnow's discussion of gossip has shown, he combines example with definition, classification, division, comparison, contrast, and analogy to make his point that gossip serves a useful function in society.

What differences does the audience make in organizing an essay? We are familiar with the ways advertisements choose details according to the knowledge that the audience is thought to possess. To cite a recent example, an advertisement for a new line of Pioneer high fidelity products in *The New Yorker* for July 13, 1981—a magazine directed to the educated general reader—contained much less information than an advertisement for the same products in *Stereo Review* for July, 1981—a magazine directed mainly to people who probably own high fidelity equipment, and understand technical specifications. Thus the *New Yorker* ad says this about Pioneer receivers:

> For instance, our receivers memorize the precise locations of your favorite stations. So you can instantly tune in any station at the touch of a button.

By contrast, the *Stereo Review* ad gives us considerably more information in technical language that is absent in the first:

> Pioneer's SX-7 Receiver brings you precise electronic control of most functions including volume. The Auto Station Scan control previews the entire

band and eight FM and eight AM Memory Presets recall the stations you prefer instantly. What's more, Pioneer's patented Non-Switching amp does away with one of the most troublesome and audible forms of distortion—the noise generated when output transistors switch on and off thousands of times a second.

The *New Yorker* ad says this about the new turntables:

New Pioneer turntables have such superb suspension our Polymer Graphite tonearms won't skip when people dance.

The *Stereo Review* ad again gives more information, including the following:

It features a linear motor that drives the tonearm across the track by electro-magnetic repulsion—another Pioneer innovation. . . . The tonearm itself is made by Polymer Graphite—an amazing material that dampens resonance. And there's a coaxial suspension system that isolates the platter and tonearm assembly.

Obviously, too much information in an ad may confuse the general reader, but this same information may persuade the reader interested in specifications that the differences noted make new equipment desirable.

The methods used in exposition may also depend on the audience. Readers lacking scientific and mathematical knowledge need definitions and analogies with everyday experience to understand special ideas like "electromagnetic repulsion." Though an audience of scientists would undoubtedly understand a reference to it without supporting definitions or illustrations, an exposition directed to general readers would have to draw on wider resources of explanation.

Organization, too, depends on the audience. For a general audience whose knowledge of the subject varies, the writer will do well to proceed from simple, somewhat familiar details and ideas to complex, less familiar ones. By contrast, a technical article directed to the specialist may proceed from one complex idea to another, with the ideas arranged in the order of their importance to the thesis. An exposition may be organized in other ways too—for example, from specific details to general conclusions as in a lab report, or from less to more interesting details and conclusions.

Exercises

1. The following explanations of the common cold are directed to different audiences—the first, to consumers who require information about the disease to distinguish effective from ineffective cold remedies; the second, to medical students and pathologists concerned with diagnosis and treatment. Discuss how much knowledge of

technical ideas and vocabulary each audience is assumed to possess:

a. In fact, the common cold, known in medical jargon as the "coryza" syndrome, is not a simple matter; rather, it is a complex of symptoms. Caused by any one of a group of viruses (currently estimated at about 100 in number), the common cold is primarily an infection of the lining membrane of the upper respiratory tract, including the nose, the sinuses, and the throat. This delicate membrane reacts to infection by swelling and by increasing the rate of mucus formation, leading to congestion, stuffiness, and probably a good deal of nose blowing. Due to loss of the nasal cavity as a resonating chamber, a characteristic change in voice quality also occurs. The increased mucus flow usually causes postnasal drip, which is irritating and contributes to the familiar "scratchy" throat and cough.

The Medicine Show: Consumers Unions' Practical Guide to Some
Everyday Health Problems

b. The common cold is a symptom complex caused by viral infection of the upper respiratory passages. Most precisely, the term applies to afebrile, acute coryza of viral origin. In the broadest sense, the common cold refers to any undifferentiated upper respiratory infection. The terms rhinitis, pharyngitis, laryngitis, and "chest cold" are sometimes used to designate the principal anatomic site of infection. The main difference between the common cold and other viral or bacterial respiratory infections is the absence of fever and the relatively milder constitutional symptoms and signs.

Beeson and McDermott, *Textbook of Medicine*

2. Examine the explanation of an economic phenomenon like inflation, or a similar psychological or sociological phenomenon, in a textbook directed to college students to determine what knowledge the readers of the book are assumed to possess. If possible, compare the explanation with that in an encyclopedia or a manual to determine how the explanations differ.

Organizing the expository essay

We have just seen how a particular audience can influence the way an essay is organized. Here we will organize an essay for a specific audience, and in the process show how essays are usually constructed. Our discussion and outline of the essay will use the methods of development reviewed in the preceding chapter.

But before considering the structure of the essay, we need first to define our purpose in writing and our audience as exactly as we can. Let us assume that we wish to describe and analyze the kinds of cheating that occur in college. Our purpose in doing so is to provide the facts needed to decide whether an honor code can and should be instituted at the college we attend. A committee consisting of administrators, faculty, and students is holding hearings on the issue; this committee will review the facts we present, but we also wish to inform the students of the college of the prevailing situation. We are writing, therefore, for a mixed audience, some of whom know the details of cheating and some of whom do not. In writing our exposition, we can be sure that the audience just described knows how assignments are made and how examinations are conducted. They also know what procedures and penalties exist to deal with cheating. We need not review all of these, but we probably will want to review some of them if only for the purpose of comparison.

Let us first write down some of the points we need to make. We will do so without concern for their organization in the completed essay:

Since there is disagreement over what constitutes cheating, we want to explain what cheating is.

As part of this explanation, we want to distinguish the kinds of cheating that occur.

Since cheating occurs for different reasons, we want to identify these carefully.

We also want to trace the effects of cheating on the students and the college, perhaps showing how cheating has tarnished its reputation.

The growth of cheating over the years can be compared to the growth of a hidden tumor, and this analogy will illuminate the problem.

It may be useful to compare the kinds of cheating that occur in college with the kinds that occur in high school.

The process of cheating during examinations must be understood before specific remedies are considered.

Other examples of cheating will show the extent of the problem.

Since existing procedures have not been successful in curbing cheating, analysis of these will give insight into what has to be done.

Planning the composition

In organizing our presentation, we need first to decide on an order of ideas. There are several possibilities. We might follow this plan:

Kinds of cheating
Reasons for cheating
Effects of cheating
Possible remedies for cheating

Or we might begin with existing remedies, explain why they have failed, trace the effects of this failure, and consider new remedies in preparation for a later argument in favor of some of these:

> Present remedies for cheating
> Kinds of cheating involved
> Reasons for cheating
> Reasons that present remedies have failed
> Effects of cheating
> Possible new remedies

The plan we choose depends on the focus we wish to give our essay. We have, however, discovered a thesis or main idea in the facts we have gathered, one that bears directly on this issue of central concern to our audience. That thesis is the following:

> Cheating at this college is so widespread and so ingenious in its methods that existing remedies have failed to curb it.

We may later want to use this thesis to make a proposal:

> Since existing remedies have failed, new ones should be adopted.

Such a proposal for a strict honor code, administered by students and their teachers together, can then be argued on the basis of the facts assembled in the exposition.

Notice that the organization depends now on the thesis we have discovered. We can, indeed, develop it through either of the two plans just outlined. Let us show in more detail how the first of them can be worked out through various methods of analysis:

I. Kinds of cheating
  A. What cheating is [**definition**]
  B. Kinds of cheating in general [**division**]
  C. Kinds of cheating at this college [**division**]
    1. Specific acts of cheating [**example**]
    2. Ingenious methods of cheating during one examination [**process**]
  D. Methods of cheating in high school and college [**comparison and contrast**]

II. Reasons for cheating
  A. Student attitudes [**causal analysis, comparison and contrast**]
  B. Pressures on students [**causal analysis**]
  C. Attitudes and behavior of teachers [**causal analysis**]
  D. Interlocking attitudes of students and teachers (**comparison and contrast)**
  E. Tumor-like growth of cheating [**analogy**]

III. Effects of cheating
    A. Effects on the student [**causal analysis**]
    B. Effects on the college [**causal analysis**]

IV. Possible remedies for cheating
    A. Nature of existing procedures [**analysis**]
    B. Reasons for their failure [**Causal analysis**]
    C. Other possible remedies [**definition and division**]

We have not broken down all of the topics shown, since we want to show the organization in broad outline. Later, we may wish to outline some of these topics further. After reviewing the outline, we may decide that not all the topics shown need be included, and of course not all of them will be developed at the same length. Thus, the effects of cheating on the college might be stated in a very few sentences, and the analogy might be developed in just one.

What topics we include and what length we require for their development depend, as we have said, on the thesis we discover as we plan the exposition. We need now to examine more closely the nature of the thesis in exposition and argument.

Exercise

Decide on a purpose and an audience for an expository essay based on one of the following topics. Work out an outline, including at least four of the following: definition, division, analysis, process, example, comparison and contrast, analogy, and causal analysis (tracing causes or effects or both):

a. the teenage driver

b. social norms governing conduct

c. unrealistic views of young and old people

d. growing up as an only child

e. relationships in a large family

f. making and losing friends

Thesis in exposition and argument

We have seen how planning the essay can lead to the discovery of a thesis, if the writer did not have one in mind to begin with. We need now to consider what the thesis is and does in more detail, in particular how it resembles the topic sentence that states the central idea of a paragraph.

Here are the topic sentences of Rosnow's paragraphs:

1   Gossip is not just "idle chatter" (the common definition) but "talk" with social purpose.

2   It is because gossip serves myriad functions that it is a valued commodity in the marketplace of social exchange.

3   Indeed, there is a close parallel between the "rules" of gossiping and the principles of economic exchange.

4   One primary psychological objective of gossiping is status or esteem.

5   For example, someone agrees publicly to divulge information about certain backstairs happenings in return for a fat fee and instantaneous notoriety.

6   Another objective of gossiping is mutual entertainment.

7   Gossiping also maps out the social environment.

8   All three varieties of gossip are prominently featured by the mass media, which compete with one another to be first with the most juicy story.

These sentences form a summary of the essay—they make, in effect, a miniature essay. They also help us identify the thesis, which is the idea that organizes them. Usually, a thesis consists of a general statement that serves as the controlling idea—like the topic sentence of the Orwell paragraph analyzed earlier (see p. 9). In Rosnow, the thesis is the first sentence of his essay.

> Gossip is not just "idle chatter" (the common definition) but "talk" with social purpose.

In this case the thesis happens to be one of the topic sentences of the essay, but in many instances it may be any sentence in the essay, coming anywhere in the piece of writing—at the beginning, middle, or end.

The thesis, then, is the central, controlling idea to which all details and other ideas connect and which they all develop together. It is roughly like the main clause of a sentence, an independent statement to which supporting details and ideas can be added. Indeed, it has the force of assertion, a declaration of a truth—what in logic we call a proposition. The word assertion is the key to what a thesis does. Arguments, as we shall see, consist of propositions, statements that affirm or deny something. A thesis is, like a proposition, a statement to which we can say yes or no, as for example in the statement quoted earlier from the Declaration of Independence on what makes a prince unfit to rule.

Some essays do not develop a thesis in this strict sense of the word. They may instead explore an idea without claiming truth for it, and the word *thesis* is also used to describe this non-argumentative idea. The word *essay,* it is worth noting, had as one of its original meanings a first attempt or trying out, the testing of an idea—in the words of one early writer, "an irregular undigested piece."

Moreover, not every piece of writing contains a thesis—either a proposition that asserts or denies a truth, or a central controlling idea. A diary entry or a rambling letter to a friend need not contain a central idea. We find a thesis only if a point is being made. Even a newspaper account of a chemical spill, which does no more than tell us that the spill occurred at a particular time in a particular way, implies a thesis. Of course the editorial that makes a point and draws a conclusion from the story's evidence makes a thesis explicit: we need to make certain that safeguards are adequate to avoid chemical spills. The thesis of the newspaper story may be non-argumentative, and may consist of a flat assertion of fact: due to inadequate safeguards there was a chemical spill at plant X yesterday. This may be the beginning of an expository article explaining what happened and how or why it happened. The editorial's thesis is the basis for an argument.

We cannot give a full account of what makes a thesis adequate until we have discussed inductive and deductive arguments, but we can make a few preliminary points. If we think of a thesis as an answer to a question, how adequate the answer is will depend on how much information the audience of the essay requires. Some will ask for more information, others for less. In other words, the development of evidence in support of a thesis will determine the adequacy of the thesis, which must not say more than the evidence warrants—or say less. Like an examination answer, it will be inadequate if it generalizes wildly, unsupported by specific examples, or if it fails to draw a sufficient conclusion, or draws none at all.

Writing Assignment

Look again at the outline you wrote, and write down several points that your exposition may be used to make. Choose one of these that best serves your purpose in writing: a conclusion that may be drawn for your audience. This point or conclusion is your thesis. If necessary, rearrange your ideas and supporting details so that the order of ideas and details develops your thesis in an effective way. You are now ready to write your essay. In writing it, keep in mind the importance of prominent topic sentences and clear transitions (see pp. 8–11).

The parts of an argumentative essay

Arguments, like expositions, can be organized in various ways. We shall consider first the form of argument that comes to us from the judicial plea and legal brief, the main form of argument in the courtroom. We will show what this form consists of through an extended example—the opening statements of prosecutors and defense attorneys at the start of murder trials.

Some prosecutors begin with pleas to juries for their attention and concern. They then present the backgrounds of their cases, the events and circumstances that in their view led to the murder they are concerned with. They are careful to present all pertinent details, because they want to fix their versions of what happened in the minds of the jurors, and they know defense attorneys will present different versions when their turn comes.

Now follow outlines of the proofs of guilt, and the universal proposition or thesis statement: "X is guilty of the crime of murder!" The first part of the presentation now completed, prosecutors present the evidence or proof of guilt—their confirming arguments. Then they anticipate the responses of defense attorneys and refute them. They are ready now to conclude their statements: they review the proofs of guilt, and make final appeals to their juries, always asking for "a just verdict."

Of course, the entire confirmation or refutation may not be given in the opening statements. As a rule, more evidence and arguments are presented later in trials, after prosecutors have heard the statements of defense attorneys.

Defense attorneys now have their turn to speak to the jury. Since their concerns are mainly with refutation, they may alter the pattern somewhat—stressing refutation more than do prosecutors. First they make their own appeals, perhaps asking jurors to keep an open mind; then they present the backgrounds as they and their clients believe them to exist. In doing so, defense attorneys have begun their refutation; that is, the narrative of the individual background forms part of the refutation. Then they outline the proofs of innocence, finishing with their own proposition or thesis, which is usually "My client is innocent of the charge!"

The confirmation that follows is a presentation of the proofs of innocence. An alternative order is possible. Defense attorneys may refute the charges first, introducing new evidence not previously stated in the narrative, or reviewing the evidence presented there. They may combine their evidence with different proofs of innocence, the confirming arguments of their own theses. Like prosecutors, they may finish with a review of the points made, and with a final plea to the jurors for their understanding and fair judgment.

Here is an outline of the form of argument we have described. We will take the prosecutor as our model:

Exhortation or plea   **Introduction**
Background or narrative
Division of proofs
Proposition or thesis statement

Confirmation or arguments in support of the   **Body**
proposition
Refutation of opposing arguments

Summary of the main arguments   **Conclusion**
Final appeal

The parts of the argument fall into a familiar division—introduction, body, and conclusion. It is worth recalling that not all of these parts need to be included in an argument, and some may be combined—confirmation with refutation, for example.

The same basic form of argument is also found in the discourse of legislatures. A speech in favor of a proposed law may make its points in approximately the same order as our outline. And so may a speech honoring or mourning someone—except that in these circumstances a refutation would probably be inappropriate. We do not expect to hear criticism of a dead person brought up during a funeral eulogy and rebutted. But we do occasionally hear criticism introduced and rebutted in a tribute to a controversial public figure.

Let us look briefly at arguments that are special forms of refutation. One of these traces the effects of a policy or attitude. Here is a paragraph from a magazine editorial that employs this kind of refutation:

> Meanwhile, every malevolent idea about crippling man or producing mass suffering is given sanction the moment the word security is affixed to it. Thus, it is considered proper and essential to mass-produce odorless and invisible gases that can inflict heart attacks, or bombs that can disseminate germs to spread the very diseases that mankind over countless generations has been trying to eliminate. But nothing is more insidious in this apocalyptic inventory than the determination of each side to convince the other that it would not have the slightest hesitation to turn it all loose if it felt warranted in doing so.
>
> Norman Cousins, *Saturday Review*, October 27, 1962

When we are shown these consequences in an exaggerated way, we say that the argument is satirical. One powerful form of refutation is the *reductio ad absurdum*, in which an idea or attitude is shown to be irrational by carrying it to its logical consequences. When these consequences are also ridiculous, the treatment will seem satirical. For example, Art Buchwald satirizes the commercialization of Christmas by having an imaginary spokesman for business interests oppose the effort to make Christmas a religious holiday. The spokesman says in part:

> "[People] can go to church on Sunday or during the week. Why do they insist on going the one day of the year when people should stay home and enjoy the fruits of our great economy?"

And he adds:

> "Look at all the traffic congestion it causes. The church bells wake up people who are trying to sleep late. Besides, why shouldn't priests and ministers have a day off like everybody else?"

Reductio ad absurdum is here combined with another satirical strategy—reversing the situation familiar to us and exploring the consequences of this reversal.

There are other forms of argument that we will have occasion to examine later in this book.

If you will look now at the following essay on smoking by Carll Tucker, you will find parts of the argument identified in the margin. Notice that the extended background or narrative leads into a division of proofs, and that the confirmation is short, and the refutation extended. Instead of presenting his thesis with his division of proofs, Tucker builds to a thesis statement at the end of the essay. The conclusion takes the form of a recapitulation or summary of the main argument.

As in the Rosnow, our analysis of the parts of the argument are indicated in the margin.

SMOKE SIGNALS

by Carll Tucker

**Introduction
Narrative background**

1   In recent weeks, the campaign against smoking has assumed new urgency and scored some impressive victories. A national No-Smoking Day evoked articles and editorials against the evil weed. The Civil Aeronautics Board has banned all cigar and pipe smoking on commercial airlines and has taken steps that could lead to the prohibition of cigarette smoking as well. Regulations against smoking in the Pentagon's dining halls and classrooms have been sent to the Army, Air Force, and Navy "for responses on how to implement them."

Use of personal experience to identify with readers holding opposing views

2   Now I am not, nor have I ever been, a smoker. At the age of eight, I stole one of my father's cigars to share experimentally with a friend; fearful that our crime was about to be discovered by an approaching adult, I swallowed the lit butt. In college, unwilling to be considered uncool by classmates, I inhaled marijuana, but never with enjoyment. (Even in that era of "do your own thing," there were pressures to conform.) Shortly after graduation, I adopted a pipe in the belief that the first step toward being a writer was looking like one; but I soon abandoned it after finding that most of my reading time was spent trying to keep my tobacco on fire.

Personal experience (cont.)

3   I am neither allergic to cigarette smoke nor fond of it. If at a lunch counter a woman asks in the middle of my meal would I mind if she smokes, I consider saying yes. I sit gratefully in the nonsmoking section of airplanes and movie houses.

Body
Division of proofs
Statement of question

4   Nonetheless, I am troubled by the attitude and success of the campaigners against smoking. It is one thing to warn consumers that cigarette smoking may be hazardous to their health; living in a world of often invisible dangers, we should be grateful for the caution. It is even arguable that given the demonstrated ability of television and radio to reach below the intelligence and to sow subliminal "needs," cigarette advertising should be banished from the airwaves. But having alerted the consumer to the danger and having protected him from subliminal seduction, what arguments can be used to justify what the antismoking militants see as their eventual goal: the outlawing of cigarettes?

Opposing argument

5   A recent editorial in *The New York Times* cited some reasons why the Carter administration ought not to be "resigned to a national addiction that will kill 300,000 Americans this year." Cost was one reason: According to Surgeon General Julius Richmond, ailments caused by smoking will cost the nation $20 billion this year. The will of the American smoker was another: Eight out of ten smokers would like to quit, said Richmond, adding, "We must help them, and they want us to."

Refutation

6   Never having smoked, I do not comprehend the force or the invincibility of an addiction to tobacco, but I do know a number of less-than-Herculean Americans who have, albeit with some discomfort, managed to shake their addiction. I wonder what it is about the purported 80 percent of smokers who want to quit that prevents them from doing so. I also wonder whether the cost of treating a sickness should be used as an argument for removing the freedom to incur the sickness and whether it is government's role to help citizens do something that they are not psychologically capable of doing themselves. (By this logic, government should limit the calories allowed to each American per day.)

Refutation (cont.)
Qualification

7   The advantage of a democracy over various more or less organized methods of government is that it allows a citizen the maximum freedom to do as he pleases up to the point at which his freedom infringes on someone else's. As the world becomes more complex and people become more interdependent, our freedoms necessarily become more restricted. Speed limits were not needed before automobile and highway manufacturers created the opportunities for serious accidents. It was not necessary to

prohibit homeowners from burning leaves until everyone's air became smoky.

Thesis
Confirmation
Conclusion

8   What we must guard against, though, is using the excuse of interdependence to enact restrictions that, however desirable, are unnecessary. I suspect that the creation of nonsmoking sections in public places answers the complaints of most nonsmokers. To ban cigarettes altogether would be to do something that, however healthful, is not strictly necessary and that would limit the freedom of those who like to smoke. Government should resist the temptation to treat its citizens like children—making us wear seat belts that buzz if we don't fasten them, forbidding us marijuana or Laetrile or tobacco simply because they haven't been proved as safe as mother's milk (which nowadays isn't safe, either). Advise us, yes; restrict us when we threaten the essential freedoms of others. But do not attempt to protect us from all the dangers of existence.

Final appeal
Restatement of thesis

9   There are two sorts of freedom: freedom *from* and freedom *to*. Given the choice, democracy should favor the latter. Whether or not one likes smoking, the freedom to smoke is a more important right than freedom from smoking or its consequences. When usually thoughtful opinion shapers like *The New York Times* start advocating laws not because they are necessary for the preservation of our freedom but because they would be good for us, it is time to worry.

In analyzing Tucker's argument we should note that he uses many of the techniques we discussed in connection with the expository essay. Let us examine his method in some detail.

Paragraph 1 states Tucker's subject in the first sentence—the campaign against smoking—and then goes on to provide three examples of this campaign. Paragraph 2 opens with a transitional topic sentence and quickly moves to a chronological narrative of Tucker's early experiences with smoking. Here Tucker establishes his credentials as a nonsmoker through the use of a number of examples. The third paragraph develops out of the second, its topic sentence parallels the opening sentence of paragraph 2, and it also relies on examples to illustrate his point.

With the transitional word "nonetheless," in paragraph 4, Tucker moves to the body of his argument and states that although he has no personal interest in smoking, he is troubled by the campaign against it. He develops the paragraph by causal analysis, giving the reasons for his concern while granting the legitimacy of cautioning the public against hazards to their health. He concludes the paragraph by raising the central issue of his argument. Paragraph 5 presents two of the chief reasons that have been given for "outlawing cigarettes."

While developing his refutation in paragraphs 6 and 7, Tucker opens with a discussion of the complexity of the issue: addiction to tobacco is hard to break. He then moves in paragraph 6 to the refutation proper when he questions the legitimacy of one antismoking argument and raises another question about the legitimate role of government in personal choice. Tucker ends paragraph 6 with an analogy between diet and smoking. He continues the refutation in paragraph 7 by opening with a definition of democracy, which he then qualifies through an analysis of the circumstances under which freedom must be restricted.

Paragraph 8 opens with Tucker's statement of his thesis, which develops out of the qualifications in paragraph 7. He then confirms or supports his thesis in paragraph 8 through a series of comparisons and contrasts. The last two sentences of this paragraph state the conclusion of his argument. Paragraph 9 opens Tucker's final appeal with his division of freedom into two kinds: freedom *from* and freedom *to*. In his restatement of his thesis, Tucker presents a parallel division of laws into two kinds: those necessary to our freedom and those necessary to our health, with the obvious choice in favor of freedom.

In Tucker's essay we have encountered many of the techniques used in persuasive writing. Later in this book, we shall examine some of these techniques in greater depth. Here it is sufficient to note that persuasive writing is directed toward what is taken by the author as the presuppositions or biases of the audience.

Alternative structures

Argument

In our outlines of the courtroom argument, the confirmation preceded the refutation. In Tucker, we saw that the refutation came first. Usually, the part of the argument coming toward the end receives the most attention, and the placement of refutation and confirmation is guided by this consideration.

Arguments may be organized as confirmations only, without identifying or dealing at length with opposing arguments. Many letters to the editors of newspapers and magazines do exactly this:

> The school levy must be passed if the schools are to remain open. The increase in students makes it impossible for them to operate without additional money.

Other writings are organized as refutations only, with opposing arguments answered within the refutation:

The argument that our schools can absorb a third more students and operate on the same budget is absurd. Additional space and teachers for a hundred more students do not now exist; fifty students would be forced into classrooms intended to seat twenty-five. Equally absurd is the argument that teachers work less than other professional people and therefore deserve less pay. The work of teachers may be different in kind from that of doctors and lawyers, but preparing children to live in the world is just as important as safeguarding their health and legal rights.

Exposition

The expository essay can follow the basic form of the argument, with omission of the refutation. Organized in this way, it will contain most of the parts of the argument we outlined earlier, in the same or a different order.

If it contains a refutation, this will correct a possible misconception or tell us what a word does not mean or what steps not to follow in performing a process.

Here is this model, with the refutation omitted:

Introduction
  Background or narrative
  Outline of the main ideas
  Statement of the thesis

Body
  Discussion of the main ideas
  Supporting detail, comparison, definition, etc.

Conclusion
  Review of the main ideas
  Restatement of the thesis
  Final reflections or comments

Rosnow follows this model roughly. His opening two paragraphs serve as an introduction. The thesis is stated in the first sentence of paragraph 1, and gossip is defined. Paragraphs 2 and 3 provide background—we are told about the history of gossip in America—and the definition of gossip is expanded through analogy.

The main discussion (paragraphs 4–9) consists of a division of the subject—a discussion of the three objectives of gossip—with supporting illustrations and definition. The concluding paragraph relates the previous analogy to the attitude of the general public toward mass media. The conclusion, in other words, applies the analysis to a current issue.

The organization a writer chooses depends largely on what will be the most effective kind of presentation, given the audience—unless the subject itself requires a particular structure. An essay describing a process must be chronological, for example. Had Rosnow decided that his thesis would be understood without careful definition, illustration, and comparison, he might have built up to these devices instead of beginning the essay with them.

A concluding statement

Having concluded this preliminary discussion of exposition and argument, let us state some basic questions to keep in mind in preparing to write:

Who is my audience? Is it a general audience, for whom my examples and details must be complete and simple enough to be understood easily? Is it a specialized audience, for whom I can select details and facts according to their particular knowledge and interests?

What is my purpose in writing? Do I want merely to explain facts and ideas—that is, identify them for the reader? Or do I want to use them to develop a thesis and to persuade my audience of it? If so, what ideas do I want them to accept? What action do I want them to take, if any?

What questions about the subject do I need to answer? What can I expect my readers to know or believe, what will I have to explain to them? How much do I have to develop an idea?

What kind of organization will best serve my purpose, given my audience?

Exercise

1. Political cartoons often treat issues satirically, while the same issues have been treated nonsatirically in editorials and letters to the editor. Bring to class such a cartoon and an editorial or a letter, and discuss the differences you find.

2. Analyze the form of argument contained in the following passage from John Stuart Mill's *On Liberty* (1859):

   There is a class of persons (happily not quite so numerous as formerly) who think it enough if a person assents undoubtingly to what they think true, though he has no knowledge whatever of the grounds of the opinion, and could not make a tenable defense of it against the most superficial objects. Such persons, if they can once get their creed taught from authority, naturally think that no good, and some harm, comes of its being allowed to be questioned. Where their influence prevails, they make it nearly impossible for the received opinion to be rejected wisely and considerately, though it may still be rejected rashly and ignorantly; for to shut out discussion entirely is seldom possible, and when it once gets in, beliefs not grounded on conviction are apt to give way before the slightest semblance of an argument. Waiving, however, this possibility—assuming that the true opinion abides in the mind, but abides as a prejudice, a belief independent of, and proof against, argument—this is not the way in which truth ought to be held by a rational being. This is not knowing the truth. Truth, thus held, is but one superstition the more, accidentally clinging to the words which enunciate a truth.

Writing Assignments

1. Write an expository essay on various ways people choose a college to attend. Then discuss the way you made a decision. Distinguish the causes that were foremost in your mind at the time of the decision and those that conditioned it.

2. Write an argumentative essay on why a certain subject should be required of high school students but not of college students. Choose an appropriate audience, and select examples that best fit it. Include a narrative drawn from your personal experience, a division of proofs, a confirmation and a refutation.

3. Write an expository paragraph and an argumentative paragraph on one of the following statements:

   a. The people who live in a dream world are always being rudely awakened. They cannot see life's surprises as sources of useful information. They must see them as attacks.

   John Holt

   b. I have never seen more true mean spiritedness among children than when they were in a school and a class in which adults tried to prevent or, if they could not prevent, to settle all their quarrels.

   John Holt

   c. In dealing with children what is needed is not logic but sense.

   G. B. Shaw

4. Write an analysis of an editorial or letter to the editor that argues a thesis. Discuss the extent to which it conforms to the model argument form—that is, contains exhortation, narrative, division of proofs, confirmation, refutation, and recapitulation or summary and final appeal. Note that the refutation may be combined with the confirmation instead of being developed separately.

Chapter Three

The Inductive Essay

Observation and personal experience

Induction is one of two important kinds of logical analysis. In logic, induction refers to the process of observing features or patterns in experience and applying these to things that have not been observed. It is a form of prediction based on incomplete evidence, a kind of reasoning we engage in every day. Noticing that several houses in my neighborhood have been coated with the same brand of paint and seem to be more resistant to peeling than before, I apply the paint to my own house, expecting it will show the same lasting quality. I have made an inference about the quality of the new paint from a limited "sample."

Inductive reasoning of this kind proceeds from part to whole—from particulars of experience to a general conclusion, although it can also proceed from particular to particular and generalization to generalization. I draw numerous inferences from my experience with people. For example, my expectations about a new boss may derive from a variety of observations, including how he or she answers questions about problems on the job and gives instructions for carrying out a task. We are constantly making inferences in our everyday lives.

To infer something is to carry over an idea from one set of circumstances to another. As we have seen, the inference can be drawn from several samples of the same kind or it can be made from a single example—from one house in the neighborhood that I know was coated with the new brand of paint. Either way we are doing the same thing. We have arrived at a conclusion as a result of a rational process of thought. Our conclusion is implied in our statement that houses coated with a new paint resist peeling. It is our ability to recognize the implications of our experience that enables us to draw inferences in daily life.

At an earlier time induction was identified with the process of accumulating facts without concern for previous findings and looking for connections between them. This was thought to be a way of discarding worn-out views of the world and of seeing it with new eyes—perhaps also of discovering new worlds and experiences, in the way John Keats describes his discovering Homer:

> Then felt I like some watcher of the skies
> When a new planet swims into his ken.

Such was undoubtedly the experience of space scientists when, in the fall of 1980, the Voyager spacecraft sent pictures to earth of a "braided" ring about the planet Saturn and of new rings not previously observed.

Usually, however, induction is a process of controlled, not random, experimentation or study of facts. Previous experience guides the scientist in the search for new facts and connections. Astronomers focus their telescopes on parts of the sky where previous observations suggest that discoveries might be made. In general, scientific investigation builds on the work of earlier investigators who leave questions to be answered and whose findings need further testing. And that is what often happens in our everyday experience. We see the world on the basis of what we have seen in the past. We see with old eyes, and see gradually with new ones as our experience is enriched and even changed by what we see, read, and are told.

As a rule, our previous experience prepares our present expectations. When we wake up in the morning on a summer day, we expect the day to be filled with light, even if it is cloudy or raining; when we go to bed at night, we expect it to be dark. If someone asked us to predict whether the following night would be dark or light, we would unhesitatingly say that it would be dark. We would make this prediction not because of any special scientific knowledge, but because we expect the present and future to resemble the past. However, we do not have this expectation with every event we have experienced. When we have an accident, such as tripping on a stone and injuring an arm, we do not expect this event to repeat itself. Otherwise we would not be able to walk the same path again. In walking the same path, however, we are now somewhat more cautious than earlier, for we have become aware of its dangers. In effect, we have adjusted our expectations to our continuing experience and have assimilated the past to the present.

Writing about personal experience resembles inductive reasoning in important ways, though they are not the same. Scientists, in recording their observations, are seeking to establish their conclusions—to prove them to the highest degree of probability warranted by the evidence. Though writers are not usually concerned with proof in this formal sense, they do much the same in seeking to establish or evoke the feelings and ideas generated by experience. And just as the scientist knows that absolute certainty is impossible when reasoning about experience and observation, so writers know that their experiences are not all that can be experienced in the world.

In the essay that follows, Kristin Knutson describes the experience of exploring a beaver pond in late November with her father and brother:

> Dad and I hobbled over to where he was and looked down. We saw, then, that we were standing on and looking through ice that was so perfectly and clearly frozen that it could hardly be seen at all. It was as if we were magically suspended above a world which ordinarily would have been unreachable to us and therefore unknown to our sight.

This is the kernel out of which an essay of personal experience grew. It is much like the experience Keats expresses in his poem. Knutson conveys the experience to us in details so specific that we see what happened at the pond and we feel the same excitement of discovery. She then generalizes from it in somewhat the same way induction generalizes from samples.

A personal essay

IN SEARCH OF A CLEAR VIEW

by Kristin Knutson

It was late in November, the first big freeze of the season, and Dad had rousted us out and bundled us up on a Saturday morning for a drive to the Sioux Rapids hills to investigate a beaver pond he had found the summer before, "perfect for skating," he had said.

He was forever looking for places to skate, supposedly for our education and enjoyment, but we always knew these trips were just as much for him as for us, for he loved to skate and to explore. His enthusiasm and delight were so great, in fact, that whenever he did discover one of his "places," he would take the small green trailer out of storage in the garage, the one he kept just for hauling wood and for our trips to the mountains in the summer, and drive through our tiny Iowa town where he was the School Superintendent. As soon as they saw him driving down the street, the children, who must somehow have known and been waiting, would dash out of their houses shouting, "Wait for me, I'm coming," and then back inside to bundle up and throw their skates over their shoulders and grab a blanket under their arm for the open air trailer ride to the Sioux Rapids hills. We thought of our dad as a genuine Pied Piper during our growing up years, for he inevitably attracted children wherever he went with the pipes of his warmth and his zest for living.

On this particular Saturday, however, it was just my dad, my brother and I, going to the latest discovery, a beaver pond that was fit into a cleft between two hills, good protection for the skaters from the cold winter wind. There was a wooded area on one end, with trees and bushes and fallen logs which were, in the summer, partly submerged with water, but now locked in ice. A perfectly executed beaver dam was at the other end, with a deep pond as the result, the dam having been made with logs gathered from the wooded area. The water in the pond had not frozen deeply enough this early in the season, so we went over to the wooded area where the water, since it was more shallow, had frozen solid.

We found a log which was halfway on the ground and halfway submerged in the ice, so we sat on the ground end to put on our skates. My brother, who was first on the ice, had skated only a few feet when he suddenly dropped down on his knees and, pointing to the ice, shouted, "Hey, look at the fish!"

Dad and I hobbled over to where he was and looked down. We saw, then, that we were standing on and looking through ice that was so perfectly and clearly frozen that it could hardly be seen at all. It was as if we were magically suspended above a world which ordinarily would have been unreachable to us and therefore unknown to our sight.

We dropped down on our hands and knees for a closer look and then finally we lay stretched-out flat on the ice, all three of us in a row, faces pressed against it as though our noses were pressed against a window that looked onto another world.

We could see everything so clearly—the gritty bottom, sandy but clean, the weeds swaying, feather-like, in the quiet water below the ice, the fish swimming, unaware of and so unconcerned by this gentle intrusion, weaving their quick way in and out of the reeds and behind the rocks.

We watched for a long time as this new world went about its daily business, fish nibbling casually on the reeds and weeds, sometimes nosing each other in silent communications, bigger fish appearing from behind a rock and then disappearing again, little tiny crabs scuttling across the sandy floor, and bubbles continually rising slowly to the surface where the water met the ice.

Finally, it was time to finish putting on our skates and so we skated then, for the rest of that short November day. We must have looked like the fish below us, effortlessly gliding over the glassy ice, weaving our way in and out from between the trees, noiselessly passing each other in our silent investigations, the bare November air pinching our cheeks and warming our breaths which rose like miniature clouds to an invisible surface.

We went back several times that year, and then other years, but the ice had either frozen with ripples in a wind, or was too thick and cloudy because it had snowed and frozen at the same time. We never found ice like that again.

But I'm still looking. To see the world like that, I've often thought, through that clear suspended vision, nothing hidden, clouded or malformed in between—that, to me, would be heaven enough!

Organizing our impressions

But the "essay" is not written just because the experience has been undergone and reflected upon. The journal or diary entry, which records the direct experience, is a reflection of the moment. We see the effort to capture its sensible qualities in the journals of Henry David Thoreau, out of which he created his book *Walden*:

> April 4, 1841. That cheap piece of tinkling brass which the farmer hangs about his cow's neck has been more to me than the tons of metal which are swung in the belfry.

We see in the entry the beginning of an idea. Knutson, too, does more than just record her impressions.

To place her readers in the experience, she creates a narrative and joins it to description; she begins at the beginning, describing the world and its people in enough detail to allow us to imagine the experience. The opening paragraphs tell us just enough for us to understand and imagine what follows. Succeeding paragraphs provide additional details, enlarging our picture of the late November world. Notice how Knutson gives us information about her father in the context of the experience, as she develops it, instead of in a single paragraph by itself. This method helps her keep the focus on the experience itself rather than on her father—a fascinating person on whom the essay might instead have concentrated.

There are times when too much detail distracts us, taking our attention away from the idea being developed. One example or instance often succeeds better than a string of examples or instances developed in so much detail that the discussion wanders. However, there are occasions when several examples can make different points or reveal different facets of an idea and therefore have a justification. What is important is that we see and feel, as we write and read, the pertinence of every detail to the experience or idea being developed.

The major consideration in writing about personal experience—as in all inductive writing—is how much detail to provide. Finding the right proportion for a particular audience is not easy to achieve. Revision is essential: rethinking and rewriting what we have originally written to assure the coherence of the essay, which is the interconnection of all the parts so as to achieve unity and satisfying proportions. Each event must be presented as a unified whole, so that the reader's understanding of it is complete. This means that details or subsidiary events are retained only if they contribute to the whole. Moreover, the right amount of detail must be given, no more and no less than is necessary, if the essay is not to sag or be incomprehensible in places. Like Knutson's well-proportioned and unified discussion, the essay must be neither overstuffed with detail nor undernourished and thin.

Writing Assignments

1. First write down your impressions of a childhood experience similar to that described in the essay. List these impressions in phrases, not in complete sentences—and do so as quickly as you can. Don't think about the order in which they happened or about their relationships. When you have put them down, select the impression that stands out above the others. Now write about the experience, centering on this impression, and relating the others to it. Provide as much detail about persons, place, and time as you need to help the reader see and experience what you did.

2. Describe the moment when you first realized a truth about the physical world—perhaps your discovery that space is immense. Lead your reader gradually to this discovery through details about what you had previously believed, seen, and felt.

3. Rewrite the following paragraph, providing sufficient detail to make it possible for an audience unfamiliar with American driving habits and rules to drive on an expressway in an American city:

> On some expressways in American cities, it is difficult to enter the road even before or after rush hours. The close proximity of entrance and exit ramps are one cause of the problem. The road itself, with the increase and decrease in the number of lanes and the large number of directional signs, can also present problems. Urban driving habits, which developed perhaps as a response to the frequent congestion of cars and traffic tie-ups, create additional problems. The driver unfamiliar with urban expressway traffic needs certain personal qualities to survive the experience.

Generalizing from observation and personal experience

Generalizing from observation and reasoning inductively are similar but not the same: we make observations and develop impressions and ideas less systematically, and sometimes without being aware we are doing so. Our ideas are modified by our daily experiences, indeed to the point where they sometimes change completely, and later we cannot recall when or how they did. By contrast, inductive reasoning is based on carefully selected samples and considered evidence. Despite these differences, we can draw some important lessons from inductive reasoning about writing about our personal experience.

The essential consideration in inductive reasoning is the point at which we are ready to generalize from the evidence we have gathered—to make what is called the "inductive leap." How many examples, or samples, must be gathered before we are able to draw a conclusion from it?

The answer depends on how strong a conclusion we want to draw. Inductive reasoning often begins with a hypothesis we have chosen to test because we think it will predict more, if our testing confirms it, than another we did not choose. In other words, we want the hypothesis to lead to a strong and reliable conclusion.

Let us consider the conditions under which we make the induction. The so-called perfect induction can be made from an easily countable sample free of exceptions. For example:

All students in my high school own blue and gold sweaters.

None of the people on my block own Buicks.

These generalizations are easily verified; we can guarantee them if we test carefully that no exceptions exist. Of course, exceptions can and do turn up. But in the examples we have just looked at we are safe in considering such inductions perfect.

The difficulty with this type of induction arises when we draw more extended conclusions from them:

Since all students in my high school own blue and gold sweaters, all previous students probably did too.

Since none of the people on my block own Buicks, probably few people in the whole city do.

Notice that in these statements the sample (students in my high school, people on my block) is asserted to be typical of a broader class (all previous students, people in the whole city), not all of whose members we can assume were counted or surveyed. In other words, the reasoning proceeds on the assumption that what is true of a limited number of objects is probably true of a larger number of like ones.

The statement about all previous students may strike you as absurd. For it would seem to imply that the students cited are alike in their needs, of which the color of sweaters is one. Changing the statement to "*most* previous students probably owned blue and gold sweaters" does not make it more credible—unless we are given the additional information that blue and gold are the school colors. If we know that, the probability that all previous students owned blue and gold sweaters increases somewhat. But notice what happens when I make a prediction on the basis of my original sample:

Since all students in my high school own blue and gold sweaters, all future students probably will too.

Given the new information about the school colors, the statement is not absurd either, but I am now making the larger claim that present circumstances will probably not change.

What of the statement about Buick owners? If I can show that people on my block are typical of people in the whole city (a very difficult assignment), the statement has a claim to truth. Two requirements must be met in reasoning of this kind. The sample chosen must be typical of the class we are talking about, and the conclusion must be properly limited or qualified. Thus, I would have to show that income and preference in cars is about the same in the whole city as on my block, and I must be careful not to say or imply that I am talking about everyone in the city.

How strong a prediction can we make about future preference or purchase of cars? Here, again, we must know that the circumstances are likely to stay the same if our prediction is to be well based. The scientist usually can make stronger predictions than is possible in the situation described, because more can be known about chemical and biological processes and the like. If sulfuric acid is always produced when a hydrogen and sulfur compound combines with water, the chemist can predict with very high probability that the same will happen in the future. If unforeseen circumstances occur and sulfuric acid is not produced in subsequent experiments, the theory of chemical process must be reformulated.

These examples tell us that we do not usually reason from perfect samples such as those cited earlier. The chemical experiments we perform are not all the experiments with hydrogen and sulfur compounds and water ever performed. And when the sample involves making a count as with sweaters and cars, then where we cannot count them all (all the sweaters owned in the past and owned today), we must be sure that we have overlooked none and have counted enough of them to permit the inference we want to make. In selecting a limited number of American cars to test for frequency of repair, that is, in selecting a representative sample, we need to be sure we have selected a sufficient number and variety, and have selected them at random to assure that no special circumstances make the sample unrepresentative. Here is how Consumers Union, a product testing organization, defended the sample on which it based its comparison of Chrysler K-cars with GM X-cars:

> To represent the K-cars in our testing, we bought a four-door *Plymouth Reliant* sedan. We compared it directly with a four-door *Buick Skylark* sedan, representative of the X-cars. We bought each with its standard engine, automatic transmission, power steering, power brakes, air-conditioning, and other popular options. Equipped that way, both cars would list for more than $8000.
>
> For a more thorough comparison of these closely competitive cars, we also bought a *Dodge Aries* station wagon and a four-door *Chevrolet Citation* hatchback, equipping each with the larger optional engine, an automatic transmission, power steering, power brakes, and air-conditioning. And we bought a two-door *Plymouth Reliant* with the standard engine, a manual four-speed

transmission, manual steering, and nonpower brakes, just to see what Chrysler is offering those who don't want power accessories.

Consumers Reports, January 1981

Although Consumers Union chose a limited sample in order to compare the two cars it was interested in, it was justified in its method for several reasons. First, automobiles are manufactured according to standard procedures, so that every car is as much like every other of its class as is possible. Therefore, it should be safe to assume that one member of a class would indicate the characteristics of all other members of that class. Second, the cars were randomly selected, thus limiting further any intentional (or unintentional) bias. Third, a number of other cars were also chosen as controls so as to provide standards of measurement. By following this method, Consumers Union could provide its generalizations about the comparative performance of K-cars and X-cars with the strongest possible support.

But most of us are not able to support our generalizations in this manner. From the point of view of inductive reasoning, one might say that we usually rush to judgment. Popular prejudices, which we hear daily and often express ourselves, are usually based on very little or no evidence whatever. Often we make hasty generalizations on the basis of incomplete knowledge. To cite an example, what evidence exists to establish that teenagers are reckless drivers?

What constitutes pertinent evidence can be a matter of dispute. The reputation of teenagers as bad drivers probably arises in part from facts like the higher insurance rates they or their parents sometimes pay, and from assumptions about the nature of adolescence, such as that it is a time of adventure and risk-taking. Though these facts and assumptions may be well supported, they may be disputed on the basis of other facts, as for example, the large number of teenagers who have received excellent driving training in high school and whose driving records show no exceptional number of arrests, accidents, or convictions for misdemeanors or felonies. Even were the record of arrests and accidents exceptionally high for all teenagers (in contrast to other classes of drivers), the evidence would not be decisive. For the popular prejudice that teenagers are reckless drivers contains a judgment about character, something that is exceedingly difficult to define or verify in any group of people, whether teenagers or Jews or Italians or women.

An inductive essay

Consider the amount and quality of the evidence presented in the following essay on children's toys. The method of reasoning used in the essay is inductive in the ways we have been discussing.

GOOD AND BAD TOYS

by Elena Gianini Belotti

Toy merchants know very well that anyone who buys a toy as a present always has the child's sex in mind. To the typical request "I would like a toy suitable for a child of two" they will generally reply, "Is it for a boy or a girl?" It is true that there are some neutral toys, that is, toys considered suitable for children of either sex. These are generally unstructured materials—like the infinite variety of constructional toys, mosaics, puzzles; modelling materials such as plasticine, etc.; crayons and paints; musical instruments, although such instruments as trumpets are regarded as purely masculine; and so on. However, as soon as the toys consist of perfectly identifiable and structured elements sexual differentiation becomes clear. For girls there is a large range of toys which consists of miniaturized household fittings, such as kitchen and toilet sets; nurses' bags equipped with thermometers, bandages, sticking plasters and syringes, interiors of rooms such as bathrooms, bedrooms, babies' rooms; outfits to sew and embroider, irons, tea-services, electrical appliances, prams, baths and endless dolls with their outfits. Toys for boys are completely different: vehicles for land, sea and air, transport of all shapes and sizes, warships, aircraft carriers, nuclear missiles, spaceships, weapons of all kinds from perfect replicas of cowboy pistols to sinister-looking machine guns which differ from the real thing only by virtue of their greater safety, swords, scimitars, bows and arrows, and cannons; a real military arsenal.

Between these two groups of toys there is no place for choice or even concession. Even the parent most anxious to follow the inclinations and desires of the child in his choice of toys will not accede to a request for a machine gun for a girl or a tea-set for a boy. It would be impossible for him, he would consider it sacrilege. In any case, the differentiation that is imposed on boys and girls is such that "peculiar" tastes in toys after the age of four or five really signify that the child has not accepted his or her sexual role and that therefore something has gone wrong. Even when it is a question of "neutral" toys, that is, those suitable for children of either sex, the fact that they are intended for use more by males than females, or vice versa, is often obvious from the illustrations on the box or packaging. Typical of this are the plastic Lego bricks on whose boxes only boys are depicted building skyscrapers, towers, armoured cars, houses, etc. Lego, however, also sell special boxes of bricks for girls in which, just for a change, are the components for constructing complete kitchen fittings, including refrigerators, washing machines, and dishwashers; or drawing-rooms, bathrooms, bedrooms and so on. Obviously in this case the picture of a boy on the box gives way to that of a girl, the future wife/mother/consumer.

For some time the packets of a well-known brand of cookies have had on them a stylized drawing of a girl and a label saying "for girls." The back of the packet explains: "Girls! this product contains a surprise gift. Inside you will find dolls, cutlery, pots and pans, barrettes, bracelets, rings, powder-compacts, combs, irons, dolls, and many other delightful toys.'' The two basic elements of a girls' upbringing are perfectly respected in this list of toys: running the house and the care of her appearance. On the corresponding packet for boys it said: ''Boys! This product contains a surprise gift. Inside you may find: soldiers, airplanes, armoured cars, kits for making model vintage cars and ships, spinning tops, cap pistols, whistles, little trains, badges of football teams, and many many other lovely toys.'' All in order as one can see.

Parents maintain that children spontaneously choose toys which are suitable for their sex, thereby showing very precise tendencies. It is fairly common for a boy in front of a shop window to demand that his parents buy him a car, airplane or gun, until he is hysterical. Often the parents refuse him, producing various reasons (that it costs too much, he already has lots, etc.), but not that they consider it unsuitable for him. The boy's fixation establishes itself therefore on the certainty that it is a *permitted* toy and comes after a whole series of offers of exactly that type of toy, and an equally long series of refusals to requests for other sorts of toys. The obstinacy of the child in insisting on that particular toy is nothing but a final pseudo-choice between the choices which have already been made by the adults. The adult, in fact, will give in sooner or later to the child's requests, but it is very rare for an adult to give in when the child tries to insist on something which is considered unsuitable. I heard a boy of about five who was following his mother round the supermarket insist all the way round that his mother buy him some soap for doing the washing. ''But when can I do the washing?'' the child kept asking insistently. ''You can't do the washing,'' answered the mother inflexibly, ''you're a boy.'' ''But I want to do the washing with soap,'' insisted the boy and the mother did not even answer, until the boy went to the shelf, took a piece of soap and put it in the cart. The mother, furious, put it back and scolded him severely; at this point the child began to weep with rage. But the mother was unmoved. Surely after such a significant and unquestionable refusal that boy will no longer try to ask for washing soap but will orient his requests towards things which he has learnt to recognize as acceptable.

A young woman told me that she could still remember perfectly the acute sense of guilt she had felt when at the age of seven she had come upon her mother complaining to a friend that she did not like playing with dolls. From that moment on she forced herself to play with them, wanting as she did to comply at all costs with her mother's expectations, to be approved by her and to please her, even though she continued to prefer more active games.

I have often had occasion to observe that in nursery schools where the child is left a free choice of games, toys, and activities, that girls will play with cars, airplanes, ships etc., until the age of about three. I have seen girls of 18 or 20 months old spend hours and hours taking a whole lot of little cars, airplanes, helicopters, boats and trains from a bag, line them up on a carpet, and move them about with the same pleasure and the same concentration as little boys. In the same way one can see boys spending the whole morning washing, cleaning the tables and polishing shoes. Later this pattern of play disappears. Children have already learnt to ask for the ''right'' toy because they know the wrong one will be denied them.

An infant school teacher who is particularly sensitive to these problems told me that when she had brought into the class a toy consisting of nuts, bolts, screwdrivers etc., an excited girl quite pink with joy, took possession of it. As she was heading towards a little table with her newly acquired treasure, a little boy of about four leapt on her and tried to snatch it away from her. The teacher intervened, saying that he could have it later when the girl had finished with it. The boy reacted by saying "But it's mine, it's a boy's game." The teacher made it clear that there is no such thing as a boy's game or a girl's game, but that all games are the same and all children can play at them. The boy was astonished. He looked at the teacher as though she were quite mad and hung around the girl for a long time with a deeply perplexed air, revealing the state of mind of one who has assisted at the violation of a law he had believed immutable, and who cannot reconcile himself to it. It would be a good thing if such violations were made more often, whether by parents or by teachers. If the teacher had not made her point of view clear, both children would have received confirmation of what they already knew about toys and all the implications of sexual discrimination in this area. Whereas the little girl would have been humiliated and driven back into a state of inferiority, the boy would have had his superiority confirmed.

Testing inductive arguments

To test the strength of an inductive argument, we need to ask a series of questions. Since the tests logicians apply are complex and technical, we will consider only a few—those that we can apply in our everyday reasoning. The questions are these:

1. How typical and various are the examples from which the conclusion is drawn?
2. Is the sample a random one? Are there obvious or important exceptions or special circumstances that affect the conclusion?
3. Would additional evidence strengthen it?
4. Is the conclusion broader than the evidence permits?

We will consider Elena Belotti's argument in light of these.

1. In a controlled experiment, the investigator begins with a sample that previous experience suggests is typical and sufficiently various. Consumers Union assumes that its sample of K-cars is both. A different process occurs in Belotti's essay. Unlike Consumers Union, she does not collect a sample of toys to test for preselected qualities; instead she describes toys she has observed in various places—all of which show that toys exist in two groups, differentiated according to the gender of the child: "Between these two groups there is no place for choice or even concession."

It is probable that Belotti's observation was conditioned by her experience with other products. In other words, she noticed the difference between the toys she describes partly because she had seen the same difference in children's books and the like. Were she to look at toys in another store—at Christmas the following year—she would have good reason to consider these typical of children's toys throughout the country, and she would describe various ones to be found in different places.

2. In making our inspection, we look for possible exceptions or special circumstances that would qualify the conclusion or show it to be erroneous. Belotti has admitted exceptions to her generalization in taking note of neutral toys like crayons and musical instruments. The reader, then, must decide first whether the characterization of them as neutral is an accurate one, and if it is, whether Belotti is correct in her implication that these are exceptional rather than typical.

   Does the answer to this question depend on how many neutral toys one finds in the store? Not necessarily. If all toys were equally popular with buyers, the number of toys we are discussing would be significant. But if we counted toys that low sales suggest were unpopular for some reason, our conclusion would be adversely affected. If buyers favored neutral toys to a considerable extent over those differentiated sharply for boys and girls, we would have good reason to question the statement that we buy toys with gender in mind.

   Special circumstances can also affect the sample and therefore the conclusions drawn from it. If one kind of toy were displayed more at one time of the year than at another, we would have reason to question whether the sample was typical. We have no reason to believe that this is the case with those Belotti describes.

3. Additional evidence can strengthen an argument if it proves difficult to show that the sample is a typical one. Belotti, in fact, presents evidence in addition to the sample discussed in her opening three paragraphs. She describes a child and a mother she observed in a supermarket, and further observations she made in nursery schools. And she cites also the personal experience of a young woman and infant school teacher. It is worth repeating that the amount and variety of evidence presented depends in part on the audience to whom the essay is directed. Were Belotti writing to an audience consisting mainly of school teachers, the testimony of other teachers would carry even greater weight. The testing of an inductive argument depends in part on the readers, who consult their own experience and observations.

4. The conclusion would have been broader than the evidence allows

if Belotti argued that children's toys prove that sex differentiation exists in other areas—for example, in books for children, textbooks and movies. A conclusion or hypothesis must limit itself to a particular area of experience and be directly related to the facts it seeks to explain. But notice that her conclusion offers good evidence that sex differentiation may exist in these other areas; in other words, her discussion generates grounds for a number of other hypotheses that can be tested inductively. Arguments often develop from smaller arguments dealing with specific and limited areas of experience to broader ones. A generalization that is too broad or seems unsubstantiated has not taken account of areas we consider important.

Out of data and findings such as Belotti presents come hypotheses. But not all hypotheses are considered valuable in reasoning about matters of fact. Only those that can be verified through empirical testing are of concern to scientists and researchers. Thus the hypothesis that milk curdles when elves are present may be of interest to poets but is of no interest to scientists, who have no way to verify it.

Not only must each term or element of a hypothesis be capable of being tested (we must be able to find elves in order to test their powers), but the whole hypothesis must be relevant to the phenomenon we are trying to explain; the processes postulated must be clearly and simply connected to the phenomenon in ways that can be shown to exist in other phenomena or at least have been offered as an explanation. This is another way of saying that the hypothesis must be consistent with hypotheses previously established by other experiences and observations.

A hypothesis must not be more complex than the facts allow; that is one failing of the hypothesis that elves curdle milk, for there is a simpler explanation of curdled milk. And the hypothesis must be capable of refutation—of being shown to be false—if it is applied to another similar set of circumstances. If we could find elves and show that they curdle milk but not other liquids, our hypothesis would have some merit. A better hypothesis—that of fermentation—can be verified in a number of separate experiments with milk but not with all other liquids. This demonstration that the hypothesis is limited in its application is an essential means of verifying it.

Finally, the hypothesis must be capable of prediction, a characteristic of inductive reasoning with which we began this chapter. The purpose of making generalizations about things we have observed is to make predictions about things that have not been observed. If we say that certain toys promote stereotypical behavior in one group of children, we are in effect predicting that they will do so in other similar groups of children. And if they do, then the hypothesis has been verified in another important way.

A better example of this capability is to be found in scientific studies, for example, those of pesticides. The hypothesis that a certain pesticide is cancer-producing is not proved conclusively if a large number of people develop cancer in an area where the pesticide has been heavily sprayed, but we can say that the prediction supports the hypothesis conditionally. In presenting a hypothesis, a researcher usually specifies what consequences or behavior it will and will not predict.

The researcher is thus setting limits to the hypothesis. More than this, he or she is dismissing other hypotheses that are too weak to make predictions or too vague to be capable of verification. A hypothesis is also weak if it is capable of explaining everything, as elves can do. It is strong if it can explain one set of facts and do so better than other hypotheses. Were other hypotheses presented to explain the high rate of cancer in areas where the pesticide was sprayed, we could test them in the ways we have just discussed.

We can apply these restrictions and tests to generalizations in writing. For example, it is easy to assert that women enjoy more (or less) protection under the law than do men, or that "the female of the species is more deadly than the male." But we would have a hard enough time proving the first statement (or its opposite); we would certainly have a very hard time proving the second. Adding a qualifier like *perhaps* or *possibly* will not really limit these generalizations, for the statements still make very broad assertions that will require a considerable amount of supporting evidence. We will do better to let our generalizations develop carefully out of our experiences and observations, or out of research that we have conducted, limiting them to what our evidence supports. And we should try to verify them in some or all of the ways we have discussed.

Exercises

1. Write down two generalizations about people your age that you consider true of most of them, then two that you consider true of all of them. Defend the evidence that you believe supports each of your generalizations, and suggest ways to verify them.

2. From letters to the editor of a newspaper identify generalizations that you believe are based on insufficient evidence or faulty reasoning. Explain what is wrong with the evidence or reasoning in each instance.

3. The following article appeared without commentary in *The Cleveland Plain Dealer,* on November 2, 1979. Using the details in the article, discuss the conclusions that you think can be legitimately drawn about youth or violence in America or the present state of law and order. Then discuss the conclusions that in your opinion

are not supported by the evidence. In writing your essay, assume that your audience has read the article but needs to be reminded about essential or striking details. Some of these may be presented through summary, others through quotation from the article.

At least eight persons were killed this Halloween, including six hit by cars while out playing "trick or treat."

A teen-ager accidentally hanged himself in a Halloween skit at a Mormon church in Plattsburgh, N.Y., and the candy given to a small child in a Los Angeles suburb sent his mother to the hospital.

A youth on Long Island hit in both eyes by eggs hurled from a passing car was in critical condition, and police in Oklahoma City got reports that somebody was handing out treats doctored with alcohol.

A man in Kansas City, Kan., opened fire with a .22-caliber rifle when a group of youths started throwing rocks through his living room window, police said. A 17-year-old youth was killed and another teen-ager was wounded.

In Louisville, Ky., a woman and her small daughter were struck and killed by a hit-and-run driver, and in Hazelton, Pa., two teen-agers were killed by a car pulling around a tractor-trailer.

A 12-year-old Brooklyn, N.Y., youth was hit and killed by a car when he ran into the street to avoid a shower of eggs thrown by other youths. In Cedarville, N.J., an 11-year-old boy was fatally injured when he ran onto a road while playing with a friend.

Vincent DeBiaso, 15, of Valley Stream, N.Y., on Long Island, was listed in critical condition yesterday after undergoing surgery for the injury to his eyes. Police said the youth apparently tossed an egg at a car and six other youths riding in the car retaliated with a barrage of eggs of their own.

Derek Jennings, 8, of Lakewood, N.Y., found straight pins embedded in his gift of chocolate candy and he was taken to the hospital for X rays. No pins were found.

In Austin, Texas, the Seton Medical Center was providing a free candy X-ray service.

"We had a lot of calls about X-raying candy last year, so this year we decided to offer free candy X-ray service," said Cathy Fontaine, who was operating the $125,000 equipment.

Patrolman James Sullivan of Tiverton, R.I., probably summed up the feelings of law officers around the country after a night that saw the stoning of seven police cars and the burning of a drive-in movie screen in the tiny community.

"It's been one hell of a night," Sullivan said. "Just unbelievable."

All of Grundy County in Tennessee, and part of neighboring Rhea County, were plunged into darkness for 45 minutes when vandals broke into a Tennessee Valley Authority substation at Coalmont and cut the main switch.

The mayor of Snow Hill, Md., imposed a 9 p.m. curfew when a group of 200 pranksters started smashing windows in the downtown area. With the help of police dogs and a helicopter, state and local officers finally managed to break up the crowd and arrest three.

By contrast, an estimated 15,000 revelers celebrated peacefully in downtown San Francisco, with only a couple of minor stabbings on Castro St. Another 15,000 to 17,000 gathered without major damage near the University of Wisconsin campus in Madison.

In Knoxville, Tenn., three masked men posing as Halloween pranksters forced their way through the front door of the home of financier Fred R. Langley, tied up the banker, his wife and two children, and fled with a briefcase containing several thousand dollars in cash and jewelry.

In Inwood, N.Y., police said two 11-year-old girls were punched to the ground and robbed of their candy. Arrested and charged with second degree robbery were Daryl Ebb, 18, and Cynthia Baxter, 19.

In Hacienda Heights, Calif., Carol Mather, 38, sampled a miniature candy bar that her 7-year-old son Matthew had collected. She spat it out because it burned her mouth, tongue and lips and she was treated at a hospital for her injuries. Authorities warned that similar candy bars may have been injected with a caustic substance.

In Plattsburgh, N.Y., Mark Halilton, 14, was pretending to hang himself with a rope wrapped around his chest and neck and looped over a pipe during a skit at the Church of Jesus Christ of Latter-day Saints.

"The boy had been doing the trick for about 30 or 40 minutes without any trouble," said Lt. Robert Carpenter. "Then someone walked by and noticed he was unconscious."

The youth died a short time later at a hospital.

"It's the kind of trick I've seen kids do on television," Carpenter said. "Something just went wrong."

Forms of inductive reasoning

Sampling

Though sampling refers to statistical surveys, the dependence on numbers in argument is more common than many realize. Consider the statement in a newspaper editorial defending the quality of life in a particular city, "More people want to live in large cities than in small towns." Many readers will assume that the statement has the support of a carefully conducted survey, like those of professional pollsters. In fact, the statement may be a mere expression of opinion—based on what the writer believes is obvious. No statistical investigation has been conducted. This is the most common form of reasoning that pretends to be based on inductive processes. We can recognize it easily when the basis of the statement is not given.

We should note, however, that we depend on such inductive samples everyday, some of them not statistical in the technical sense. Our past experience gives us reason to believe that we can stretch a tank of gas until the end of the week because we have gotten the same gas mileage under the same circumstances in previous weeks. We act on such presumptions in other instances, without thinking about them at all. When we are forced to reason about our experience—perhaps in looking for an explanation for why we have run out of gas—we may give the basis of our past inferences some thought.

And we probably would give more thought to the newspaper statement if a surprising reason had been given: "More people want to live in large cities, where life is safer than it is in small towns." Let us suppose that the evidence for the word "safer" is the following: statistics on felonious assault for a particular year show that cities with populations below a million had a higher arrest ratio than cities above a million. In other words, the number of arrests per each one thousand people was, let us say, greater in Akron, Ohio than in Chicago or Los Angeles. Larger cities are therefore taken to be safer places to live because this accords with the popular view that the fewer the arrests the safer the city, despite the impression we may have of large cities. The same conclusion would be true if we based our sample on the number of convictions reported in newspapers.

To decide how strong the evidence is for the statement in our hypothetical example, we must first ask whether the cities included in our survey are representative of all cities in the United States. People will disagree on the definition of "representative": some will insist that cities with high unemployment be excluded from the sample, others may wish to include suburban areas from which many cities draw their labor force. In order to arrive at adequate support for our generalization, we must assure ourselves that our sample is typical of the cities we are concerned with.

Let us examine in a little more detail a familiar instance of sampling. Pollsters who predict the outcome of elections on the basis of sample precincts in various cities seek a distribution of characteristics in the population: sufficient variations of income, white- and blue-collar employment, race, ethnic and religious backgrounds, political affiliations, and the like. The distribution of characteristics justifies our considering the sample population typical of Americans generally. The pollsters' decision to seek certain qualities in their sample population and not others is itself determined by previous elections. The view that such a population is a likely predicter of an electoral outcome is warranted by what happened in the past. However, the presidential election of 1980, in which most pollsters failed to predict the Reagan landslide, shows that no prediction is certain; moreover, it also tells us that the degree of probability or the margin of error is sometimes hard to determine.

In deriving a fair sample relating to safe cities, special circumstances may affect the sample in unexpected ways. One of these might be the efficiency or integrity of the police department: a city with a history of police corruption would not be comparable to one without such a history. Because of corruption, the arrest rate for certain crimes might well be lower, though not necessarily the number of convictions.

The sample might also be affected by a hidden correlation that challenges the whole body of evidence, for example, a correlation between size and efficiency. Thus, a city as large as Los Angeles may be harder to police than one the size of Akron, regardless of the quality of the police department. Akron may be a desirable place to live because the lower traffic allows for a faster response time than is possible in cities with dense traffic. A careful gathering of evidence and interpretation of it may show, then, that the extent of crime in Akron is lower though the number of arrests is high.

Some further points need to be made about statistical reasoning. First, such reasoning about a group in general can affirm nothing about a particular member of it: statistics about groups or types of cities cannot tell us that any particular city is a safer place to live than any other particular city. It tells us nothing, then, about Akron or Los Angeles. It tells us only that the particular city falls into a group that may be a relatively safe or unsafe place to live.

Secondly, statistical evidence must be explained in light of other information the investigator possesses. A word like "safer" refers in this particular argument, let us say, to felonious assault. But clearly the word can refer to other conditions that affect safety, and the reader is entitled to know about these. Thus, the author of a statistical comparison of American cities, in 1975, notes that in the "amenities" of living, Seattle and Tulsa rank highest and Detroit, Chicago, St. Louis, and Newark the lowest. However, he does not assume that his ranking speaks for itself. Here is part of his interpretation:

Seattle's position at the top of the list seems plausible enough. As one who has been there, I can attest that it is an appealing and immensely civilized place. The high standing of Tulsa, however, may surprise most people who don't live there. It can be partly explained by the fact that the city has annexed substantial amounts of suburban territory. More than 93,000 Tulsa residents counted in the 1970 census—about 28 percent of the total population—would have been outside the city limits at the time of the previous census. By absorbing suburbs, with their lower crime rates, greater affluence and better health and housing conditions, a city can dramatically improve its vital statistics. Vigorous expansion into the suburbs in recent decades also enhanced the rankings of Indianapolis, Nashville, and Oklahoma City—to cite a prominent few.

Arthur M. Louis, *"The Worst American City," Harper's Magazine,* January 1975

Third and most important, statistical evidence must be presented as exactly as possible: the reader should know the basis of the sample. To say that Los Angeles has "more" crime than Akron, or "relatively less," is inexact and unclear. We need to know what kind of crimes are included in the generalization, and also the basis for defining "safe." As part of the exact presentation, we also must know the purpose of the reasoning, that is, the breadth of the generalization or conclusion—not just what kind of crime the statement refers to, but also what prediction if any the statement is making about future prospects.

Exercises

1. Pollsters, in seeking an accurate sample of opinion, try to phrase questions that do not contain a hidden bias. The bias in the following question is plain: "Is instant coffee the kind that a proud cook would serve friends or family?" The question clearly encourages a response that favors the brewed, though proud cooks may not necessarily be opposed to convenience in preparing foods. Be ready to explain how the following questions contain bias or avoid it, and to suggest alternatives for those that do contain it:

   a. "Wouldn't you rather own a Buick?"

   b. "How widespread is cheating in American high schools?"

   c. "Would you help a friend cheat on an examination if asked?"

   d. "Are taste and convenience of equal importance to you in deciding between instant and ground coffee?"

   e. "Have you made up your mind whom you will vote for?"

   f. "Is this a book you want on the shelves of a school library?"

2. Gregory A. Kimble describes the problem of estimating the population of Boulder, Colorado:

> When you look up a city's population in *The World Almanac*, you will find a comfortably definite number. For Boulder, Colorado, where I live, the number is 66,870. But what exactly does this mean? For example, does it include students at the university? Probably not, unless they have established residence in Boulder. How many additional people does this add to the population? There is no real way to answer the question because a student at the university turns out to be a statistical abstraction. The university operates under a legislated limit of 20,000 students per year. But this does not mean 20,000 human beings; it means 300,000 student credit hours. For purposes of limiting the size of the university, a "student" is 15 credit hours of work. Since the average student takes fewer than 15 credit hours of courses, the number of people is some indefinite number greater than 20,000. Some unknown fraction of them (those who are not Boulder residents) should be added to 66,870 to produce a more accurate figure for the population of the city.
>
> *—How to Use (And Misuse) Statistics*

Cite special problems that might well arise in estimating the population of the following:

a. a skiing resort town in Colorado

b. a port city

c. a town close to an army base

d. a city containing a junior college that has no dormitories

Writing Assignment

First analyze the appeals made to the audience in the cigarette ad on page 67. Consider what attitudes toward smoking the ad both states and implies. Then compare this ad with cigarette ads in a magazine with a general readership (*Time, Newsweek*) and with a more specialized readership (*Field and Stream, Ms.*) to determine how typical these appeals are in ads directed to general and special audiences. Include discussion of the problems you dealt with in making this comparison.

Analogy

Arguments by analogy are controversial when they are used alone in an effort to provide conclusive evidence. For example, if we argue that a nation is like a human being in moving through a life cycle from birth to death and then draw from this analogy *alone* the conclusion that the

New Belair... all the way to fresh!

NOW 30% LESS 'TAR'!
Just the right touch of menthol.
Never heavy. Never harsh.
The taste is pure fresh!

BELAIR

Now only 9 mg.!

9 mg. "tar", 0.8 mg. nicotine av. per cigarette by FTC method.

United States must decline as a world power, we have done two things. One, we have argued deductively about an inductive matter, for whether a nation is indeed like a human being, or whether the United States is at the height of its power or in decline can only be determined empirically. Two, we have claimed that our conclusion follows necessarily from our analogic premise. Since nations are not biological creatures and are very different from human beings, it may happen that the United States will not decline as a world power and therefore our argument cannot have the force of logical necessity (an idea we shall consider in the following chapter on deductive reasoning).

Properly used and qualified, however, an analogy can provide *some* evidence for a conclusion. Analogies are a common form of argument in inductive processes and occur frequently in our everyday reasoning. If we were in the process of buying a new car, we might reason that a new make would probably serve our needs as well as our previous car because of similar features. The new car, for example, has the same kind of engine (and the promise of higher fuel efficiency), the same body size, the same kind of transmission and dashboard accessories. These are points of similarity that influence our decision. We take account also of the points of dissimilarity—for example, the difference in color and body design—and decide that these differences are not important. In reasoning this way, through the series of parallels just cited, we have left open the possibility that the new car may turn out to be unsatisfactory. By using the word "probably," we recognize that the analogy does not guarantee that the car will be satisfactory and will serve our needs.

We more or less follow the same process when we formally present analogic evidence in an inductive argument. The main difference is that our formal argument is constructed more rigorously. We use many more samples, and more carefully insure that those samples are representative, than we do in everyday situations. We also look for many more points of resemblance in an analogy, and try to reduce or account for the differences between the objects or concepts that are being compared. Most of all, we make sure that our comparison is relevant, for, as we know from the old saying, "It's not right to compare apples with oranges." That is precisely what was wrong with our analogy between nations and human beings—we were comparing apples and oranges.

We said earlier that an analogy may be partial or limited, based on a few similarities only. It may also be total, based on all points of similarity. We had an example of partial analogy in Rosnow's essay on gossip:

> Indeed, there is a close parallel between the "rules" of gossiping and the principles of economic exchange. Thus the value of news increases in direct proportion to its scarcity. When the market for news expands, the amount of gossip in circulation will proliferate. Consumers of gossip have their own brand loyalties—columnists, tabloids, magazines.

This analogy is expanded later in the essay:

> The two-step flow of "non-essential news" from the news media to interme-
> diary opinion leaders who redistribute it to the public at large is another way
> in which gossip delineating the social environment is distributed. This can
> be compared to the economic trading pattern in which resources are brought
> to a central operation and from there dispersed.

The vividness of the extended comparison depends on the fundamental difference between the rules of gossip and the principles of economic
exchange. The sharper the differences, the more the similarities stand
out. In argument, we must be careful that the differences are not relevant
to the point at issue. If I am arguing by analogy that having been captain
of the football team makes me the top candidate for president of General
Motors, the difference in size and organization between the team and a
large corporation is a relevant difference that weakens the analogy to the
point of absurdity, though the similarities may be striking ones.

A good analogy instead begins with a defense of the basic analogy
itself, a statement explaining why it is warranted. George Bernard Shaw,
for example, builds an argument against vivisection—the practice of ex-
perimenting on living animals—and uses analogy in doing so. He begins
with the preliminary argument that people have a right to knowledge as
they have a right to live. Indeed, the two rights are analogous:

> The right to know is like the right to live. It is fundamental and unconditional
> in its assumption that knowledge, like life, is a desirable thing, though any
> fool can prove that ignorance is bliss, and that "a little knowledge is a dan-
> gerous thing. . . ."

But if they are analogous, Shaw continues, then the right to know cannot
be any more absolute than the right to live:

> But [a man] is by no means free to live unconditionally. In society he can
> exercise his right to live only under very stiff conditions.

And he drives his point home with a striking illustration:

> No man is allowed to put his mother into the stove because he desires to
> know how long an adult woman will survive at a temperature of 500° Fahr-
> enheit, no matter how important or interesting that particular addition to the
> store of human knowledge may be. A man who did so would have short work
> made not only of his right to knowledge, but of his right to live and all his
> other rights at the same time. The right to knowledge is not the only right;
> and its exercise must be limited by respect for other rights, and for its own
> exercise by others.
>
> Preface to *The Doctor's Dilemma*

Shaw's final statement argues that the analogy between the right to
know and the right to live is relevant to the issue of vivisection. And by

allowing us to test it by our own experience, Shaw allows us to regard it as a hypothesis or theory that we may qualify or reject if we wish.

To employ an analogy in argument, the writer must show that the analogy applies to the issue under discussion. If we do not as readers believe that the things being analogized are in fact comparable, we reject the analogy as false. To cite another example, we may not want to accept the argument that college freshmen need no more explanation of the curriculum they are undertaking than Army recruits need of their course of training. To see what may be wrong with the analogy, we will have to make its terms explicit and carefully examine the points of difference.

Exercise

Analyze the analogy employed in the following arguments, and evaluate them, stating whether the points of difference between the things being analogized limit or weaken the analogy:

a. Surely men who can manufacture a moon can learn to stop killing each other; men who can control infectious disease can learn to breed more thoughtfully than guinea pigs; men who can measure the universe can learn to act wisely in handling the materials of the universe. Why are we so pessimistic?

> Marston Bates, *The Forest and the Sea*

b. Violence begets violence. I believe that many policemen lost their lives in this country in the last ten or fifteen years because the police used excessive force, including deadly force, in making arrests. By analogy, I think that when the state applies the death penalty, this supports violence in a way which tends to increase violent crime.

> Patrick V. Murphy, *U.S. News and World Report*, April 6, 1981

c. We must eat if we want to live, and therefore we have a natural right to secure food. We must shelter ourselves if we want to live, and we therefore also have the right to seek adequate housing. In the same way, we have the right to own firearms. For we must also be able to protect ourselves if we want to live: we must be able to protect our persons, our property, and our means of livelihood from those who want to deprive us of them.

Writing Assignment

Let us work out an analogy based on the following:

driving an automobile
growing into adulthood

Here are a few similarities that should get the analogy started. We will put them side by side:

Driving an Automobile	Growing into Adulthood
the need of instruction	the need for parents and teach-ers
learning the steps of a process one at a time	learning the skills of life one at a time
the importance of trial and er-ror	learning by making mistakes
the first driving experience alone	first ventures into life without the help of others

Take the analogy from this point, and add to this list other similarities that you can think of. And then write down *significant* differences that show the limits of the analogy.

Now think of a topic idea or a thesis which this analogy will help you develop. You may wish to develop a second analogy in support of the same idea or thesis. Indicate in the course of your paragraph or essay the limits of the analogy—the extent to which the significant differences you have noted qualify it.

Cause and effect

A common way of thinking about cause is to look for something imme-diate and remarkable that precedes an event, an unusual occurrence that we think must be the explanation just because it is unusual. Although the cause may be immediate and extraordinary, these features are not what define the cause, and indeed they may be absent.

For example, the Japanese attack on Pearl Harbor is often cited as the cause of the American entry into the Second World War. The attack was the immediate cause, but we can cite it as one event that led America to enter the war since we know other facts. We know, for example, that Pearl Harbor had its not so immediate causes—long developing circum-stances that led to the Japanese aerial attack. We know that a complex series of decisions, acts, and conditions led to the attack. Indeed, events like Pearl Harbor are usually the result of a whole series of events and circumstances. It is common, however, to single out one of these events and speak of it as the "cause," as we just did of the attack on Pearl Harbor. For example, the American policy toward Japanese immigration into the United States and widespread stereotypes of orientals, in the decade before Pearl Harbor, has each been cited as a "cause." No doubt each of them did contribute to the growing hostility of the Japanese gov-ernment toward the United States in these years and later to the outbreak of war, but in citing them as causes we need to remember that they are circumstances or conditions that probably could not and did not alone result in the attack on Pearl Harbor.

Usually in identifying one or more circumstances or conditions like those just cited, we have not uncovered all the conditions that comprise the cause. All of these probably can never be known. And none may be remarkable or unusual. But we may have identified conditions in whose absence the event might not have occurred, and whose elimination might prevent future wars or lessen their impact on soldiers and civilians.

Nevertheless, the striking and unusual occurrence may play an important role in the *search* for causes. Consider how Rocky Mountain Spotted Fever (or Texas Fever) was thought about in the last century, before the role of ticks in the dissemination of the disease was understood. It was natural for scientists to look at all conditions to which cattle had been exposed, and it was also customary to seek unusual conditions, or perhaps one single condition or circumstance that would uniformly explain why some cattle contracted Spotted Fever and other cattle did not. In the absence of any knowledge whatever, all conditions that may have contributed to infection were dealt with: fields where herds became sick were burned, infected cattle were destroyed, healthy cattle were quarantined from other livestock.

In searching for a cause, we seek one or more conditions that are uniformly and invariably related to an effect. This means that we are seeking conditions that are always present when an event occurs. We call these necessary conditions, those in whose absence the event cannot occur. For example, Theobald Smith identified the cattle tick as the necessary condition of Spotted (or Texas) Fever, though he did not use this term:

> We may now consider it demonstrated that Texas . . . fever outbreaks in the North *are not possible without the cattle tick.* Isolated cases may occur through other agencies, perhaps, but no general infection of fields or pastures is possible without the cattle tick. Hence, in any doubtful disease where Texas fever is suspected, ticks should be looked for, and in doing so all the facts concerning the size of the ticks on animals in the acute stage and during recovery and their location on the body must be borne in mind. . . . But even when great care is exercised the ticks may be overlooked, or in a late fall infection they may have speedily disappeared. [a report published in 1893; italics added]

It is much harder to discover or formulate the sufficient condition of something that happens. For to do so is to claim that we know what condition will produce an effect. Defined simply, a condition is sufficient if the event must happen when the condition is present. Smith was not claiming to have discovered the sufficient cause of Spotted Fever, for he did not know all the agencies that might transmit the disease, as he observed in our excerpt. But complete knowledge is not needed to eradicate or reduce the incidence of a disease. Discovering one necessary condition may be enough to do so. Those seeking to prevent Spotted Fever needed only to prevent the infestation of cattle, but those seeking the cure of the fever needed to know more—specifically, what conditions together were sufficient to produce it. The sufficient cause in this instance is the sum of necessary conditions.

Scientific investigation continually increases our knowledge of necessary and sufficient conditions, and knowing this, scientists seldom claim to have discovered all the conditions of a disease or natural phenomenon. There is no way to be certain that all necessary conditions have been discovered, and for this reason causal analysis—like all inductive reasoning—can make a claim to probability only, a very high degree of probability sometimes, but only probability. New and unsuspected ways of looking at the physical world open new possibilities of investigation. Scientists, for example, have just recently begun to investigate genetic factors in cancer.

In seeking to establish a cause, we must define carefully the aim and scope of our investigation so readers will understand why the evidence presented is relevant. In stating that we are seeking evidence of a genetic factor in a class of cancers, and that some evidence exists to support this possibility (our justification for proceeding), we will have qualified our discussion in the proper way. We will have reason to proceed to a broader investigation if our limited experiment provides further evidence suggesting a broader hypothesis.

We have been discussing causal analysis in science. What about cause and effect reasoning in everyday life? Suppose we wish to trace our decision to attend college. We will cite the conditions we believe were present—and had to be present—to make the decision. We may separate the remote causes (events or influences occurring much earlier) from the immediate ones (those occurring close to the decision). Here is a short list of remote and immediate causes that might be included in such an analysis:

> the general respect for education at home
> the example of college-educated parents, brothers or sisters
> the advice of high school teachers and counselors
> the experience of older friends attending college
> the wish to become a doctor or engineer or lawyer or chemist
> a letter from a college offering a scholarship

Notice that the influence of any one of these does not depend on whether it is remote or immediate. All affect the decision but one of them may have been decisive, and we may want to emphasize this influence. Notice also that the weight given to any of the causes in analysis depends on our purpose. If we are writing to persuade a brother or sister to make a similar decision, we may emphasize the remote causes, for example, long-standing wishes and goals of the whole family.

Exercise

Find an argument or an exposition that traces the causes of an event or physical occurrence—the outbreak of the First World War, the Vietnam War, rainbows, photosynthesis, combustion. Analyze the causal reasoning, perhaps the distinction between remote and immediate causes, or the necessary and sufficient conditions that are stated or implied.

Writing Assignments

1. Trace the remote and immediate circumstances for a decision or event comparable to the decision to attend college. Discuss which of these circumstances were necessary—that is, had to be present for you to have made the decision.

2. First analyze the kinds of evidence used to support the statement, "team sports exert their deepest psychological appeal on males still." Then present evidence of your own to support or qualify or refute the statement:

   The appeal of mass spectator sports, even those thus conspicuously male-styled, can reach to women as well as to men, for there are women sports buffs, and intensive cultural conditioning, such as is being undertaken now in some places, will doubtless produce more. But team sports exert their deepest psychological appeal on males still. Those who go to a stadium to watch football are attending a social as well as a sports event, and for a wide variety of reasons: as a result the stadium crowd is very mixed. Those who watch football on television are captivated by the sport itself, and they appear to be overwhelmingly male, not only in fact but also, more important, in symbolic interpretation. The male television sports addict has become a near-mythological character in hundreds of cartoons . . . slumped alone with his can of beer before the screen under the glare of his justifiably outraged sports widow, who, according to one story, found that the only way to attract her husband during the World Series or a Super Bowl game was to dress in Astroturf. . . . The appeal of football has roots in the distant sociobiological past: the two sides are gaming for territory like two male robins or two Uganda kob bucks. The wife proposing to dress herself like a bit of territory shows greater wisdom than perhaps she consciously knows, although it is not at all impossible that she senses the deep relevance of her proposal.

Walter J. Ong, *Fighting for Life*

3. Analyze the reasoning in the following editorial from the *Akron Beacon Journal,* March 1, 1977. Give particular attention to the use made of sampling and analogy:

In several test drives on area interstate highways, a Beacon Journal reporter, who kept his car speedometer at 55 miles per hour, found he was overtaken by about seven vehicles for every one he passed.

From that and similar reports around the country, some might conclude that, because most motorists exceed the speed limit, the limit should be hiked back to 60 or 65 or 70. That way, everybody would be driving within the law once again.

That logic makes about as much sense as urging that would-be bank robbers be given a pile of cash by the government to rid them of their desire for more money.

No matter how rich people become, there will always be those who will attempt to obtain additional wealth through extra-legal methods. And no matter how high the speed limit, there will always be those who routinely will exceed it. So what else is new? Perhaps the only effective way to halt the mad rush on the highways would be to prohibit automakers from building cars capable of exceeding the speed limit. Matter of fact, it always has puzzled us why Detroit builds cars capable of 110 mph—twice the speed we're legally permitted to drive.

The arguments for a national 55-mph limit haven't changed one bit from the time the lower ceiling first was established by Congress on a temporary basis in 1973, and then made permanent in 1974. Backers said the lower limit would reduce gas consumption and cut highway fatalities.

The figures bear out those assertions. In 1973, the U. S. traffic death toll reached 55,096, but fell 16 percent to 46,049 in 1974. Even though average speeds have been inching back up since then, traffic fatalities have held fairly constant—44,782 in 1975 and 44,807 in 1976.

Although drivers no longer feel the urge to conserve gasoline that they did in 1973 during the Arab oil embargo, it has been amply demonstrated that lower speeds mean more miles to the gallon. In 1974, Americans cut gasoline consumption by 4.2 percent from 1973 levels, primarily by driving fewer miles at lower speeds.

In our view, it's not the speed limit that should be changed. It would be shortsighted for this nation to boost its gasoline consumption at a time when energy supplies are diminishing, and to follow a policy that would mean the deaths of thousands more motorists annually, just so some drivers could get from here to there faster.

Rather, we believe federal and state governments and highway user groups should do a better job of alerting the public to the benefits of the lower speed limit.

Law enforcement officials also need to keep the heat on. The pressence of patrol cars strategically stationed in median strips of superhighways usually serves as a reminder to most drivers to reach for their brakes.

Organizing the inductive essay

Exposition and argument are most closely related in the inductive essay. This is because an argumentative point may develop out of, or be supported by a gathering of details; it may also develop out of a causal analysis, or a statistical report. All of these are expository in form. For example, we may trace the effects of a certain pesticide (exposition), then argue that on the basis of these effects the pesticide is safe or that it should be banned.

We saw in the argumentative essay outlined in the previous chapter that the narrative or background is expository. Similarly, the confirmation or refutation may contain exposition, a presentation of facts in support of the argument being made.

The methods of research we use to gather these facts are often discussed as part of the presentation. In this section, we will focus on a particular organization of the inductive essay that includes discussion of research methods. To summarize these methods briefly: if our essay is on the effects of pesticides, facts may be discovered in the laboratory or field, in analyzing the chemical properties of pesticides and examining their effects on plants and animals, or in the library, in books and articles on pesticides by scientists and other authorities. The evidence itself may be experimental, as in a report on the use of a pesticide over a particular area of cultivated land; or statistical, as in the report on cancer deaths in areas of high and low use of a particular pesticide; or it may simply consist of conclusions reached by an informed observer who visited an area thought to be affected by pesticides. And, as we have seen, the evidence may consist of reasoning from analogy or causal analysis.

Here is an outline of how an essay on the effects of pesticides might be organized, with attention to the methods of research used to gather the facts of the essay:

Stating the topic of the essay—the problem or question under consideration. The problem may be stated in general terms, as for example, through a statement of the widespread concern about the effects of pesticides on the environment; or in terms of a particular event or controversy, like the use of a pesticide to control the infestation of California farms and orchards by the Mediterranean fruitfly. General concerns and particular controversies may, of course, both be stated.

Providing background on the problem or question. Before introducing current research, we may review the history of the controversy and methods of research used in the past. The use of Malathion to combat the Mediterranean fruitfly has aroused controversy in California. In her pioneering study of the effects of pesticides, *Silent Spring,* Rachel Carson, in 1962 reviewed the current research on Malathion and other pesticides like Parathion and D.D.T., and predicted the impact of their continued use on the environment and food supply. Additional research has been conducted since the publication of *Silent Spring,* and though much of it has been superseded by current research, a review of past research may help the reader to understand better the present debate over Malathion and other pesticides.

Explaining the methods of research used. The inductive essay may be a report of a laboratory or consumer agency concerned merely with stating the findings of experiments with Malathion. Or it may be an argument for or against the use of the pesticide, based on findings of various investigators. The method of investigation may be described briefly or at length. A report appearing in a scientific journal will usually present a more detailed account and defense of methods than an article in a popular magazine like *Time* or *Newsweek.* In its published reports, Consumer's Union usually gives a detailed explanation of the methods used to test a particular product.

Presenting data or findings. The presentation of data usually constitutes the largest part of an inductive essay or report. How detailed this presentation is depends on the audience—on its knowledge of the subject and the information it already possesses. Sometimes all findings are reviewed, and sometimes only those considered decisive to a particular issue.

Stating qualifications. As we noted earlier, scientists usually state the limits of their research and the hypotheses they derived from it. In presenting statistical information on cancer rates in areas where pesticides are widely used, researchers will state the size and nature of the sample studied, indicate special circumstances that may affect correlations, and describe clearly how the data applies to a current issue. They may also defend hypotheses on the basis of their ability to make important predictions. By doing so, researchers are showing how these hypotheses can be verified. In highly technical papers, more advanced methods of verification may be discussed. Where contradictory experimental or statistical evidence exists, researchers may explain why their evidence and methods are better than those of other researchers. Objections to their methods and findings may also be anticipated, stated, and answered.

Stating further questions raised by data. No research undertaking is capable of answering all questions or even of formulating all those that may prove important. It is customary for researchers to state at the end of essays or reports what further questions need to be answered and what data secured.

Providing summary. It is customary also to summarize the results of the investigation—the methods used, the data found, the hypotheses based on the data and applied to particular questions or problems. Sometimes this summary appears as an abstract of the discussion appended to it.

The concerns we just outlined may appear in a different order from that shown here. Even the "inductive order" in which facts are presented and conclusions are drawn can vary. Thus, an account of a scientific experiment may present the steps of the experiment in the order performed, then may draw conclusions about what was done or discovered. But the steps need not be presented chronologically. They may be presented instead in the order of their importance to the discovery made. In the same way, the various observations made during a walk down a city street may be presented in the order of their occurrence, or instead in the order of rising importance or interest—what we call the order of climax.

Prewriting

The advertisements that appear on the following pages are taken from an issue of a widely read magazine. Examine them first in the light of the following questions:

1. Do the three ads on the following pages seek to capture your attention in the same way? Are there differences in how they each do so?

2. In general, are they seeking to sell bicycles or biking equipment through the same appeals? What are these appeals?

3. Notice that the ads are for different kinds of equipment. Are the claims for each different—or are they similar? For example, is each claiming that the product shown is the best that can be bought for the money?

The easiest way to rack 'n roll.

Your ordinary, roof-mounted bicycle carrier can be, to say the least, a problem.

Even if you manage to survive lifting your bike up, over and onto the carrier, it's no picnic strapping it down securely.

If you're tired of all that hassle, Schwinn Dealers now stock a line of remarkable, new carriers called Top Decks™.

They're everything ordinary carriers aren't.

First off, Top Decks are incredibly easy to rack and unrack, thanks to a bit of ingenious engineering.

A unique loading tray attaches to your bike. The whole shebang—tray, bike and all—slides snugly into the carrier.

Depending on your car, you can carry up to six bikes, each on its own tray, so they won't rub together.

There are Top Decks that fit roofs, trunks and hatchbacks. With trays that fit virtually any kind of bike, except tandems.

There are even special trays for skis or luggage or canoes or, yes, kayaks.

What's more, Top Decks even look nice empty because they ride so low.

So now you can see why we think these are, by far, the best carriers around.

And why we think they'll be a hit with you, too.

See the Yellow Pages for your nearest dealer.

SCHWINN

© Schwinn Sales Inc. 1981

Morgan Grips™ Keeps You Ahead...by Fitting Your Hands.

Transamerican record holder John Marino *will be using Morgan Grips in his challenge race against the British road champ this summer.*
LA to New York — 12 days, 3 hours, 41 minutes.

Designed for hands, not handlebars. Morgan Grips™ are comfortably large where the palm needs a broad surface, yet intelligently slender where precise fingertip control is desired. The result is increased control and feeling of oneness with your bike. The grips' unique internal ribbed shock absorption system cushions your hands from tiring, nerve damaging road vibrations. Installation is simple. There's no need to remove hand brakes nor are special tools required. Lightweight, aerodynamically designed Morgan Grips™ will enhance even the most custom bike. Get control of your bike with Morgan Grips™. John Marino did.

morgan grips

morgan concepts

June 1981   79

4. What conclusions can you reach about the readership of the magazine? Can you determine anything from the three ads about the sex or the age or general interests of these readers? Would you expect to find the same kind of presentation in other ads for biking equipment in the magazine?

5. Is it safe to infer from these ads that *all* magazines that contain ads for biking equipment would have the same kind of ads—that is, ads that make the same kind of appeals?

6. How much do such magazines tell you about people who own bicycles in the United States?

You have now done some preliminary thinking about these ads, and it is time to test some of the conclusions you have drawn about them. Here are some that you may have reached about the readership:

> The readers of the magazine are probably interested in the technical features of biking equipment.
> These readers are interested in performance more than in appearance.
> These readers are probably bicycle dealers.
> Most of these readers are men.

The first of these conclusions we probably would agree is supported by this limited amount of evidence. But the conclusion is a trivial one: it will not take you very far, in your inductive essay, because few if any other conclusions can be drawn from it and tested inductively by the ads and other evidence from the magazine.

Consider the other three conclusions. Look again at the ads, and write down some of the evidence that would support or refute them. Having done this, select the conclusion that in your opinion is most strongly supported by the evidence. And give a few minutes to considering why the remaining two are, in your opinion, less well supported or not supported at all. Notice that you are drawing your evidence from the three ads for equipment, and not from assumptions like the following:

> People generally care more about performance than about appearance.
> Only bicycle engineers and manufacturers care about performance specifications.
> Women care more about looks than performance, and therefore would not read a magazine that focused on performance specifications.

Though one or more of these statements might be supported by the ads, notice that they are *beliefs* held prior to examination of the ads—beliefs that may have derived from other experiences and observations and are thought to be well founded. Or they may be held as true without ever having been examined.

We can, however, talk about the readers to whom the three ads are directed without generalizing about all bicycle engineers or all women.

And we can draw from a well-founded inductive generalization several *limited* conclusions that can be tested inductively. Let us do this now. Write a trial opening paragraph, introducing your discussion and stating a generalization that you consider supported by the incidence of the ads. You may want to choose one of those given above. Develop this conclusion in one or more paragraphs—giving details from the ads in support of it. Be sure to select these details carefully. The more relevant the evidence you cite, the less of it you will need.

One way to test this evidence—to show the reader that it is well supported—is to discuss it in light of the four questions stated earlier:

1. How typical and various are the examples that support the conclusion?
2. Are there obvious or important exceptions that qualify it?
3. Would additional evidence strengthen it?
4. Is the conclusion broader and is greater probability claimed for it than the evidence warrants?

Of course, you need not discuss these questions directly as they are stated here, nor do you need to discuss all of them. But you can discuss what seem possible exceptions to your conclusion, and you can defend the breadth of the generalization—your justification for drawing as broad a generalization as you have. For example, if you are defending the proposition that the ads appeal to an interest in performance, you might show how the illustrations do so. And you can argue that the amount of detail relating to performance gives weight to the conclusion.

Here now is your opportunity to draw further hypotheses that can be tested inductively. Consider this proposition:

These readers are interested more in performance than in looks.

Let us assume that you have been able to support this proposition through details from the ads. The following conclusion might be derived:

Interest in performance extends to various kinds of biking equipment.

But what about the following conclusion?

The articles and reviews of the magazine appeal to this interest in performance, and give specific details that satisfy this interest.

We clearly have enough variety in the advertisements to test the first of the conclusions, and the details of the ads also allow us to test the second. But to test the third, we need to look at the whole magazine. These ads appeared in a recent issue of *Bicycling,* and you need only examine an issue published in the last two years to test the generalization. You have now enlarged the scope of your investigation: from an examination of a limited number of ads you have proceeded to examination of the whole magazine. You may if you wish compare *Bicycling* with another widely read magazine, identical to it in the kind of articles or reviews published, and the kind of advertising presented. If you limit your examination to *Bicycling,* you will be characterizing the readership of that magazine only, but this limitation does not mean that you have to restrict your speculations about all such magazines. On the basis of this limited generalization, you can formulate a hypothesis:

> Readers of biking magazines are more interested in performance than looks.

And you can test this hypothesis through comparison with similar magazines including *Consumers Reports* which contains occasional articles on biking equipment.

A wider study will produce hypotheses and finally generalizations that can serve the purposes of argument. We have focused so far on the general readership of one type of magazine. What if we widened our study to contrast magazines directed mainly to women (*Redbook, Ladies' Home Journal, Ms.*) and those directed mainly to men (*Male*)? Would evidence drawn from these support the view held by some that, in clothes or cars or other products, women are interested in appearance, men in quality or performance? Or is it possible to conclude from the feature stories or fiction that men are more interested in adventure or conflict than are women? If we examined a magazine directed to both men and women, could we distinguish ads on the basis of possible appeals to one or the other sex exclusively?

In choosing a magazine, or a group of magazines, to examine for your essay, let your selection be guided by an argumentative question such as those we have just asked. You may wish to formulate a hypothesis before beginning your search, or you may begin with an initial hypothesis that can be retained or reformulated as your examination proceeds. Choose an idea for investigation that can be supported by the evidence at hand. Do not try to overreach your resources. For example, do not try to determine the interests of men or women in the last forty years, for that would require an examination of a wider variety of evidence than either time or facilities would generally allow, especially for a student paper.

A sample outline

Here is an outline of the inductive essay we have been planning:

Statement of the topic
Statement of the background—a description of evidence studied
Statement of the initial generalization
    Details that support this generalization

Defense of the generalization and perhaps of the methods of research
Statement of other generalizations suggested by the evidence
  Details supporting these generalizations
Discussion of other evidence drawn from the same magazine in support of generalizations presented so far
  Comparison with evidence from a second magazine to test broader generalizations
Summary of findings

To this outline may be added the following:

Statement of qualifications
Further questions for investigation

Notice that the outline moves toward increasingly broader generalizations, tested inductively at each stage of the argument. These generalizations result in a final conclusion, perhaps an argumentative point such as we raised earlier, or a summary of the ideas and evidence presented if the essay is purely expository.

Instead of organizing the essay in the way we have just illustrated, we may decide to move from descriptions of the ads to descriptions of other features of the magazines, and conclude with a series of generalizations drawn from this evidence.

We have now seen several possible ways of analyzing evidence, deriving conclusions, and organizing the evidence and conclusions. There are still other ways of doing so—ways suited to different audiences. In choosing an organization for our essay, we generally keep a possible audience in mind. In writing our essay, we choose details appropriate to this audience. An audience of bicycle owners will not require the same amount of detail or the same kind of information that an audience unfamiliar with bicycles would require.

Exercises and Writing Assignments

1. Keep a journal in which you record observations of people and experiences. Organize these observations into an essay, selecting those details which relate to a central impression or idea.

2. Write an autobiographical essay in which you describe an unexpected discovery. Join this description to a narrative that places the reader in the experience. Provide as much detail as is necessary to allow the reader to experience what you did.

3. Evaluate Belotti's argument (pp. 55–57), with attention to the processes of inductive reasoning present in her article. Develop your ideas in a well-organized essay that contains the following:

   an introduction to Belotti and explanation of her approach and evidence;

a consideration of her reasoning;

your response to her conclusions, including supporting or coun-
ter-evidence from your experience and observation.

4. Examine letters to the editor of a newspaper or news magazine to
classify the kinds of evidence that have been given for the conclusions drawn.

5. Perform the same classification for a series of magazine advertisements. Discuss how seriously the evidence is meant to be taken.

6. Evaluate the use of sampling in a series of advertisements. Indicate
whether the various samples meet the inductive tests presented in
this chapter.

7. Distinguish the uses of statistical evidence, analogy, and causal
analysis in the following passage from a contemporary discussion
of population and food supply:

> Let us return to the question of food. Responsible agronomists report
> that before the end of the year millions of people if unaided might starve
> to death. Half a billion deaths by starvation is not an uncommon esti-
> mate. Even though the United States has done more than any other na-
> tion to feed the hungry, our relative affluence makes us morally
> vulnerable in the eyes of other nations and in our own eyes. Garrett
> Hardin who has argued for a "lifeboat" ethic of survival (if you take all
> the passengers aboard, everybody drowns) admits that the decision not
> to feed all the hungry requires of us "a very hard psychological adjust-
> ment." Indeed it would. It has been estimated that the 3.5 million tons
> of fertilizer spread on American golf courses and lawns could provide
> up to 30 million tons of food in overseas agricultural production. The
> nightmarish thought intrudes itself. If we as a nation allow people to
> starve while we could, through some sacrifice, make more food available
> to them, what hope can any person have for the future of international
> relations? If we cannot agree on this most basic of values—feed the hun-
> gry—what hopes for the future can we entertain? Technology is imitable
> and nuclear weaponry certain to proliferate. What appeals to trust and
> respect can be made if the most rudimentary of moral impulses—feed
> the hungry—is not strenuously incorporated into national policy?
>
> James R. Kelly, "The Limits of Reason," Commonweal, September 12,
> 1975

8. Identify the causes and effects discussed in the following passages
from one of the most influential essays ever written on population
and food supply. Then suggest what other effects and conclusions
might be derived from the analysis:

Through the animal and vegetable kingdoms, nature has scattered the
seeds of life abroad with the most profuse and liberal hand. She

has been comparatively sparing in the room and the nourishment necessary to rear them. The germs of existence contained in this spot of earth, with ample food and ample room to expand in, would fill millions of worlds in the course of a few thousand years. Necessity, that imperious all pervading law of nature, restrains them within the prescribed bounds. The race of plants and the race of animals shrink under this great restrictive law. And the race of man cannot, by any efforts of reason, escape from it. Among plants and animals its effects are waste of seed, sickness, and premature death. Among mankind, misery and vice. The former, misery, is an absolutely necessary consequence of it. Vice is a highly probable consequence, and we therefore see it abundantly prevail, but it ought not, perhaps, to be called an absolutely necessary consequence. The ordeal of virtue is to resist all temptation to evil.

Thomas Robert Malthus, *An Essay on the Principle of Population* (1798)

Distinguish what Malthus would have considered necessary and sufficient conditions of vice and virtue, on the basis of his analysis.

9. Develop an inductive argument relating to a current social problem with which you have had personal experience, for example, the consumption and waste of energy. Suggest what might be done to solve the problem through an account of practices you have observed. Introduce a supporting analogy in the course of the argument.

Chapter Four

The Deductive Essay

Inductive and deductive arguments

Inductive arguments attempt to establish factual truths. In such arguments, particulars of experience, analogies, samples and other inductive evidence are used to reach general conclusions. Their concern, then, is with the material truth of the conclusions they propose and the degree of probability the evidence establishes. The better the evidence, the higher the probability.

Deductive arguments, by contrast, begin with statements assumed to be true and look to see what other statements these imply. These statements, to be more specific, are always propositions—statements that we can claim as true or deny as false. Here is an example of how a deduction is made from such statements. We begin as follows:

All freshmen at this university are Texans.

We then state another proposition:

All residents of my dorm are freshmen.

From these propositions we infer that all residents of our dorm are Texans. We call propositions used to reason in this way premises.

We shall see that there are correct and incorrect, or valid and invalid ways, of reaching conclusions in deductive arguments. In all such arguments, if the premises are true and the reasoning is valid, then the conclusions must be true also. This is the great strength of deductive reasoning: it allows us to see what truths can be derived from other statements we believe to be true.

Deductive reasoning is much more familiar than the arrangement of statements above may suggest. We stated the argument about freshmen, above, in a formal way, but this is not how we usually hear it. This is the familiar expression of it:

> Since all freshmen at this university are from Texas, and all those in my dorm are freshmen, all of them must be Texans.

It may even be stated in an abbreviated way, with one of the propositions implied:

> Since all those in my dorm are freshmen, all of them must be Texans.

Or even the following:

> Everyone in the freshman dorm must be from Texas.

We encounter deductive arguments in everyday conversation, in newspapers and magazines, in textbooks. Here are two brief arguments, deductive in different ways:

> For if the brain is a machine of ten billion nerve cells and the mind can somehow be explained as the summed activity of a finite number of chemical and electrical reactions, boundaries limit the human prospect—we are biological and our souls cannot fly free.
>
> Edward O. Wilson, *On Human Nature*

> Individuals have rights, and there are things no person or group may do to them (without violating their rights). So strong and far-reaching are these rights they may raise the question of what, if anything, the state and its officials may do.
>
> Robert Nozick, *Anarchy, State, and Utopia*

Propositions

Wilson and Nozick offered two different kinds of arguments. We can recognize the differences very quickly just by examining the sentences in both arguments. Wilson's sentence says in effect that *if* it is true that the brain is a machine, *then* humans are limited in what they can do. By contrast, Nozick's two sentences say in effect that *all* individuals have rights, that *no* person can do certain things to them without violating these rights, and therefore *no* government or official can do certain things, perhaps anything, to individuals. We have just converted the sentences of Nozick and Wilson into propositions.

A proposition, as we noted earlier, can be defined as a statement that claims something is true or denies it as false. It is the basic element in an argument and is different from other kinds of sentences, such as exclamations, commands, or questions. For example, we would never ask a person who said "hooray" whether he or she was speaking the truth, just as we would not raise that question with someone who shouted "halt" or asked "where do you keep the beer?" But underlying the exclamation, command, and question are ideas or experiences that can be expressed as propositions which are either true or false and therefore can be argued.

In logical discourse, propositions follow certain formulas. Wilson's statement, for example, follows the formula of "if . . . then," although the "then" part has been suppressed. This sort of statement is called a conditional or hypothetical proposition, and is often used by scientists in constructing arguments. A conditional proposition never makes an absolute claim that its subject is true, although, as in Wilson's case, it may be presented as having a high degree of probability. Nozick, by contrast, follows the formula for a certain kind of categorical proposition.

Categorical propositions are absolute statements that allow for no exceptions, which is to say that they are unconditional statements. All categorical propositions are either true or false; they cannot, for obvious reasons, be both or a little of one and some of the other. In short, there are no degrees of truth in categorical propositions, as there may be in hypothetical generalizations. If there is one example that contradicts a categorical statement, the statement is false. For this reason, great care is exercised in writing categorical propositions.

In traditional logic, there are four basic propositional forms. These were derived from the ancient Greek philosopher Aristotle. Here are examples of these forms:

1. All airline pilots are experienced flyers.
2. No thieves are honest people.
3. Some insurance companies are responsible firms.
4. Some politicians are not liars.

Each of these propositions has certain features in common. All of them contain a subject that is linked through a form of the verb *be* to a predicate. In our examples, the verb "are" links the subject, such as "all airline pilots," to the predicate of the proposition, which here is "experienced flyers." All of the propositions also make a claim about two classes (collections of people or things that have common characteristics), which are represented by the subject and predicate: for example, our second proposition asserts that no individual member of the class of thieves belongs to the class of honest people. Finally, all four propositions can be divided according to whether they are affirmative or negative statements and whether they are universal or particular ones.

Our first proposition is a universal affirmative statement. It says that the first class (all airline pilots) is included within the second (experienced flyers). This propositional form always begins with the word "all" or implies it, as in our example from Nozick. The word "all" is called a *quantifier* and serves in all propositions of this kind as a signal indicating that a universal statement is being made. Our second proposition is a universal negative statement indicating that no member of the first class (all thieves) is a member of the second class (all honest people). In this form, the word "no" serves to indicate the universal quantity of the proposition as well as its negative quality. Our third proposition is a particular affirmative statement indicating that some members of the class of insurance companies are included within the class of responsible business firms. The quantifier "some" asserts that fewer than all members, perhaps only one member, of a class named by the subject belong to the class named in the predicate. The quantifier "some" serves also to make our fourth proposition a particular negative statement. In this case, our proposition is saying that at least one member of the class of politicians is not a member of the class of all liars.

You will by now have noticed that our quantifiers make assertions about all or some of the members of the class indicated by our subject terms. Our predicate terms, however, do not have corresponding signals indicating whether the classes they name include all members. For example, our universal affirmative proposition made an assertion about *all* airline pilots but it did not claim anything about *all* experienced flyers for a very good reason. There are experienced flyers that are not airline pilots, yet it is conceivable that some day they may be. Therefore, universal affirmative propositions say nothing about *all* members of the class named in the predicate. Particular affirmative propositions make no assertions about *all* the members of either class named in the statement. In other words, affirmative statements, whether universal or particular, do not assert anything about *all* members of the class named by the predicate. The opposite is true for the negative propositions, both universal and particular. Our universal negative proposition says in effect that there are no honest people who are thieves, just as there are no thieves that are honest people. So too, our particular negative proposition says that *every* member of the class of liars is *not* one of the particular politicians included within the quantity designated by "some." In other words, we can infer from negative propositions a universal quantity for the predicate.

Categorical propositions are the basic elements of categorical syllogisms. These syllogisms are for many people the models of deductive, indeed of all logical reasoning. In categorical syllogisms, the propositions we have been discussing provide the forms for the two premises and the conclusion. The categorical nature of these propositions makes the syllogism have absolute force. When or if the propositions are accepted as true, and the form or pattern of the syllogism is correct, then the reasoning is compelling and can be resisted only with the utmost difficulty.

Forms of deductive arguments

When propositions are arranged according to a specific pattern we have a syllogism, the basic form of deductive arguments. The term "syllogism" is derived from Greek and has as its root the word *logos*, which in ancient Greece meant both "word" and "reason." *Logos*, as we can easily see, is the origin of our term "logic," and is the underlying concept of deductive reasoning.

Strict deduction in ordinary language is mainly concerned with the careful arrangement of words in a certain order to make propositions and then the equally careful ordering of these propositions in specific patterns to make an argument, the conclusion of which can be judged as either true or false. We have just seen how some propositions are structured. Syllogisms, the patterned form of deductive arguments, use two propositions as premises and one as a conclusion. There are several kinds of deductive arguments, two of which we have already glanced at in our examination of propositions: hypothetical arguments of the "if . . . then" form and categorical arguments. We will now look more closely at these and at several others.

Categorical arguments

Traditional logic was concerned primarily with categorical syllogisms. Here is a categorical syllogism:

> All individuals are people who have rights.
> Children are individuals.
> Therefore children are people who have rights.

In everyday discussions, we find such arguments stated informally:

> Though we seldom think of children as individuals, they are individuals like ourselves, and as individuals have rights like we do.

The logician words the argument as exactly as possible to test its soundness. Notice that the premises would be asserting other matters if they said that all individuals *enjoy* rights or that children are *potentially* individuals. In wording our statements, we must say exactly what we mean.

The predicate of the conclusion (*people who have rights*) is called the major term; the subject (*children*), the minor term. The premise containing the major term is called the major premise; the premise containing the minor term, the minor premise. The term that appears in the premises but not in the conclusion (*individuals*) is called the middle term.

When the premises are so stated that if true the conclusion cannot be false, the argument is said to be valid. The conclusion follows necessarily. The pattern we illustrated above is only one of many valid forms a syllogism may have (in our discussion we will consider this one only). *Validity* is a judgment we make about the process of reasoning, not about the truth of any statement; we say that the argument is valid if the premises force the conclusion.

But notice what happens in the following argument:

All adults are gamblers.
All smokers are adults.
Therefore, all smokers are gamblers.

Both premises are obviously false, yet the argument is valid because the conclusion follows necessarily from the premises. Since even false premises can form a valid argument, we require that an argument be true in its premises as well as valid in its reasoning. Because true premises guarantee that the conclusion will be true also, arguments that have only true premises are called "sound." It is important here to recognize that the terms *valid* and *sound* are used only with reference to the entire argument, and the words *true* and *false* are used only with reference to the statements or propositions that make up the argument, in other words, with reference to the premises and the conclusion.

Arguments that contain even one false premise are unsound, although they can be valid and lead to true and convincing conclusions. For example:

All adults are gamblers, and some smokers are adults.
Therefore some smokers are gamblers.

Valid but unsound arguments can also lead to false conclusions. Here too we can have but one false premise, as in:

Mathematics is an exact science.
Astrology is wholly based on mathematics.
Therefore, astrology is an exact science.

As we can see from the last argument, valid syllogistic reasoning has great persuasive force, even when it is unsound. Valid syllogisms are so convincing that we may feel compelled to accept their conclusions even when they are false. Conversely, when an argument is invalid, even if all statements within it are true, it is unconvincing. We will choose a famous instance from American history to illustrate our point.

Some presidents of the U.S. have been assassinated.
Abraham Lincoln was President of the U.S.
Therefore, Lincoln was assassinated.

Obviously, the conclusion does not follow from the premises, since neither premise states that all presidents of the U.S. have been assassinated. In other words, the conclusion is not logically or structurally implied by the premises. An argument of this sort is unsound. Thus, we say an argument is unsound when at least one of its premises is false or its structure is invalid and that it is sound when both its premises are true and its form is valid.

A common structural fault in syllogistic reasoning involves what is known as the undistributed middle. In a valid argument, the middle term must be distributed in at least one of the premises—that is, it must refer to all members of the class that is named. Here is a valid argument:

> All gamblers are optimists.
> All smokers are gamblers.
> Therefore all smokers are optimists.

The middle term *gamblers* in the major premise refers to all members of the class of gamblers and is therefore distributed. But if the syllogism is stated as follows:

> All gamblers are optimists.
> All smokers are optimists.
> Therefore all smokers are gamblers.

the middle term has become *optimists*.

Notice that the new middle term in the two premises does not necessarily refer to *all* optimists; that is, it is undistributed in both premises. A term is distributed when it refers to all members of the class that it names. Though all gamblers are optimists, not all optimists need be gamblers, the major premise implies. They may or may not be. Nor, the minor premise implies, need they all be smokers. They may or may not be. Yet the conclusion that all smokers are gamblers is deduced from the assumption that both gamblers and smokers are optimists. But if some optimists are not necessarily gamblers and some are not necessarily smokers, the conclusion does not follow. For the subject and predicate (smokers and gamblers) to be connected as they are in the conclusion, they must be connected through the middle term (optimists). And in order to be connected through the middle term, either the subject or the predicate must relate to all members of the class named by the middle term. Neither one does so. The argument is therefore invalid.

The following diagrams show how these relationships work. Here, first, is a diagram of the original valid syllogism:

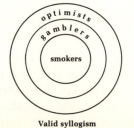

Valid syllogism

Smokers here are clearly included in the class of gamblers and hence of optimists. The invalid syllogism shows, by contrast, only that both smokers and gamblers belong separately to the class of optimists, not that smokers are necessarily gamblers:

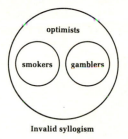

Invalid syllogism

In stating that all smokers are gamblers, the conclusion asserts more than the premises do, making the argument invalid.

We will not consider here the complex procedures logicians employ to test the validity of arguments. Our purpose has been merely to illustrate what makes a deductive argument valid.

Exercise

Analyze the following arguments to distinguish the conclusions from their grounds. Then decide whether the argument is deductive or inductive, and defend your judgment.

a. Whatever intrudes upon the peace of mind and comfort of people, particularly in public places, is a public nuisance. Smoking on buses certainly intrudes upon the peace of mind and comfort of many people, and therefore must be considered a public nuisance.

b. Smoking presents a health hazard to citizens of this country. The Surgeon General of the United States has claimed that smoking is injurious to health, and cigarette packages are required by law to state this fact. Recent scientific studies have linked smoking not just to lung cancer but to cardiovascular disease. Indeed, the increase in smoking among women has been correlated with the increase in lung cancer and the decrease in life expectancy of women in recent years. Thus, smoking will probably be the subject of legislation in future years—legislation stronger than now exists.

c. Well, the moon was there. The moment there was a chance to get on it, someone was bound to try. The process was accelerated by national rivalries, but it would have happened even if the U.S. or the Soviet Union alone had had a monopoly of rocketry. For any great country has a supply of brave and spirited men who would have been ready for any adventure technology might give them. That is grand: it makes one proud of belonging to the same species. But there is something else that is perhaps not so grand, that is unarguable and also sinister. That is—there is no known example in which technology has been stopped being pushed to the limit. Technology has its own inner dynamic. When it was possible that technology could bring off a moon landing, then it was certain that sooner or later, the landing would be brought off. However much it cost in human lives, dollars, rubles, social effort.

C. P. Snow, *"The Moon Landing"*

d. The state is by nature clearly prior to the family and to the individual, since the whole is of necessity prior to the part.

Aristotle, *Politics*

e. What is the education which can do this? What is the furniture which makes the only place belonging absolutely to each one of us, the world within, a place where we like to go? I wish I could answer that question. I wish I could produce a perfect decorator's design warranted to make any interior lovely and interesting and stimulating; but, even if I could, sooner or later we would certainly try different designs. My point is only that while we must and should change the furniture, we ought to throw away old furniture very cautiously. It may turn out to be irreplaceable. A great deal was thrown away in the last generation or so, long enough ago to show some of the results. Furniture which had for centuries been foremost, we lightly, in a few years, discarded. The classics almost vanished from our field of education. That was a great change.

Edith Hamilton, *"The Lessons of the Past"*

Hypothetical and disjunctive arguments

The following is an example of a hypothetical argument, stated informally:

> If Wilson is telling the truth in saying that chemical dumping will end, then it will. For Wilson is a truthful person.

Here is the argument stated formally:

> If Wilson is truthful, chemical dumping will end.
> Wilson is truthful.
> Therefore, chemical dumping will end.

The second premise—stated categorically—affirms the antecedent of the first or hypothetical premise: it affirms that Wilson is truthful. The conclusion affirms the consequent: it tells us that chemical dumping will end. The argument is invalid when the second or categorical premise affirms the consequent rather than the antecedent:

If Wilson is truthful, chemical dumping will end.
Chemical dumping will end.
Therefore, Wilson is truthful.

Clearly, the dumping will end whether or not Wilson is truthful.

If instead the antecedent is denied in the conclusion, the argument is valid:

If Wilson is truthful, chemical dumping will end.
Chemical dumping will not end.
Therefore, Wilson is not truthful.

Here the second premise denies the consequent, the conclusion denies the antecedent. The invalid form of this argument is the following:

If Wilson is truthful, chemical dumping will end.
Wilson is not truthful.
Therefore, chemical dumping will not end.

Here is a valid hypothetical argument that forms part of a report on a scientific experiment:

> If memory is a function of the cerebral cortex as a whole—a kind of dynamic reverberation or electrical standing wave pattern of the constituent parts, rather than stored statically in separate brain components—this would explain the survival of memory after significant brain damage. The evidence, however, points in the other direction: In experiments performed by the American neurophysiologist Ralph Gerard at the University of Michigan, hamsters were taught to run a simple maze and then chilled almost to the freezing point in a refrigerator, a kind of induced hibernation. The temperatures were so low that all detectable electrical activity in the animals' brains ceased. If the dynamic view of memory were true, the experiment should have wiped out all memory of successful maze-running. Instead, after thawing, the hamster remembered. Memory seems to be localized in specific sites in the brain, and the survival of memories after massive brain lesions must be the result of redundant storage of static memory traces in various locales.
>
> Carl Sagan, *The Dragons of Eden*

The experiment Sagan describes proved that memory is not a function of the cerebral cortex as a whole. Though the cortices stopped functioning when the hamster brains were chilled almost to freezing, memory was not wiped out, proving that memory is localized in specific brain structures. Here is the argument stated in a formal syllogism:

If memory is a function of the cerebral cortex as a whole, memory of successful maze-running will be wiped out when the cortex stops functioning.

Memory of successful maze-running is not wiped out when the cortex stops functioning.

Therefore, memory is not a function of the cortex as a whole.

Notice that the experiment provides indirect evidence, and nothing else: no specific structures are identified and named. And a conclusion is drawn: surviving memories must be the "result of redundant storage of static memory-traces in various locales." Much reasoning about science takes this form because direct evidence is not always available.

In contrast to hypothetical arguments, disjunctive arguments present alternatives in the first premise. A disjunctive statement merely asserts that one of the alternatives is true, not that the other must be false:

Either the road is flooded or they decided not to come.

Both statements may be true. But if we deny the first statement, then the second must be true:

Either the road is flooded or they decided not to come.
The road is not flooded.
Therefore they decided not to come.

In both disjunctive and hypothetical syllogisms, the first premise consists of a compound proposition, which has two statements that are linked together. Linkage is generally signaled by a word or a punctuation mark. To use our earlier example: "If Wilson is truthful, chemical dumping will end," actually has two separate propositions, "Wilson is truthful" and "chemical dumping will end" joined by the comma. Here, the comma serves in place of the word "then." The signals that usually indicate a hypothetical proposition, and thus a hypothetical argument, are the words *if* and *then*. Since "then" is often suppressed, look for the word "if" in trying to decide whether a proposition is hypothetical or not.

The "either . . . or" proposition of the disjunctive syllogism is also made up of two separate statements, in this instance linked by the word *or*. In disjunctive propositions, "either" is sometimes suppressed, as in "The road is flooded or they decided not to come." Hence, the crucial signal in recognizing a disjunct is the word *or*.

As with categorical propositions and syllogisms, the important features to recognize in both hypothetical and disjunctive statements and arguments are the signal words and the positions of independent clauses or phrases. For categorical syllogisms, we should look for the words "all," or the implication of it, and "no," or "some," as well as for the positions of subjects and predicates; for hypothetical syllogisms, we should look for the words "if" and "then," or some substitute for the latter, and whether the antecedent, the clause before *then*, or whether the consequent, the clause after *then*, is affirmed or denied; in disjunctive syllogisms, we should look for the word "or" and for which of the alternatives is denied.

Because syllogisms are patterned arrangements of language, we rarely use them directly in writing. But they are important devices for analyzing the kinds of arguments we encounter in our reading, and for organizing our written arguments. In the following section, we will examine two variations of the syllogism that are frequently used in writing.

Exercises

1. Use one of the following statements as the major premise of an argument. Supply the minor premise and the conclusion:
   a. All human beings are individuals who differ in their conception of happiness.
   b. Knowledge of a second language is a way to sharpen knowledge of our own language.

2. Use one of the following statements as the minor premise of an argument. Supply the major premise and the conclusion:
   a. New Yorkers are inhabitants of a large city.
   b. Joggers are health enthusiasts.

3. Using the hypothetical premises given below, construct a short hypothetical argument, following the model in the discussion:
   a. If the weatherman forecasts rain for the weekend, we are not driving to Cleveland.
   b. If Congress lowers the speed limit to fifty miles an hour, some drivers will be angry.

4. Using the following disjunctions as major premises, construct arguments that are valid in form:
   a. Either we find new oil reserves or the price of gas will rise.
   b. Either a conspiracy existed or President Kennedy was killed by an assassin acting alone.

5. Construct a deductive argument, supplying your own major and minor premises, and testing their soundness. Then use it to write a brief paragraph in which you present the argument informally.

Sorites and enthymemic arguments

In certain extended arguments, a series of syllogisms may be connected in such a way that the conclusion of one syllogism serves as a premise in another immediately following:

1. Institutions that promote social conformity are institutions that produce intellectual conformists.

American high schools are institutions that promote social conformity.
Thus, American high schools are institutions that produce intellectual conformists.

2. Institutions that produce intellectual conformists are institutions that do not understand the real purpose of education.

   American high schools produce intellectual conformists.
   American high schools do not understand the real purpose of education.

3. Institutions that do not understand the real purpose of education need reform.

   American high schools do not understand the real purpose of education.
   American high schools need reform.

We can restate the arguments above by combining them into what is called a sorites—an interlocking series of syllogisms in which intervening conclusions (the first two italicized above) and perhaps some of the premises are omitted. In the sorites, the predicate of the first proposition becomes the subject of the second, and its predicate becomes the subject of the third, down to the conclusion, the subject of which is the subject of the first proposition. Here is that sorites:

American high schools are institutions that promote social conformity. Institutions that promote social conformity produce intellectual conformists. Institutions that produce intellectual conformists do not understand the real purpose of education. Institutions that do not understand the real purpose of education need reform. American high schools need reform.

There is an advantage in omitting the intervening conclusions and some of the premises. These are readily understood, and therefore do not need to be stated for the audience; their omission makes the long and complex argument easier to follow. We call an argument which omits one of the premises or the conclusion an enthymeme. The sorites illustrated above is enthymemic in both of these ways.

Here are three kinds of enthymemic argument:

1. *The Deer Hunter* is violent because it is a movie about Vietnam.
   [*major premise implied:* All movies about Vietnam are violent.]

2. Because all movies about Vietnam are violent, *The Deer Hunter* is violent.
   [*minor premise implied: The Deer Hunter* is a movie about Vietnam.]

3. All movies about Vietnam are violent, and *The Deer Hunter* is a movie about Vietnam.
   [*conclusion implied: The Deer Hunter* is violent.]

Enthymemic arguments are among the most common we encounter, yet we may not be aware that we have done so. Advertising provides numerous examples. Here are two examples:

When good friends and bad cigars get together, it's time to get out the Lysol Disinfectant Spray.

People who want more out of life want more out of their vitamins and minerals, too. Like Myadec.

And here is part of the introduction to President John F. Kennedy's June, 1963 statement on the integration of the University of Alabama:

If an American, because his skin is dark, cannot eat lunch in a restaurant open to the public; if he cannot send his children to the best public school available; if he cannot vote for the public officials who represent him; if, in short, he cannot enjoy the full and free life which all of us want, then who among us would be content to have the color of his skin changed and stand in his place?

The absent premise presumes what all people would be unhappy with. They would not be happy to be denied the full and free life others enjoy. The absent premise is obvious, but omitting it here forces attention upon it.

Writers frequently develop extended arguments using enthymemic techniques. The sorites, although rarely used in its pure form, is an excellent device for controlling such arguments when writing.

Exercises

1. Decide whether the reasoning is valid and the premises true in the following. Reword the statements as you find necessary:
   a. Apes are mammals, and so are whales. So apes and whales are members of the same class of vertebrates.
   b. Apes are mammals, and horntoed lizards are apes. So horntoed lizards are mammals.
   c. Lizards are not primates, and rainbow trout are not lizards. So rainbow trout are not primates.
   d. All apes are primates, and all chimpanzees are apes. So some chimpanzees are primates.
2. Complete each of the following enthymemic arguments, supplying the missing premise or the conclusion:
   a. Many women had trouble getting accepted as writers in the nineteenth century, and Emily Bronte was a woman.
   b. Emily Bronte had trouble getting accepted as a writer because she was a woman.

    c. Since women had trouble getting accepted as writers in the nineteenth century, Emily Bronte had to publish her novel under a pseudonym.

    d. French should be required in American schools because English and French are the languages of Canada.

    e. French is spoken widely in Canada, and the United States and Canada will grow closer in the coming years.

An argumentative essay

Most arguments contain unstated assumptions. These assumptions are usually inherited from earlier stages of the controversy that gave rise to the arguments. As a rule, the latest arguments do not review all of the arguments, assumptions, or premises that preceded them.

Alan Wertheimer, in the argument that follows, identifies some of his assumptions, in particular "uncontroversial assumptions" that he believes his audience will accept without debate. One of these is that "competitive elections are desirable." Another is that compulsory voting—which he is urging in the essay—would not be hard to enforce. It is important for us to weigh the truth of seemingly obvious assumptions such as these, and it is doubly important to identify important unstated assumptions if any and weigh them too.

Wertheimer's basic argument is that many people do not vote because voting is, like public highways, national defense, and police protection, a "public good." It is a right we enjoy rather than a duty we are forced to perform. Just as people do as little as they can to provide for public highways or police protection, so they "ride free" when it comes to another such public good, voting, because they want to avoid the costs. This at least is what the "rational citizen" would do. It follows, then, that voting must be compulsory if certain benefits are to be gained.

Each of these statements contains assumptions that need careful examination. Here are a few questions that will identify some for you. There are others for you to consider, too:

Is voting actually a right rather than a duty, and need we regard it as a duty so as to increase the number of voters?

If it were a right, is it the role of government to force us to vote?

Do rational citizens in fact take a free ride in the way described? Is a free ride, indeed, a rational response?

What is a "public good"? Is it a good that people cannot be prevented from enjoying free of charge? How else might it be defined?

The essential question for Wertheimer is whether voting is a duty we should be compelled to perform, because a broader electorate will benefit the nation. Notice that this question does not depend on what, in fact, is the truth about the present attitude of voters. Wertheimer would be making the same argument even if people were now voting in larger numbers. His discussion of voting habits today is intended to show that the problem he describes is a serious one and in need of a solution.

FOR COMPULSORY VOTING

by Alan Wertheimer

Introduction
Narrative
An appeal to interest of general reader: "right to vote" has been of concern to Americans in the past. *Exhortation* combined with background of issue.

As the Presidential election approaches we will no doubt be asked to recall that it was, in part, the demand for the "right to vote" that led to independence. Editorial writers throughout America will predictably bemoan the low level of participation and implore us to feel doubly guilty for failing to vote in this Bicentennial and Presidential election year.

Thesis

Rather than conduct these ritual "get-out-the-vote" dances, why not simply make voting compulsory?

Thesis explained. Additional narrative or background.

That we even seem compelled to urge citizens to exercise a right (what other *rights* do we need to urge citizens to exercise?) indicates that we may err in thinking of voting as a *right* at all. If citizens have a duty to vote, we should penalize those who fail to do their duty.

Division of proofs
Statement of "uncontroversial" assumptions

My argument for compulsory voting makes several (I think uncontroversial) assumptions: Competitive elections are desirable—for all their problems and deficiencies they are preferable to alternative methods of obtaining political leaders; it is technically possible to administer a compulsory-voting program (nonvoters would pay a tax or fine as in Belgium, the Netherlands and Australia); compulsory voting works—it *does* increase the percentage of eligible voters who actually vote.

Definition of "public good"— used to establish a "given"— premise or assumption Wertheimer considers certain enough to establish truth of what follows.

Elections can be understood as "public goods." A public good is any good that if made available to *any* member of a community must be made to *all* members, generally because there is no feasible way to exclude noncontributors from enjoying the good. Public highways, national defense and police protection are examples of public good.

Confirmation
Conclusions deduced from definition of "public good."

Appeal to experience: inductive evidence, or well-established facts.
Further deduction from facts signaled by "it follows."

Refutation
Answer to objections:
Wertheimer is not saying that people should not vote;
he is saying that it is not in their interest to do so.
Further objection: why do so many vote—if what he says is true.

Answers:
some people altruistic.

Some people think voting is more important than it is.
Some vote to relieve feeling of guilt.

Conclusion
Appeal to benefits that would accrue from compulsory voting.
Continuation of refutation: objection to proposal, and answer.

Now if the benefit of a public good is available to all, it is irrational for one to *voluntarily* contribute to its provision, in terms of money, time or energy. The rational citizen will attempt to "free ride," to enjoy the benefits while minimizing or avoiding the cost, as when we attempt to pay the lowest tax possible (or none at all).

All Americans benefit from the peaceful change of leadership and the fact that elections keep all elected officials (even those we do not support) at least somewhat responsive to our preferences. Voters and nonvoters alike receive these benefits and receive additional benefits if their preferred candidate wins. It follows that the rational citizen will not vote but will ride free by avoiding the costs (including information costs) involved in voting.

I am not suggesting that we should not vote, merely that it is not in one's *individual interest* to vote, because no single vote will affect the outcome of the election and the electoral system will not crumble if any one of us fails to vote. We get the same benefits regardless of what we do.

It is not surprising that many citizens fail to vote. Rather, why do so many act irrationally (if altruistically) and vote?

First, some people are simply willing to sacrifice their interest for the public good.

Second, many people overestimate the importance of their vote. Third, many vote to assuage their sense of guilt. But this hardly happens spontaneously. We systematically encourage citizens to overestimate the importance of their vote and to feel guilty when they do not vote—and it works.

What would compulsory voting do? First we would be spared the ritual propaganda campaigns in which we lie to ourselves about the significance of our individual votes and drum up our feelings of guilt. Second, we could be allowed to abstain, and thus citizens could specifically indicate that no candidate was satisfactory. Third, because it is largely the poor who tend not to vote, compulsory voting would increase their political power, as candidates would be forced to become more responsive to their interests. Fourth, since those who prefer candidates who are unlikely to win often do not vote, elections would provide a more accurate description of the nation's political preferences.

Writing Assignments

1. Write an essay in which you either agree or disagree with Wertheimer. In your introduction, summarize his basic assumptions and conclusions, and in your division of proofs, state the assumptions that will serve as the basis of your argument. As part of your confirmation, you may want to introduce your experiences and observations as an illustration of these assumptions. Do so in narrative form. If you agree with Wertheimer, use your refutation to discuss objections that can be made to his ideas. If you disagree with him, use this part of the essay to explain why.

2. Using Wertheimer as a model, write an argumentative essay on another law that you think should be created and enforced. Draw on your experience and observation to support your reasoning: these might be presented as an introductory narrative. Your confirmation should state the basic assumptions that support your recommendation. In your refutation, answer those who may object to such a law. Before composing your essay, write down objections that can be raised to it.

Sources of premises

Logicians have long disagreed about the nature of premises and possible sources of them. Perhaps the most ancient controversy is between those who claim intuition as their ultimate source for premises and those who insist on experience only. Aristotle, who is considered the father of logic, stated both positions at the conclusion of his *Posterior Analytics,* a work that examines the nature and origin of premises. There he said, ". . . it is clear that we must get to know the primary premisses by induction; for the method by which even sense-perception implants the universal is inductive." But since induction yields only hypothetical conclusions, or as Aristotle would have put it, "truths that admit of error," we need a kind of thought "more accurate than scientific knowledge." He then went on to say: "From these considerations it follows that there will be no scientific knowledge of the primary premisses, and since except intuition nothing can be truer than scientific knowledge, it will be intuition that apprehends the primary premisses. . . ." Generally, those logicians who are considered rationalists hold that the ultimate source of our premises is intuition and those who are empiricists usually deny this and claim that only experience can yield the significant truths that make up our premises.

There are also other ways of defending premises that it is important to be aware of. The premises, we may be told, are "self-evident," or "axiomatic," or "reasonable." "It's plain common sense," someone says in defense of a statement we have challenged. If we defend our own statements or premises in this way, we may find ourselves in disagreement over the source of our ideas rather than over the conclusions we draw from them.

Let us consider what these various terms mean. The term "self-evident" was used by Aristotle to describe the axioms of geometry, a deductive science familiar to many of us. Axioms are basic and necessary truths used to connect statements in proofs. For example:

The whole is greater than its parts.

So obvious or "self-evident" a statement was assumed not to require demonstration or proof, and this is what we sometimes mean in calling a statement "axiomatic." We said "was assumed" because not all axioms have been accepted as self-evident by later mathematicians or philosophers. In fact, different geometries have been developed from axioms and definitions completely opposite to those known by Aristotle and Euclid, who systematized the earliest geometry known to us.

The term "self-evident" has also been used to describe statements of a different kind, those relating to human beings and human life:

We hold these truths to be self-evident, that all men are created equal, that they are endowed by their Creator with certain unalienable rights, that among these are life, liberty, and the pursuit of happiness.

Declaration of Independence

We will not try to distinguish the many views of what "self-evident" means in this famous statement. One important view is that the author of the Declaration, Thomas Jefferson, held these truths to be inherent in us by nature, in Jefferson's words, "impressed on the sense of every man." If this was his view, then he was perhaps referring to the same "common sense" we sometimes refer to in defense of truths we hold. As with axioms, truths based on "common sense" are thought by some not to require demonstration because they are rooted in "what we all know."

It is also frequently argued that we need not offer proofs or demonstrations for truths derived from Scripture or other sources of "revealed truth." In this case the ultimate source is considered to be God, who is conceived of as all knowing. Many arguments on religious and ethical matters will cite the Scriptures or revelation as the source for their premises. For example, one might argue that "It is wrong to use trickery in business, for as Leviticus 19:11 says, 'Ye shall not steal, neither deal falsely, neither lie to one another.' "

Other truths that are thought by some not to require proof are those derived from "reason," the faculty of thought capable of giving us ideas clear and free of contradiction. This seems to be the assumption of the writer in the following passage:

> Let us concede that every society must have some system that attempts to adapt the young to their social and political environment. . . . But it seems to me clearer to say that, though it may be a system of training, or instruction, or adaptation, or meeting immediate needs, it is not a system of education. It seems clearer to say that the purpose of education is to improve men. Any system that tries to make them bad is not education, but something else.

Robert M. Hutchins, The Conflict in Education

Notice that the definition of education is justified on the basis of its clarity ("it seems clearer to say"), not on the basis of its conformity to experience. For we may live in a world where such an ideal education does not yet exist. For the person who relies on "reason" in this way, experience may give supporting evidence, but the truth of an idea is determined by its clarity and consistency.

Finally, premises may originate in experience itself, and, as we noted earlier, for some can only originate there. This was the view of an ancient philosopher who pointed out that we would not know the statement "All humans are mortal" is true unless we observed the deaths of friends, members of our families, and other humans. In other words, the truth of the premises must previously have been established inductively. As we have discussed, much disagreement exists about how to classify arguments based on inductive evidence. What is not in dispute is that deduction plays an important role in inductive reasoning.

We shall not pursue this matter further here, but we will point out that inductive evidence gives us hypotheses from which we may deduce a number of ideas, as we have seen in several of our examples in this chapter. We seek then to verify these through further observation and experiment. Deductive and inductive processes work together in this way in science. Thus, there is no one single source of truth in science, nor is there for us in our daily life. We continually develop hypotheses from our daily experience, draw conclusions from them, and test them by other experiences. We shall return to this point in the next section.

We know that there is always disagreement about what experience tells us. And so is there, let us note, about ideas assumed to be "self-evident" or "axiomatic" or "reasonable" or "based on common sense." As recent controversies over abortion and ERA show, few ideas go unchallenged regardless of the source cited in their defense. There is, in fact, no general agreement on what "axioms" or "common sense" or "reason" are. And even where there is agreement on their nature and authority there may be disagreement about what they tell us. Scriptural texts have been interpreted in different ways, and, as the different geometries mentioned earlier show, what is obvious or "self-evident" in one system of thought is not necessarily obvious or "self-evident" in another.

Exercise

Writers sometimes indicate the source of their premises or of assumptions that have conditioned their thinking about particular issues. The following deductive and inductive arguments give such an indication. Identify the sources in each:

a. There now is sophisticated research that strongly suggests a deterrent effect [of capital punishment]. Furthermore, the principal argument against the deterrent effect is weak. The argument is that in most jurisdictions where capital punishment has been abolished there has been no immediate, sharp increase in what had been capital crimes. But in those jurisdictions, the actual act of abolition was an insignificant event because for years the death penalty had been imposed rarely, if at all. Common sense—which deserves deference until it is refuted—suggests that the fear of death can deter some premeditated crimes, including some murders.

George F. Will, *Cleveland Plain-Dealer*, March 13, 1981

b. Vast as the universe is in its four dimensions, it represents but a single order of being based on uniformity of composition and uniformity of the processes that go on throughout it. A star in some other galaxy, even though 6,000 million light-years away, is composed like our sun of hydrogen, helium, carbon, nitrogen, and other elements that we are at home with on our own little earth. All the stars are so composed. And in all of them the interactions of the elements are the same as in our sun, producing the same radiation (which is how we know it to be so). The laws of nature that prevail in our own little sphere prevail equally at the distance in space and time of the most remote star. The order that overlies chaos there is the order that overlies it here.

The universality of the single order is surely the most significant and hopeful fact about the realm of being. It is a fact that we have had no choice but to assume from the beginning, even though we did so on faith alone, because any alternative assumption would have implications of chaos that could not be contemplated simply because they would erase the distinction in principle between sanity and insanity on which we depend in our thinking and our living alike. It is of immeasurable importance, therefore, to have, as we do have, experimental confirmation.

Louis J. Halle, *Out of Chaos*

c. Now God, our good Master, teaching us in the two great commandments the love of Him, and the love of our neighbor, to love three things, God, our neighbor, and ourselves, and seeing he that loves God, offends not in loving himself; it follows that he ought to counsel his neighbor to love God, and to provide for him in the love of God, sure he is commanded to love him, as his own self. So must he do for his wife, children, family, and all men besides: and wish likewise that his neighbor would do as much for him, in his need: thus shall he be settled in peace and orderly concord with the world.

St. Augustine, *The City of God*

d. If the increased power which science has conferred upon human volitions is to be a boon and not a curse, the ends to which these volitions are directed must grow commensurately with the growth of power to carry them out. Hitherto, although we have been told on Sundays to love our neighbor, we have been told on weekdays to hate him, and there are six times as many weekdays as Sundays. Hitherto, the harm that we could do to our neighbor by hating him was limited by our incompetence, but in the new world upon which we are entering there will be no such limit, and the indulgence of hatred can lead only to ultimate and complete disaster.

Bertrand Russell, "*The Expanding Mental Universe*"

Discovering our own basic premises

We have just seen that there is considerable disagreement about the sources and nature of premises. It is therefore important to know where our own premises come from. In a dispute, we must be able to state— and if necessary, illustrate or defend—the sources of the truths from which we reason. This means that we need to question our own basic assumptions, as well as those of others.

In our daily conversations, we reason easily from ideas or beliefs that we take as "givens," truths we presume most other people share with us and that could therefore serve as the unquestioned bases of our thinking. When these givens are challenged, we are often disturbed. Most of us have had the experience of bristling at the suggestion that our statements have hidden assumptions and that these are untrue or fallible.

We bristle at the suggestion because we believe our ideas are in accord with "the way things are." It is hard to know, however, whether we came to hold these ideas through long acquaintance with facts that suggested them, or absorbed them from parents, teachers, and the prevailing climate of thought—that is, the prevailing view of the world we find in newspapers and on television. It is just as hard to know where the evidence and premises in some arguments come from.

Let us consider the following statement by Malthus, the early nineteenth-century Englishman who developed the famous idea that population always exceeds the available resources for its support:

Man cannot live in the midst of plenty. All cannot share alike the bounties of nature. Were there no established administration of property, every man would be obliged to guard with force his little store. Selfishness would be triumphant. The subjects of contention would be perpetual. Every individual mind would be under a constant anxiety about corporal support, and not a single intellect would be left free to expatiate in the field of thought.

Essay on the Principle of Population (1798)

The opening sentences may be taken as conclusions drawn from the statements that follow—statements based on experiences with people in times of hardship. In other words, they may be regarded as inductive generalizations, derived from experience and observation. But they can also be regarded as unquestioned truths that Malthus holds and from which he reasons about what people would be like in a world without property laws. They might, in other words, be for him premises arising from ingrained beliefs about human nature in general and "the way things are."

In examining our own ideas, we occasionally know which came first—experiences with people or our ideas about them. We can point to experiences that led to a decisive change in our way of viewing people. Most of the time, however, changes in how we think and view the world happen gradually. We are always testing our ideas by experience, and we may change them unthinkingly when new experiences occur. They may, in fact, be changes we do not want to admit. In everyday reasoning, this mutual testing and reinforcement is extremely common. Indeed, this is one way that inductive generalizations established by long and continued observation become the premises of deductive arguments. Another way premises originate, we saw, is in ideas we have been taught. These, like the Golden Rule, we hold whether or not we find them confirmed by experience: the Golden Rule thus would be true whether or not we found people who followed it, or whether we found any *practical* reason to justify it. For, to those who believe it, the Golden Rule is a moral law that stands regardless of what experience may say about it. It is different, then, from a maxim that derives from experience and stands or falls according to what happens in the world, such as:

Do as you would be done is the surest method that I know of pleasing.

Lord Chesterfield

Defending our premises

A point to notice, and one that bears on the writing of deductive essays, is that when the Golden Rule is stated as a proposition and used in an argument some people insist on presenting it without defense or illustration. They do so because they want to avoid the implication that the

Rule, or any truth they revere, *needs* defense. Here is how the Golden Rule might be stated as a categorical proposition:

> Moral actions are those in which we act toward others as we would want them to act toward us.

To qualify the statement with a *maybe* or a *probably* would indeed change what we mean. But illustration or defense need not and would not produce a change. We could, for example, illustrate a given truth from experience, showing what it means to act toward others in the way indicated, and we could defend it as a truth worth living by, in contrast to other maxims that fall short in some way.

Indeed, we often do illustrate and defend such beliefs in the course of arguing with friends who do not share our view of the world or hold the same beliefs. And we must. For there are few beliefs that everyone will accept in an argument without backing or defense, and few physical "laws" that can be presented with the assurance that they have never been questioned and will never be changed.

Most arguments occur in a particular context, against a background of assumptions. Between participants, there is usually a mutual give and take in which ideas are explained, disputed, rejected, modified, or accepted. And this is so whether the ideas originate as "given" truths or as inductive generalizations. Thus, when we reason deductively we do illustrate and defend our ideas. And we do so perhaps more in spoken than in written arguments, because in spoken arguments people are present to demand illustration or defense. They may say to us, "We can't say whether we agree with you until we know what you mean!"

In writing arguments, we may not think of illustrating or defending our ideas. But if we want to make our thinking understood to a wider audience than just the people who hold exactly our opinions and have had the same experiences, and more important if we want to persuade this wider audience, then we do need to provide illustration and support. For what may be true or obvious to us, as we said in the previous section, is not necessarily true or obvious to others—even to those who hold the same opinions and have had the same experiences.

In doing more than just presenting bald premises and conclusions, we are presenting several kinds of evidence—the premises themselves, and illustrative and qualifying detail, just to name a few. We need now to distinguish these kinds more exactly.

Exercises

1. Find an example in one of your textbooks in the sciences or the social sciences of a stated assumption and one or more conclusions deduced from it.

2. All of us make assumptions about people in general—assumptions that govern our behavior toward others. The following are such assumptions made by great thinkers and writers of the past. Decide whether you agree or disagree with the assumption, then decide whether you do so on the basis of long observation and thought or of other assumptions absorbed from your world without your having given them any thought:

> In the misfortune of our best friends, we find something which does not displease us.
>
> La Rochefoucauld

People use thought only to justify their wrongdoings, and speech only to conceal their thoughts.

Voltaire

The reward of a thing well done, is to have done it.

Ralph Waldo Emerson

I have lived some thirty years on this planet, and I have yet to hear the first syllable of valuable or even earnest advice from my seniors.

Henry David Thoreau

Everyone is a moon, and has a dark side which he never shows to anybody.

Mark Twain

Everything is funny as long as it is happening to somebody else.

Will Rogers

Writing Assignments

1. Discuss the conclusions that may be drawn from one of the statements just quoted. You may want to discuss ideas related to the statement that also have important consequences. You need not state your agreement or disagreement with these ideas.

2. The following essay presents different arguments on the purpose of imprisonment. Each argument is based on different assumptions about human nature or about the nature of society or punishment.

   Write an analysis of these arguments, identifying these assumptions, and the conclusions that Gaylin shows are derived from them. Then discuss which of these arguments on imprisonment you most agree and disagree with, and why you do. Be careful to identify your own assumptions and to explain their origin—for example, as given truths, or inductive generalizations based on your experience and observation.

UP THE RIVER, BUT WHY?

by Willard Gaylin

Criminology is in a transition phase, and transitions are notoriously unsettling. When the experts themselves are unsure, the public will be confused. The past year or so has witnessed the introduction of measures that seem to represent a hardening of attitudes toward the prison population. Talk of punishment now seems to be replacing the previous dominance of the concept of rehabilitation. There is movement to do away with parole, eliminate the discretionary sentence and tighten the rules on juvenile justice. All of these, traditionally championed by the liberal community, are under attack by that same group. Yet the reversal of intention and motive is not so great as the methodological shift might imply.

There are five traditional purposes of imprisonment: prevention, general deterrence, individual deterrence, rehabilitation and punishment.

• The simplest is prevention, often referred to as confinement or incapacitation, which means that at least while a man is confined, he is unable to commit crimes.

An argument against prevention is that such a small percentage of criminals are apprehended and sent to prison that this purpose alone would affect the level of crime very little. This has recently been debated: Some studies have suggested that perhaps six percent of all criminals are responsible for two-thirds of all violent crime.

• General deterrence. It is assumed that if a man is punished for a crime, that example will intimidate others. It is a difficult concept to prove, but it is part of common assumptions about human nature. Certainly in some societies general deterrence seems to work. The success of the Scandinavians in controlling drunken driving by harsh treatment of all offenders is one example.

The argument has been that general deterrence probably works best for white-collar crimes but is limited in other areas by the very nature of certain criminal types who are incapable of learning anything by example, or who resist the assumption that they themselves will be caught.

• Individual deterrence. This principle assumes that once having been punished for an act the individual himself will not be likely to repeat it. Again, common sense is misleading. Recidivist rates seem to indicate that imprisonment does little if anything to reform the criminal.

• Rehabilitation. During the last century and a half this concept has dominated penal philosophy. It is part of the humanistic tradition, which in pressing for ever more individualization of justice has demanded treatment for the criminal. The concept borrowed heavily from psychology and medicine, defining the criminal as, if not sick, at least less than evil, and somehow less "responsible" than he had previously been considered. Inherent in the definition of a sick person is presumption of nonculpability for his disease. To say "It is not his fault. He is sick," is to define the patient as victim, not victimizer.

When, however, society switched from a frame of reference that was judgmental and punitive to one that was medical, a whole range of corollaries, some unexpected, came into play.

The rehabilitative model, despite its emphasis on understanding and concern, has been more punitive than a frankly punitive model would probably have been. Medicine, after all, is allowed to be bitter; inflicted pain is not cruelty if it is treatment rather than punishment. Under the rehabilitative model it is possible for society to abuse prisoners, without disabusing its conscience. Beneath this cloak of benevolence, hypocrisy has flourished, and each new exploitation has been introduced as an act of grace.

It is this failure that has caused liberals to question rehabilitation. Inevitably abandonment of rehabilitation as the cornerstone of penal logic leads to a reassessment of the entire concept of discretionary justice in sentencing, parole and probation. The supporters of rehabilitation, those few who are left, say it was never given a chance, that it was accepted in theory while punishment continued in practice. On the other hand, the question remains whether it is reasonable to expect anything different from rehabilitation, given the extended trial period it has had.

• Punishment. One consequence of the use of the term "law and order" as a disguise for racist feelings was that the intellectual community turned away from the legitimate rights the words law and order implied. Instead intellectuals focused almost all their attention on the neglected rights of the criminal offender. It is now sometimes argued that in so doing they forget that although this was a compassionate pursuit, the welfare of the community was the real concern of the criminal justice system.

With this readjustment of focus came a return of interest in the concept of punishment. When viewed in terms of just desserts, the purpose of punishment is not to satisfy a desire for vengeance but to restore a sense of moral order. The argument runs like this: Certain things are simply wrong and ought to be punished. There is a sense of moral outrage when crimes go unpunished. This outrage can be disorganizing and destructive to the social system, which operates with the tacit understanding that there is—if not absolute fairness—some normal order in life. It simply seems wrong and unfair—almost unbearably so—for evil to triumph and good to be punished.

Some liberals now think it is time for the concept of desserts. But they also believe that in its devotion to moral principle society must be careful not to turn its back on generosity, charity, compassion and love. Desserts emphasized justice, not mercy, and while the idea of desserts need not rule out tempering justice with mercy, shifting the focus from concern for the individual to devotion to moral right may lead to abandonment of the former altogether.

The current re-evaluation of the criminal justice system may be seen as part of a cycle that will continue until society goes beyond the treatment of the offender and begins to have some better understanding of the causes of crime. Without that, everything else is palliative; every solution temporary.

The Toulmin model

We said earlier that well established inductive evidence may be generalized to provide premises of deductive arguments. The logician Stephen Toulmin has given us a highly useful way to analyze and construct such arguments, and we shall consider its main features as a way of distinguishing various kinds of evidence in arguments.

Toulmin points out that, though some arguments merely deduce or analyze what their premises imply, most do more than this and make substantial claims including predictions about the future—claims about what really is. For Toulmin these arguments are deductive in a wider sense than this term traditionally implies. We shall not review his reasoning on this matter or his own classification of arguments, which cuts across the traditional one between deductive and inductive; we will merely note that "substantial" arguments, which we will now describe, contain elements of deductive and inductive reasoning as we have described it.

Basic to Toulmin's theory of argument is that the grounds presented for conclusions in arguments differ from field to field, whether mathematics, law, medicine, or politics. And so do "the ways in which these grounds bear on the conclusions."[1] Indeed, the probability of these arguments varies according to the evidence, the probability sometimes reaching near or practical certainty. In short, the criteria we use to judge arguments is, in Toulmin's words, "field dependent."

Toulmin points out further that most arguments are based on data—on observed facts, experiments, common knowledge, and the like: "Data of some kind must be produced, if there is to be an argument at all: a bare conclusion, without any data produced in its support, is no argument."[2] This data is presented, he continues, in support of a "claim"—a conclusion or thesis that we wish to have accepted. But data is not enough. Bare data means nothing until we know why it should be accepted as evidence for the claim.

This defense is called the "warrant," a guarantee that the data is relevant to the claim. A warrant in this sense is a kind of license or permit, something which gives us authority to proceed to an action. For example, I may say that I am warranted (that is, I have authority) in claiming that John will be prosecuted for tax evasion because (statement of the warrant) tax evasion is subject to prosecution. And if there is a question about the truth of my warrant, I can give it the "backing" of pertinent legal statutes that govern the payment of taxes. "Warrants are of different kinds," Toulmin points out, "and may confer different degrees of force on the conclusions they justify."[3]

[1] Stephen Toulmin, *The Uses of Argument* (Cambridge: Cambridge University Press, 1958), p. 42.
[2] Ibid., p. 106.
[3] Ibid., p. 100.

The backing for warrants is also different from field to field, and the weight or force of the backing therefore varies also. Thus legal statutes, which change slowly, have greater force as evidence than telescopic observations, which change with advances in astronomy.

In addition to data, warrants, and backing, an argument may contain what Toulmin terms "qualifications." These specify the "degree of force" or probability through familiar words like "maybe," "perhaps," and "very probably." An argument may also contain "reservations," which take account of exceptional or special circumstances, perhaps making the warrant ineffective. Here is an illustration of a "substantial" argument analyzed according to this model:

Data	John failed three courses last semester, and did just as poorly the previous semester.
Warrant	Since a person who fails three courses may be dismissed from the university,
Backing	because of the university requirement that students maintain at least a 2.5 average,
Qualification	it is probable that,
Reservation	unless John earns grades in other courses high enough to compensate for his failing grades, or can prove that special circumstances affected his work,
Claim	he will be dismissed from the university.

Here is Wertheimer's argument on compulsory voting, analyzed according to this model. The backing here comes not from laws and precedents or well established scientific facts, but rather from well established political truths and observations that Wertheimer believes his audience will accept as sufficient evidence for the warrant. We have kept the original wording where possible:

Data	Many Americans do not exercise their right to vote. [Interpretation of this fact: They take free rides when they can, and believe voting is not in their individual interest.]
Warrant	Since a compulsory voting system is technically possible, and does increase the percentage of voters (no **backing** given), and since voting is essential to democracy,
Backing	because all Americans benefit from a public good available to all, and because elections keep officials at least somewhat responsive to our preferences,
Qualification	though it will not achieve perfect results—
Reservation	with the understanding that citizens will be able to abstain when no candidate is satisfactory to them—
Claim	voting should be made compulsory.

The "warrants" distinguished by Toulmin are sometimes similar to the premises in the deductive arguments we have been discussing in this chapter. Clearly, the strength of these warrants depends on how strong the backing for them is taken to be. As the Wertheimer argument shows, that backing is sometimes assumed: the facts or evidence may be considered obvious, or as in the first of Wertheimer's warrants, not pertinent enough to the whole argument to require discussion.

The particular strength of the Toulmin model is that it allows us to distinguish and analyze arguments, where inductive evidence provides premises or is used to support them. It also helps us organize such arguments, in particular the data, warrants, and background in our confirmation.

Exercises

1. The following passage makes a claim about what market behavior will be in the 1980s, presents data in support of this claim, and states a reservation and a qualification—the degree of probability for the claim. What is that data, claim, reservation and qualification, and what is the stated or implied warrant that connects the data with the claim?

   It was not until after the gasoline price rise of 1979 that the American public took advantage of the large fuel savings that could be achieved by shifting to a fleet better suited to modern patterns of usage. As a result sales of five- and six-passenger cars and the larger light trucks have dropped sharply. In the first half of 1980 four-passenger cars captured 45 percent of the passenger-car market, compared with 33 percent in 1978. Even this shift, however, leaves vehicle capacity and actual transportation requirements badly mismatched. Surveys show that on about 80 percent of all trips American cars carry no more than two people and that in a little more than half of all trips the driver is alone. Therefore it is likely that if inexpensive, fuel-efficient two-passenger cars become available in the 1980s, many will be sold. (Today the only such vehicles available are relatively expensive and energy-inefficient sports cars.)

   It is hazardous, of course, to predict market behavior when complex social factors enter in, but assuming that periodic gasoline shortages and price increases will continue to occur over the next decade, a passenger-car sales mix in the mid- to late 1980s might have a breakdown something like the following: two-seaters 25 percent, four-seaters 50 percent and five- or six-seaters 25 percent. In addition the demand for light trucks might drop to a ratio of only one truck to every six cars sold instead of the current one to every four.

   Charles L. Gray, Jr., and Frank von Hippel, *"The Fuel Economy of*
   Light Vehicles," Scientific American, May, 1981

2. Construct an argument of your own, following either illustration given in the Toulmin model. Then write this argument in the form of a paragraph or essay. In the margin, identify the various parts (data, warrant, backing, qualifier, claim).

Prewriting

For the planning and writing of a deductive essay, we will consider two articles that we hope will stimulate your interest and thinking about an important current issue. The analytic method described below can be used for preliminary thinking about any interesting issue on which comparable materials exist.

In short, we propose to examine the assumptions of an editorial opposing capital punishment, then contrast these assumptions with those of an argument in favor of capital punishment. The purpose of this examination is to help you identify your own assumptions and trace their origins—in social and religious training, or some other process by which beliefs are generated.

The editorial in *The Journal of the American Judicature Society* introduces the argument for capital punishment based on its deterrent effect on would-be criminals, and then argues against it on the ground that it is contradictory. For the state that enforces this penalty declares murder "an act of crime," then makes it a policy of the state to commit the same crime. We can easily identify the assumptions on which the argument is based, for these are stated directly. Note that several of these assumptions are presented as true without further proof or support:

1. There are better ways of obtaining that assurance [that the murderer will commit no more crimes] than by committing another homicide.
2. The state, representing organized society, should apply a higher standard to itself, not a lower one.
3. Every time human life is intentionally destroyed by fellow man . . . mankind is degraded and admits kinship with the beasts.
4. Any homicide, however committed or under whatever auspices, is an act of violence.

The first is obviously an assumption based on long observation and experience and considered to be so well supported that it can serve as a premise in a deductive argument. The second and third are different in origin. Both are based on beliefs about what makes a society good and what makes a human being "human." Neither of these assumptions is argued; we know that the writer considers them so well established that they can serve as the basis for the conclusion. The fourth is based on the logical principle of noncontradiction: a statement cannot be true if it

contradicts itself, and since it is contradictory to consider capital punishment as anything other than a homicide, it must be a false solution
to a problem for which other solutions exist. The main argument against
capital punishment is clearly based on this same logical principle.

We now have a basis to weigh the arguments of Barzun. But to do so
we must decide whether we agree with these four assumptions. Before
reading Barzun, write down your reasons for agreeing or disagreeing
with each of the assumptions; then write down other beliefs that you
hold concerning the taking of human life and the punishment you think
should be meted out. For each of these beliefs, write down what you
think is the origin of it.

Now read Barzun, and as you read write down assumptions you find
stated or implied. Note that Barzun's assumptions may not be stated as
directly as those in the editorial are. Thus Barzun states in his second
paragraph:

> But a man's inability to control his violent impulses or to imagine the fatal
> consequences of his acts should be a presumptive reason for his elimination
> from society.

Consider what the statement implies: individual rights—the right to drive
while drunk, the right to race on public highways—do not have precedence over the rights of the society as a whole. Barzun might also believe
that society as a whole is composed of individuals, each of whom has
the right to live so long as he does not harm others.

Look to see whether these assumptions are stated explicitly later in
the passage. And look for and write down other such assumptions. On
the basis of his statements, do you think Barzun would disagree with all
four assumptions stated as arguments against capital punishment? On
what essential matters do Barzun and *Judicature* disagree? Such a comparison will help you to think out some of the major arguments for and
against capital punishment, and to identify both explicit and implicit
assumptions that you hold. But it is important to write these down, considering as you do so the origin of the belief and the strength with which
you hold it.

You have now identified assumptions that can serve as the premises
of a deductive argument of your own on capital punishment. Before trying
to construct such an argument, you need to test one or more of the assumptions on which you will base your response to ideas in one of the
essays. To do so, first decide which of the two you wish to respond to,
in part or in whole. If, for example, you wish to challenge the assumption
that society, in order to protect the right to life of its individual members,
is justified in taking the life of someone who has violated that right, you
will need to show why an opposite conclusion is true—that is, why individual rights, including those of a murderer, have precedence over
those of society considered as a collection of individuals.

Though you may hold as an unquestioned belief that individual rights are supreme, you must be prepared to show that conclusions derived from it must be true also. Assume that you have been challenged by a proponent of capital punishment and are forced to defend your assumption in this way. Think of conclusions he or she may suggest, and consider how you would answer this person in an actual face-to-face discussion. Anticipating objections and answering them is the way refutation is managed in developing an argument. You may, for example, anticipate the objection that in protecting the rights of a murderer you are interfering with the rights of innocent people. You may then wish to qualify your assumption. But you must exercise care in assuring that your qualification does not undercut your argument, or you are perforce under an obligation to give up that argument.

In examining your assumptions and beliefs, you are in effect looking to see whether one assumption you hold contradicts another. The advantage of engaging in this examination before constructing or entering into the actual argument, or writing one, is obvious. The prosecutor in a murder trial, for example, anticipates the arguments of an opponent and may seek to answer them in the opening statement; he or she usually does so in the closing one. And there is one additional step that you need to take. Consider what specific rights would be implied by the assumption that individual rights are absolute with the following qualification:

> If individual rights have precedence over those of society, so long as the rights of other individuals are not interfered with,
> then parents have the right not to educate their children,
> the right to own firearms is absolute,
> people have the right to use drugs not approved by the FDA,
> people have the right to risk their lives in dangerous stunts, even to commit suicide.

You may agree with some of these conclusions, but those you do disagree with provide an important test of the assumption.

If, for example, you disagree that parents have the right not to educate their children, you need to look closely at your assumption, including the qualification "so long as the rights of other individuals are not interfered with." The word "rights" needs exact definition: it will probably be the center of debate in the argument over capital punishment and related issues.

In constructing a deductive argument of your own, remember that arguments do not exist apart from actual controversies. It would be best to develop your argument in response to an editorial or letter to the editor, or an essay like that of Barzun, with which you disagree in part or in whole. We have suggested here the stages that might be followed in constructing the argument. We need also to organize it. Here, again, is the pattern of the argumentative essay discussed earlier. You may want to adapt it to your own essay.

Introduction, stating the issue to be argued, and identifying your opponent—Barzun or "Judicature"

Narrative or background, summarizing the ideas of your opponent, with attention to particular assumptions you disagree with. Notice that even those assumptions with which you agree need to be identified and discussed. Keep this narrative moderate in length: don't try to cover all of the points made and examples given.

Division of proofs, and *thesis statement:* your position on capital punishment, and the arguments you will present in support. Again, keep this "division" short: its purpose is to provide a map of the discussion to follow. Like a map it must be simple to follow.

Confirmation, stating your assumptions and the conclusions you deduce from them, your illustrations, and discussion of other important assumptions and conclusions (perhaps specific rights that these assumptions entail)

Refutation, anticipating objections to your argument, and answering them

Conclusion, summarizing your main argument, and perhaps commenting on a current controversy (perhaps debate over an impending execution) to which it is pertinent

Remember that your refutation might precede your confirmation or be combined with it.

THOU SHALT NOT KILL

Judicature

Capital punishment is one of a number of controversial issues on which the Supreme Court of the United States may hand down a ruling during its present term. The time has come for this relic of barbarism to be banished from the United States courts.

Nobody should take seriously the contention that the death penalty is necessary for the sake of its deterrent effect on other presons who may be tempted to commit crime. Centuries of history leave any deterrence at all a matter of doubt, and psychology confirms that persons contemplating commission of crime are either not thinking of punishment or are confident that it will not happen to them.

A murderer who is hanged is not going to commit any more murders, true enough, but there are better ways of obtaining that assurance than by committing another homicide.

No alleged justification of capital punishment can excuse or disguise the inconsistency and the horror of the state declaring an act a crime and then making it a part of the state's policy to commit the same act itself. Those who think it does should be willing to concede the right of a prosecuting attorney to use fraudulent evidence in court although the defense may not do so, or the right of Internal Revenue to cheat to increase a taxpayer's tax while forbidding him to cheat to reduce it. If there is to be any difference between moral standards for the individual and for the state, then the state, representing organized society, should apply a higher standard to itself, not a lower one.

Old Testament scripture is cited in defense of capital punishment. The same authority may be used to support bigamy and genocide. We need not condemn Solomon for his thousand wives, or Samuel for utterly destroying the Amalekites and hewing Agag to pieces, but neither do we have to emulate them. Every time human life is intentionally destroyed by fellow man, whether in anger, in war, or in execution of a sentence of a court of justice, mankind is degraded and admits kinship with the beasts.

Any homicide, however committed or under whatever auspices, is an act of violence. There is abundant evidence, psychological and sociological, that violence begets violence. At a time in our national history when crimes of violence have increased to the point of becoming a national emergency, let us tell the world, but mostly let us tell ourselves, that we are too civilized to tolerate the death penalty in our courts any longer.

IN FAVOR OF CAPITAL PUNISHMENT*

Jacques Barzun

The four main arguments advanced against the death penalty are: *1.* punishment for crime is a primitive idea rooted in revenge; *2.* capital punishment does not deter; *3.* judicial error being possible, taking life is an appalling risk; *4.* a civilized state, to deserve its name, must uphold, not violate, the sanctity of human life.

I entirely agree with the first pair of propositions, which is why, a moment ago, I replaced the term capital punishment with "judicial homicide." The uncontrollable brute whom I want put out of the way is not to be punished for his misdeeds, nor used as an example or a warning; he is to be killed for the protection of others, like the wolf that escaped not long ago in a Connecticut suburb. No anger, vindictiveness or moral conceit need preside over the removal of such dangers. But a man's inability to control his violent impulses or to imagine the fatal consequences of his acts should be a presumptive reason for his elimination from society. This generality covers drunken driving and teen-age racing on public highways, as well as incurable obsessive violence; it might be extended (as I shall suggest later) to other acts that destroy, precisely, the moral basis of civilization.

But why kill? I am ready to believe the statistics tending to show that the prospect of his own death does not stop the murderer. For one thing he is often a blind egotist, who cannot conceive the possibility of his own death. For another, detection would have to be infallible to deter the more imaginative who, although afraid, think they can escape discovery. Lastly, as Shaw long ago pointed out, hanging the wrong man will deter as effectively as hanging the right one. So, once again, why kill? If I agree that moral progress means an increasing respect for human life, how can I oppose abolition?

*From the essay of the same title.

I do so because on this subject of human life, which is to me the heart of the controversy, I find the abolitionist inconsistent, narrow or blind. The propaganda for abolition speaks in hushed tones of the sanctity of human life, as if the mere statement of it as an absolute should silence all opponents who have any moral sense. But most of the abolitionists belong to nations that spend half their annual income on weapons of war and that honor research to perfect means of killing. These good people vote without a qualm for the political parties that quite sensibly arm their country to the teeth. The West today does not seem to be the time or place to invoke the absolute sanctity of human life. As for the clergymen in the movement, we may be sure from the experience of two previous world wars that they will bless our arms and pray for victory when called upon, the sixth commandment notwithstanding.

"Oh, but we mean the sanctity of life *within* the nation!" Very well: is the movement then campaigning also against the principle of self-defense? Absolute sanctity means letting the cutthroat have his sweet will of you, even if you have a poker handy to bash him with, for you might kill. And again, do we hear any protest against the police firing at criminals on the street—mere bank robbers usually—and doing this, often enough, with an excited marksmanship that misses the artist and hits the bystander? The absolute sanctity of human life is, for the abolitionist, a slogan rather than a considered proposition.

Yet, it deserves examination, for upon our acceptance or rejection of it depend such other highly civilized possibilities as euthanasia and seemly suicide. The inquiring mind also wants to know, why the sanctity of *human* life alone? My tastes do not run to household pets, but I find something less than admirable in the uses to which we put animals—in zoos, laboratories and space machines—without the excuse of the ancient law, "Eat or be eaten."

It should moreover be borne in mind that this argument about sanctity applies—or would apply—to about ten persons a year in Great Britain and to between fifty and seventy-five in the United States. These are the average numbers of those executed in recent years. The count by itself should not, of course, affect our judgment of the principle: one life spared or forfeited is as important, morally, as a hundred thousand. But it should inspire a comparative judgment: there are hundreds and indeed thousands whom, in our concern with the horrors of execution, we forget: on the one hand, the victims of violence; on the other, the prisoners in our jails.

The victims are easy to forget. Social science tends steadily to mark a preference for the troubled, the abnormal, the problem case. Whether it is poverty, mental disorder, delinquency or crime, the "patient material" monopolizes the interest of increasing groups of people among the most generous and learned. Psychiatry and moral liberalism go together; the application of law as we have known it is thus coming to be regarded as an historic prelude to social work, which may replace it entirely. Modern literature makes the most of this same outlook, caring only for the disturbed spirit, scorning as bourgeois those who pay their way and do *not* stab their friends. All the while the determinism of natural science reinforces the assumption that society causes its own evils. A French jurist, for example, says that in order to understand crime we must first brush aside all ideas of Responsibility. He means the criminal's and takes for granted that of society. The murderer kills because reared in a broken home or, conversely, because at an early age he witnessed his parents making love. Out of such cases, which make pathetic reading in the literature of modern criminology, is born the abolitionist's state of mind: we dare not kill those we are beginning to understand so well.

If, moreover, we turn to the accounts of the crimes committed by these unfortunates, who are the victims? Only dull ordinary people going about their business. We are sorry, of course, but they do not interest science on its march. Balancing, for example, the sixty to seventy criminals executed annually in the United States, there were the seventy to eighty housewives whom George Cvek robbed, raped and usually killed during the months of a career devoted to proving his virility. "It is too bad." Cvek alone seems instructive, even though one of the law officers who helped track him down quietly remarks: "As to the extent that his villainies disturbed family relationships, or how many women are still haunted by the specter of an experience they have never disclosed to another living soul, these questions can only lend themselves to sterile conjecture."

The remote results are beyond our ken, but it is not idle to speculate about those whose death by violence fills the daily two inches at the back of respectable newspapers—the old man sunning himself on a park bench and beaten to death by four hoodlums, the small children abused and strangled, the middle-aged ladies on a hike assaulted and killed, the family terrorized by a released or escaped lunatic, the half-dozen working people massacred by the sudden maniac, the boatload of persons dispatched by the skipper, the mindless assaults upon schoolteachers and shopkeepers by the increasing horde of dedicated killers in our great cities. Where does the sanctity of life begin?

It is all very well to say that many of these killers are themselves "children," that is, minors. Doubtless a nine-year-old mind is housed in that 150 pounds of unguided muscle. Grant, for argument's sake, that the misdeed is "the fault of society," trot out the broken home and the slum environment. The question then is, What shall we do, not in the Utopian city of tomorrow, but here and now? The "scientific" means of cure are more than uncertain. The apparatus of detention only increases the killer's antisocial animus. Reformatories and mental hospitals are full and have an understandable bias toward discharging their inmates. Some of these are indeed "cured"—so long as they stay under a rule. The stress of the social free-for-all throws them back on their violent modes of self-expression. At that point I agree that society has failed—twice: it has twice failed the victims, whatever may be its guilt toward the killer.

As in all great questions, the moralist must choose, and choosing has a price. I happen to think that if a person of adult body has not been endowed with adequate controls against irrationally taking the life of another, that person must be judicially, painlessly, regretfully killed before that mindless body's horrible automation repeats.

Exercises

1. In the following excerpts, identify the explicit assumptions and the conclusions drawn from them. Be ready to discuss your opinion of the arguments:

   a. The extreme vulnerability of a complex industrial society to intelligent, targeted terrorism by a very small number of people may prove the fatal challenge to which Western states have no adequate response. Counterforce alone will never suffice. The real challenge of the true terrorist is to the basic values of a society. If there is no commitment to shared values in Western society—and if none are imparted in our amoral institutions of higher learning—no increase in police and burglar alarms will suffice to preserve our society from the specter that haunts us—not a bomb from above but a gun from within.

   James Billington, *"The Gun Within"*

   b. To fully believe in something, to truly understand something, one must be intimately acquainted with its opposite. One should not adopt a creed by default, because no alternative is known. Education should prepare students for the "real world" not by segregating them from evil but by urging full confrontation to test and modify the validity of the good.

   Robert Baron, *"In Defense of 'Teaching' Racism, Sexism, and Fascism"*

   c. In a free society, man exercises his right to sustain his own life by producing economic values in the form of goods and services that he is, or should be, free to exchange with other men who are similarly free to trade with him or not. The economic values produced, however, are not given as gifts by nature, but exist only by virtue of the thought and effort of individual men. Goods and services are thus owned as a consequence of the right to sustain life by one's own physical and mental effort.

   Robert M. Sade, *"Medical Care As a Right: A Refutation"*

2. Identify the form of deductive argument—categorical, hypothetical, disjunctive—employed in the following arguments. Note that premises in the arguments may be omitted:

   a. Again, if the United States be not a government proper, but an association of states in the nature of contract merely, can it, as a contract, be peaceably unmade by less than all the parties who made it? One party to a contract may violate it—break it, so to speak; but does it not require all to lawfully rescind it?

   Abraham Lincoln, *First Inaugural Address*

b. If the United States is a government proper, then it cannot be terminated by any of the parties who made it. But the United States is a government proper. Therefore, it cannot be peaceably terminated by any of the parties who made it.

c. Either the U.S. is an association of states related by contract, or it is a government proper. But the U.S. is not an association of states related by contract. So it must be a government proper.

d. If the object of education is the improvement of men, then any system of education that is without values is a contradiction in terms.

Robert M. Hutchins, The Conflict in Education

e. If it is true that slang is short lived, and studies of language prove this to be so, tomorrow's youth will not understand the slang of today's youth.

3. The following passage contains a chain of arguments—a sorites. Show the connection between each of the statements, supplying intervening conclusions and premises where omitted. The author, Lewis Mumford, is discussing the impact of mass technology, particularly its new affluence, on the scientists who previously did not have to justify their research on practical grounds:

> As an operator in this power-oriented technics, the scientist becomes a servant of corporate organizations intent on enlarging the bounds of empire—by no means always Bacon's "human empire." Increasingly the "gross national product" of industry reflects the gross national product of science. Every theoretic innovation, however innocent in intention, automatically miltiplies the number of practical products—and, more significantly, profit-making wants. By participating in this transformation, the scientist has forfeited the qualities that were exalted in the past as his special hallmark: his detachment from worldly gains and his disinterested pursuit of truth.

The Pentagon of Power

Chapter Five

Argument and Audience

The uses of argument

Audiences are different, and the kinds of proof and organization suited to one may not be suited to another. Thus an audience of scientists brings different presuppositions to scientific arguments than theologians bring to religious ones. And each wider audience contains particular audiences—each with their special frame of reference or context, shared knowledge, values, language, and attitudes.

For this reason, arguments seldom reason baldly to conclusions. Writers do more than merely state the premises, as happens in a plain geometrical proof. They explain and defend them, and build the argument step by step, choosing proofs and ways to present them that grip the attention of audiences. They hope that they will earn not only the understanding of the audience, but also their conviction and good will. This need to maintain the interest and good will of audiences explains why the Greek philosopher Aristotle added to the proof of reason the proof of character—the demonstration that the speaker of an oration is a good person whose words can be believed—and also the proof of emotion or *pathos*, which invites the audience to listen to their own feelings.

We see this shaping of arguments in three kinds of discourse with which Aristotle and other rhetoricians have been concerned. In the prosecutor's indictment we discussed in an earlier chapter, the argument is fitted to suppositions about the jury. Prosecutors know that some of the premises require no defense: they need not argue that murder or theft are crimes deserving punishment. They can assume general agreement on these at least. But in arguing for the death sentence, they cannot assume that juries will agree on the kinds of punishment to be meted out. Further, they will not merely present the evidence of guilt in bare detail, but will organize this evidence, perhaps beginning with facts that will seem obvious to the jury and will require no explanation or commentary, and then moving to less obvious ones that do require explanation. The refutation will clearly depend on what doubts the jury may have and on what objections the defense attorney may introduce in addressing the jury later.

Were the arguments for reinstituting the death penalty presented to a legislature, the evidence and assumptions introduced and argued would also be shaped by an estimate of the audience. Since legislators are usually people educated in the law, certain precedents probably need not be reviewed in detail. More than this, juries are concerned with what happened in the past; legislators, mainly with what will happen in the future. This difference also influences the presentation of evidence and its discussion. The kinds of proof presented will also be different. Though both juries and legislators are concerned with precedent, judicial discourse is concerned with proofs relating to justice and injustice, deliberative discourse with policy governing the whole of the nation, to cite just one difference.

A third kind of discourse, the ceremonial (the funeral eulogy, patriotic addresses, public tributes and presentations of awards) is shaped by different considerations. Though the speaker wants to convince the audience that the person being honored is worthy, greater agreement can be assumed on a range of matters—from beliefs about what is deserving of honor to the facts of the case. In his Gettysburg Address, Lincoln reminded his audience of what they already knew and believed: he did not have to defend or review them at length. And it would have been out of place to engage in refutation of any kind. He was not addressing an audience opposed to the war then in progress.

By contrast, many speakers eulogizing the dead during the Vietnam War did engage in a defense of it—to counter the widespread belief that soldiers in Vietnam were dying in vain. The funeral eulogy in this case did contain a refutation.

Much depends on how special the audience is thought by the speaker or writer to be. The more general the audience, the more various will be its interests, values, and biases, and therefore the less appropriate will be appeals directed at length to one segment of it. The less various its interests and the more unified or special its concerns, the more appropriate and convincing will be appeals narrowly focused and developed at length. We would be surprised if a new President, in his inaugural address, spoke only about the needs of farmers or blue-collar workers or large corporations, though his principal concern during the election campaign had been with these special interest groups.

General and particular arguments

Another illustration of different approaches to various audiences is that speakers and writers often look beyond a particular audience and speak to people living in the future. The Declaration of Independence addresses the American colonists as well as the government of Great Britain, and in addition deals with issues that Jefferson probably believed would be of concern to later generations of Americans. Though Lincoln was memorializing soldiers who had died in the war still in progress, the Gettysburg Address is concerned with issues important to us today.

To cite another example, Henry David Thoreau's essay on civil disobedience is concerned with the justice of the Mexican-American War of 1846–48, yet Thoreau states the issues of that war in general terms:

> The objections which have been brought against a standing army, and they are many and weighty, and deserve to prevail, may also at last be brought against a standing government. The standing army is only an arm of the standing government. The government itself, which is only the mode which the people have chosen to execute their will, is equally liable to be abused and perverted before the people can act through it.

Thoreau is addressing American citizens in 1848, but he also has Americans of the future in mind. The particular issue is of concern to people in 1848; the general issue is of concern to them and to people later. In the whole essay he takes up the broader issue. He is, in fact, developing an argument sometimes called *a fortiori*: the Latin name for "from the stronger argument." Thus, if I can make the case that a standing government does not always deserve the support of the citizen, and that civil disobedience is sometimes warranted, then it must follow that the citizen need not give support to a standing army—a seemingly less important issue than that of a standing government, but the central issue to Thoreau because it is directly related to the issue of the Mexican War.

We see, then, that there are not just general and particular audiences but also general and particular issues. But note that general audiences are not concerned only with general issues, or particular audiences necessarily with particular issues. The general issue may be of less immediate concern, and may deal with general policy, perhaps one that will concern the nation long after the particular issue (the Mexican War, Vietnam) is forgotten.

Though also concerned with a general policy or principle, the particular issue deals with an immediate problem that demands solution. The national debate on the American hostages held in Iran during 1979 and 1980 illustrates the difference. The debate focused on the specific actions that should have been taken to free the hostages (particular issue), but it also included the questions of what should be done by any country facing a similar situation and whether negotiations to free hostages should be undertaken at all (general issues).

A writer has to decide whether to state the issue in general or particular terms. The occasion of the argument sometimes settles the question. A letter to a newspaper protesting a restrictive parking policy may seem pretentious if general issues of freedom are addressed. A principle may be involved, but the writer may choose not to raise it, and instead may attack the policy as impractical and expensive. In most arguments, the decision of which issue to emphasize depends on what the participants agree is the point of disagreement.

Exercise

For each of the particular issues below, list two or three general issues that might be raised in the course of an argument. For example, if the particular issue is the right of the American colonists to resist paying the Stamp Tax, one general issue might be the right of the governed to resist laws they did not help make:

a. eliminating a university physical education requirement

b. reimposing the draft for selective service

c. requiring yearly examination of persons over 65 for driving licenses

d. graduating automobile taxes on the basis of gas consumption

e. legalizing marijuana for medical uses

f. legalizing marijuana

g. denying high school diplomas to those who cannot pass competence tests in English and mathematics

Writing Assignments

1. Analyze a series of letters to newspapers and news magazines on a particular issue of the moment to distinguish general and particular arguments. Draw a conclusion from this analysis about the major concerns of the various writers.

2. Analyze your own concerns about an important issue of the day, perhaps one of the issues suggested above. Distinguish particular from general issues.

Point at issue

In ordinary arguments, we usually establish the point at issue in the preliminary give and take that opens it. We discover on what matters and basic assumptions we agree and disagree. Each participant states his or her views, and out of this discussion emerges what is to be argued specifically—the point at issue.

In an argument over restoring the draft, everyone may agree that the United States requires an army; in fact, this need may be taken for granted, and may not even be mentioned. The point at issue may rather be whether military service must be compulsory to maintain a strong army. And if there is agreement that it must be compulsory, the argument may center on the issue whether only men should be drafted. As with general and particular issues, the occasion of the argument may determine the point at issue, or at least limit the possible issues.

For example, one recent writer on the subject begins an essay with a statement of the events that have prompted a national debate:

> The signing into law by President Carter of a program of registration for draft-age young men this past summer was shortsighted and, at best, uninspired. Registration implies the possibility of a peacetime draft and the certainty of a wartime draft. In either case, if President Carter simply "revitalizes" and "reimposes" the draft, as he indicated he might in his State of the Union speech, a valuable opportunity for America will have been missed.
>
> Leon Botstein, *"The Debate over the Draft: We Need a Fresh Approach,"*
> *Chronicle of Higher Education*, September 2, 1980

Botstein then narrows the debate to what he believes should be the point at issue:

> President Carter and Congress ought to enlarge on their responses to the current international predicament, to the residual and potentially strong feeling of national solidarity and patriotism since Iran and Afghanistan, and move forward with a constructive program of mandatory national service for young people. Rather than a meaningless, if not inflammatory, first step to a draft, we need a new approach, a new service opportunity for the young, which can and should include the option of military service for men *and* women.

When we write for a particular audience, we need to know what concerns it at the moment, even if we intend to argue a point of less immediate concern, such as mandatory national service. We may begin with a statement about an issue that involves our readers directly, and then try to persuade them that the point we wish to argue is more pressing than that issue or is indirectly related to it. In the current debate over nuclear power, the issue for some is whether the benefits are worth the alleged risks, to others whether nuclear power has benefits at all, and to still others whether risks exist at all. In arguing the benefits of nuclear power, we will not gain the attention of its opponents unless we address their concerns first.

Botstein does exactly this later in his essay, first granting the need of a strong citizen army—a major concern of those who are asking for a return of the draft—then showing why mandatory national service is preferable to the draft. Young people will be alienated, Botstein argues, making the issue divisive:

> We need a service program that can help succeeding generations form a strong civic bond, that can help transform our nation of individuals into a nation of citizens. Military service has done that in the past only for some males.

Writing for an audience holding a variety of views as Botstein is doing, we sometimes need to define the issue as broadly as possible and narrow the discussion gradually. For we do not have the advantage of the give and take of ordinary conversation. We cannot be sure how broad or narrow the concerns of any segment of the audience we want to reach are. If Botstein wants to persuade men and women, young and old, he must take their special concerns into account. He must decide what presuppositions they share—presuppositions that affect the point at issue.

We shall turn to this matter of presupposition next. What we have been saying is that the point at issue has a context—one defined by the circumstances of the argument, the nature of the audience, the available evidence, the extent of agreement on basic assumptions (the presuppositions to be discussed next), and the intentions of the writer or speaker.

Exercises

1. Identify the point at issue in each of the editorials or the letters to the editor in a newspaper you read.
2. State what you consider to be the point at issue in two or three current disputes of the moment—perhaps the public debate over nuclear power or women's rights.

Writing Assignments

1. Compare two of the following magazines to find out how different the audiences of each of them are. Base your comparison on more than one kind of evidence—not just ads, but cartoons, editorials, letters to the editor, the focus and content of articles. Note that the two audiences may have much in common, but may differ in social or economic class, in age, or in profession.
   a. *Sports Illustrated*
   b. *Field and Stream*
   c. *The Smithsonian*
   d. *National Geographic*
   e. *The New Yorker*

    f. *New York Magazine*

    g. *Ms.*

    h. *Better Homes and Gardens*

    i. *Mademoiselle*

    j. *Esquire*

2. Choose one of the public issues you dealt with in Exercise number two and discuss how you would adapt an argument to the audiences you chose in Writing Assignment number one. Outline each of your presentations of the argument.

Presuppositions

In thinking out the basic argument, the question each speaker and writer asks is, Where do I begin? We can best understand what the question means by looking again at how Botstein opens his essay on the draft (see p. 131). We see here how much information Botstein presumes his audience possesses. He does not review the circumstances that led President Carter to reimpose registration; he does not, for example, take note of criticisms that had been made by military people, Congressmen and others concerning recruitment of army personnel, reenlistment of servicemen, pay incentives and the like. And he says little in the rest of the essay about increasing threats to the United States that, in the opinion of many, require a vastly increased national defense. He might also have reviewed published statements of government officials who were responsible for the reimposed registration and previously supported it. Though he does not presume his audience knows all of this background, he does assume they know some of it.

    Botstein also presupposes certain beliefs or assumptions. Presupposition, in logic, usually refers to a general, underlying assumption that is taken for granted. Unless the parties are totally at cross-purposes, there are common presuppositions that are never brought up in the course of the argument. In the Toulmin analysis given earlier, presuppositions are part of warrants or are very general warrants (or premises) that remain unstated.

    A presupposition in Botstein's argument is the following: "Provided the world situation remains as it is. . . ." Botstein presupposes this much, and something more. For he assumes there will be agreement that a strong national defense is necessary, and he begins his argument without defending this belief. If in the course of an oral argument he were to discover that an opponent held a different view of the world situation or national defense, he would have to take several steps back and argue his own belief.

    Most of the time we form presuppositions from the context of the argument. In everyday arguments with friends, we soon discover when we have assumed too much. In writing, it is difficult to know how wide agreement is on basic assumptions. Some writers assume more than others, and begin with the specific issue without reviewing or defending wider issues and assumptions. Others assume a variety of concerns, opinions, and beliefs in their audience, and begin with essential facts and beliefs—a wider background needed to understand the issue, and a wider ground for discussion.

For example, the psychiatrist Karl Menninger opens an essay on punishment with a general review of common attitudes:

> Few words in our language arrest our attention as do "crime," "violence," "revenge," and "injustice." We abhor crime; we adore justice; we boast that we live by the rule of law. Violence and vengefulness we repudiate as unworthy of our civilization, and we assume this sentiment to be unanimous among all human beings.
>
> *"The Crime of Punishment"*

Menninger might have omitted this review and begun with this later paragraph:

> The inescapable conclusion is that society secretly *wants* crime, *needs* crime, and gains definite satisfactions from the present mishandling of it! We condemn crime; we punish offenders for it; but we need it. The crime and punishment ritual is a part of our lives. We need crimes to wonder at, to enjoy vicariously, to discuss and speculate about, and to publicly deplore. We need criminals to identify ourselves with, to envy secretly, and to punish stoutly. They do for us the forbidden, illegal things we *wish* to do and, like scapegoats of old, they bear the burdens of our displaced guilt and punishment—"the iniquities of us all."

This latter view shows why Menninger can presume no more agreement than he states in the paragraph quoted earlier. The major part of his essay, not surprisingly, is given to arguing the assumptions stated in this later paragraph. None of these assumptions is presupposed.

In other arguments, too narrow a presupposition or presumption of background can be as ineffective as too broad a one. An essay that assumes its readers possess no background whatever on the subject and begins at the beginning, reviewing the history of crime in America or of changing ideas on punishment, will quickly lose its reader's attention.

Exercise

Identify one or more presuppositions that underlie a television news report or magazine article. Explain what part presupposition plays in the argument.

Writing Assignments

1. For one of the following propositions below make (1) a list of general arguments that can be directed to everyone affected by it, (2) a list of particular arguments that can be directed to one segment of this group—for example, motorcyclists, and (3) a list of facts and assumptions that may be made in arguments directed to *one* of these audiences. Then write an essay defending or attacking the proposition. Direct the essay to this audience, and make the presuppositions that you consider fitting:

   a. The legal drinking age should (not) be 21.

   b. Education should (not) be compulsory beyond the age of 14.

   c. Motorcyclists should (not) be required to wear helmets.

   d. High school or university administrators should (not) control the contents of the school newspaper.

2. Examine the cartoon below. What presuppositions do you suppose the magazine shares with its readers? How much knowledge or information is the reader assumed to have? What details does the cartoon assume the reader will find humorous?

"I assure you, sir, that we in management at Allied Energycorp are ever mindful of our debt to Old Sol."

Drawing by Donald Reilly © 1981 The New Yorker Magazine, Inc.

The amount and choice of evidence

The backing for the premises of deductive arguments may consist of inductive evidence used for illustration. The amount and kind of evidence presented depends on the audience. Thus Menninger describes public attitudes and behavior in the following passage:

> Time and time again somebody shouts about this state of affairs [the national disgrace of crime and the criminal justice system], just as I am shouting now. The magazines shout. The newspapers shout. The television and radio commentators shout (or at least they "deplore"). Psychologists, sociologists, leading jurists, wardens and intelligent police chiefs join the chorus. Governors and mayors and Congressmen are sometimes heard. They shout that the situation is bad, bad, bad, and getting worse. Some suggest that we immediately replace obsolete procedures with scientific methods. A few shout contrary sentiments. Do the clear indications derived from scientific discovery for appropriate changes continue to fall on deaf ears? Why is the public so long-suffering, so apathetic and thereby so continuingly self-destructive? How many Presidents (and other citizens) do we have to lose before we do something?
>
> *"The Crime of Punishment"*

This inductive evidence serves as backing for a deductive argument that immediately follows. Menninger first draws a conclusion from the evidence just presented:

> The public behaves as a sick patient does when a dreaded treatment is proposed for his ailment.

He goes on to explain that the sick patient fights against a cure because of

> traitorous impulses that fight against the accomplishment of any change in himself, even recovery!

Indeed, the patient is like Hamlet in preferring to suffer familiar aches and sorrows rather than have to deal with new and complicating experiences. From these ideas Menninger infers the following:

> The inescapable conclusion is that society secretly *wants* crime, *needs* crime, and gains definite satisfactions from the present mishandling of it!

For an audience of psychiatrists—a special audience whose knowledge and concerns are perhaps roughly the same—only the deductive argument just given might have been enough. Psychiatrists may or may not have profited from the long description of public attitudes and behavior that served as backing for the statement that the public behaves like a sick patient.

But notice that the decision to develop a deductive argument depends on the belief that ideas are well enough established to offer conclusive grounds. Menninger's initial statement about the public and the "inescapable conclusion" he draws—a conclusion stated without qualification—show that he is developing a deductive argument. But the amount of illustration, support, or defense he provides, as in the long description just discussed, is another matter.

That amount varies from audience to audience, and it varies also according to the strength of the appeal the writer wishes to make. Menninger's careful mounting of evidence in his description gives the argument considerable force. Menninger knows that he must not just open the minds but also the hearts of his audience, and vivid examples of the kind he provides here and elsewhere in his essay serve this purpose. The choice of supporting evidence, in the form of analogy and sampling and the like, may also be determined by these considerations.

The nature of the discourse, we have seen, also determines the kind of reasoning employed. Inductive reasoning is essential in scientific discourse. The nature of the evidence may be in dispute, however. Thus the theory that the earth circles the sun can be given direct corroboration from sightings taken by astronauts. Before the advent of space travel, indirect corroboration came from observations and mathematical calculations made on earth: no person had actually seen the earth move. In earlier centuries, another kind of evidence was presented for the opposite belief:

> Theology teaches that the sun has been created in order to illuminate the earth. But one moves the torch in order to illuminate the house, and not the house in order to be illuminated by the torch. Hence it is the sun which revolves around the earth, and not the earth which revolves around the sun.
>
> Besian Array, 1671

The analogy here is clearly false, but what is considered to be a true analogy is often a cultural matter. Many in the seventeenth century agreed to consider the analogy a just one. This dependence on the culture as a basis for verifying hypotheses is one reason for the low repute of analogy in scientific reasoning, when it serves as the primary or only evidence. Nevertheless, it plays an essential role when processes in various areas are seen to be analogous and hypotheses for testing can be derived from these similarities.

Writing Assignment

Analyze the kinds of reasoning in the following dissent of Justice William O. Douglas, in *Public Utilities Commission v. Pollak* (1952). In this important case, the Public Utilities Commission of the District of Columbia ruled that the privately owned transit company of Washington was within its rights to broadcast the programs of a local radio station in its vehicles. The ruling was appealed to the Supreme Court on the grounds that the system violated the privacy of passengers under the due process clause of the Fifth Amendment ("No person . . . shall be deprived of life, liberty, or property without due process of law"), and that passengers were entitled under the First Amendment not to listen to ideas they disagreed with. The Court ruled against the Commission but said the constitutional amendments cited had not been violated. In his dissent, Douglas combined deductive with inductive arguments:

MR. JUSTICE DOUGLAS, Dissenting

This is a case of first impression. There are no precedents to construe; no principles previously expounded to apply. We write on a clean slate.

The case comes down to the meaning of "liberty" as used in the Fifth Amendment. Liberty in the constitutional sense must mean more than freedom from unlawful governmental restraint; it must include privacy as well, if it is to be a repository of freedom. The right to be let alone is indeed the beginning of all freedom. Part of our claim to privacy is in the prohibition of the Fourth Amendment against unreasonable searches and seizures. It gives the guarantee that a man's home is his castle beyond invasion either by inquisitive or by officious people. A man loses that privacy of course when he goes upon the streets or enters public places. But even in his activities outside the home he has immunities from controls bearing on privacy. He may not be compelled against his will to attend a religious service; he may not be forced to make an affirmation or observe a ritual that violates his scruples; he may not be made to accept one religious, political, or philosophical creed as against another. Freedom of religion and freedom of speech guaranteed by the First Amendment give more than the privilege to worship, to write, to speak as one chooses; they give freedom not to do nor to act as the government chooses. The First Amendment in its respect for the conscience of the individual honors the sanctity of thought and belief. To think as one chooses, to believe what one wishes are important aspects of the constitutional right to be let alone.

If we remembered this lesson taught by the First Amendment, I do not believe we would construe "liberty" within the meaning of the Fifth Amendment as narrowly as the Court does. The present case involves a form of coercion to make people listen. The listeners are of course in a public place; they are on streetcars traveling to and from home. In one sense it can be said that those who ride the streetcars do so voluntarily. Yet in a practical sense they are forced to ride, since this mode of transportation is today essential for many thousands. Compulsion which comes from circumstances can be as real as compulsion which comes from a command.

The streetcar audience is a captive audience. It is there as a matter of necessity, not of choice. One who is in a public vehicle may not of course complain of the noise of the crowd and the babble of tongues. One who enters any public place sacrifices some of his privacy. My protest is against the invasion of his privacy over and beyond the risks of travel.

The government may use the radio (or television) on public vehicles for many purposes. Today it may use it for a cultural end. Tomorrow it may use it for political purposes. So far as the right to privacy is concerned the purpose makes no difference. The music selected by one bureaucrat may be as offensive to some as it is soothing to others. The news commentator chosen to report on the events of the day may give overtones to the news that please the bureau head but which rile the streetcar captive audience. The political philosophy which one radio speaker exudes may be thought by the official who makes up the streetcar programs to be best for the welfare of the people. But the man who listens to it on his way to work in the morning and on his way home at night may think it marks the destruction of the Republic.

One who tunes in on an offensive program at home can turn it off or tune in another station, as he wishes. One who hears disquieting or unpleasant programs in public places, such as restaurants, can get up and leave. But the man on the streetcar has no choice but to sit and listen, or perhaps to sit and to try *not* to listen.

When we force people to listen to another's ideas, we give the propagandist a powerful weapon. Today it is a business enterprise working out a radio program under the auspices of government. Tomorrow it may be a dominant political or religious group. Today the purpose is benign; there is no invidious cast to the programs. But the vice is inherent in the system. Once privacy is invaded, privacy is gone. Once a man is forced to submit to one type of radio program, he can be forced to submit to another. It may be but a short step from a cultural program to a political program.

If liberty is to flourish, government should never be allowed to force people to listen to any radio program. The right of privacy should include the right to pick and choose from competing entertainments, competing propaganda, competing political philosophies. If people are let alone in those choices, the right of privacy will pay dividends in character and integrity. The strength of our system is in the dignity, the resourcefulness, and the independence of our people. Our confidence is in their ability as individuals to make the wisest choice. That system cannot flourish if regimentation takes hold. The right of privacy, today violated, is a powerful deterrent to any one who would control men's minds.

"Presence" in arguments

It is not enough to state our ideas cogently and reason soundly. We need to give the argument we are developing "presence"—that is, keep its importance before the reader, with our focus on its main points throughout the essay, as in successful advertising that draws on the resources of image and color and a highlighting of key words.

How is this highlighting accomplished in the essay? As in the advertisement, the writer can depend on emphasis of key words at pivotal points—at the beginning and end of paragraphs, for example. This is how Menninger introduces his thesis—at the end of this short paragraph and in italics:

> Offenders with propensities for impulsive and predatory aggression should not be permitted to live among us unrestrained by some kind of social control. *But the great majority of offenders, even "criminals," should never become prisoners if we want to "cure" them.*

Italics are, however, the rare exception. We help the reader recognize the thesis when we place it prominently in the essay. It is also highlighted when it is restated in the course of the essay, perhaps in different words and in light of new considerations. Thus Menninger restates his thesis toward the end with reference to public attitudes he identified earlier:

> For before we can diminish our sufferings from the ill-controlled aggressive assaults of fellow citizens, we must renounce the philosophy of punishment, the obsolete, vengeful penal attitude.

Vivid imagery and metaphor also contribute to "presence," indeed are perhaps the most important means of achieving it:

> Pain cannot be photographed; grimaces indicate but do not convey its intensity. And wounds—unlike violence—are rarely shown. This phony quality of television violence in its mentally unhealthy aspect encourages irrationality by giving the impressions to the observer that being beaten, kicked, cut, and stomped, while very unpleasant, are not very painful or serious. For after being slugged and beaten the hero rolls over, opens his eyes, hops up, rubs his cheek, grins, and staggers on. The *suffering* of violence is a part both the TV and movie producers *and* their audience tend to repress.
>
> *"The Crime of Punishment"*

Of course, too much vivid writing—like the overuse of italics—works against the effect the writer is trying to achieve. If everything is present, then nothing is. For this reason, metaphor and other figurative language must not call attention to itself in such a way that the idea it is developing is obscured or lost.

Presence is best achieved through the ethical appeal noted earlier: the belief of writers in what they have to say, and showing the reader that they are expressing their thoughts honestly. Sincerity will be evident if writers say exactly what they believe, instead of trying to hedge or disguise the implications of their ideas. Fitting arguments to particular audiences does not mean saying less than one wants to, or altering ideas to make them acceptable. There is a fine line to be observed here, and one not easy to define. An essay that lacks conviction or is written in clichés will hold the attention of few readers if any.

Exercise

Advertisers give "presence" to the product in various ways—for example, through repetition of the product name in the course of a television commercial. Examine the ads for bicycles earlier in this book to determine how similar the means are by which "presence" is achieved. Be ready to discuss how effective you find these devices.

Writing Assignment

Analyze an argumentative essay in a recent issue of a newspaper or magazine to show how the writer gives presence to the thesis and the main arguments and evidence. Comment on how effective you find this presence or highlighting.

Ways of organizing the argumentative essay

"Deductive" and "inductive" are sometimes used to describe ways of organizing the argumentative essay. We may find an essay that does the following: a truth or series of premises are presented, and a series of deductions made from them; that is, the writer shows what the truth or premises imply. The Declaration of Independence is organized very much in this way. The sorites illustrated in the previous chapter is a model of this kind of organization.

The inductive essay proceeds in the reverse order, developing a series of details or factual statements to a general conclusion based on them. We might, for example, list the wrongs done to the American colonists and build these wrongs to the conclusion that the colonists have a justifiable grievance against the British government that inflicted them. Notice that we use the inductive order when we wish to arrive at a probable truth such as we just stated. We could not use it to arrive at the general truths that open the Declaration.

We have seen that both orders can work together in arguments. In the model of the argumentative essay discussed and illustrated earlier we see that they may occur as part of the confirming arguments. Here again is the basic structure:

Introduction
Background or narrative
Division or proofs and thesis
Confirmation
Refutation
Conclusion

As we said earlier, this basic plan varies from writer to writer. The refutation, for example, may come before the confirmation or be combined with it. Here is an essay in which the latter is done:

OUR YOUTH SHOULD SERVE

by Steven Muller

Introduction
Background of
issue

Too many young men and women now leave school without a well-developed sense of purpose. If they go right to work after high school, many are not properly prepared for careers. But if they enter college instead, many do not really know what to study or what to do afterward. Our society does not seem to be doing much to encourage and use the best instincts and talents of our young.

On the one hand, I see the growing problems of each year's new generation of high school graduates. After twelve years of schooling—and television—many of them want to participate actively in society; but they face either a job with a limited future or more years in educational institutions. Many are wonderfully idealistic: they have talent and energy to offer, and they seek the meaning in their lives that comes from giving of oneself to the common good. But they feel almost rejected by a society that has too few jobs to offer them and that asks nothing of them except to avoid trouble. They want to be part of a new solution; instead society perceives them as a problem. They seek a cause; but their elders preach only self-advancement. They need experience on which to base choice; yet society seems to put a premium on the earliest possible choice, based inescapably on the least experience.

Thesis

On the other hand, I see an American society sadly in need of social services that we can afford less and less at prevailing costs of labor. Some tasks are necessary but constitute no career; they should be carried out, but not as anyone's lifetime occupation. Our democracy profoundly needs public spirit, but the economy of our labor system primarily encourages self-interest. The Federal government spends billions on opportunity grants for post-secondary education, but some of us wonder about money given on the basis only of need. We ask the young to volunteer for national defense, but not for the improvement of our society. As public spirit and public services decline, so does the quality of life. So I ask myself why cannot we put it all together and ask our young people to volunteer in peacetime to serve America?

Refutation and confirmation
(1) Not compulsory

I recognize that at first mention, universal national youth service may sound too much like compulsory military service or the Hitler youth or the Komsomol. I do not believe it has to be like that at all. It need not require uniforms or camps, nor a vast new Federal bureaucracy, nor vast new public expenditures. And it should certainly not be compulsory.

(2) Compelling incentives
  a. job training
  b. education
Further advantages
  a. end of tuition tax credits
  b. earned assistance
  c. simple grant program

A voluntary program of universal national youth service does of course require compelling incentives. Two could be provided. Guaranteed job training would be one. Substantial Federal assistance toward post-secondary education would be the other. This would mean that today's complex measures of Federal aid to students would be ended, and that there would also be no need for tuition tax credits for post-secondary education. Instead, prospective students would *earn* their assistance for post-secondary education by volunteering for national service, and only those who earned assistance would receive it. Present Federal expenditures for the assistance of students in post-secondary education would be converted into a simple grant program, modeled on the post-World War II GI Bill of Rights.

Refutation (cont.)
(3) Question: What would high school graduates do?
  a. intern in agencies
  b. work in various programs
  c. serve in military service or Peace Corps

But what, you say, would huge numbers of high school graduates do as volunteers in national service? They could be interns in public agencies, local, state and national. They could staff day-care programs, neighborhood health centers, centers to counsel and work with children; help to maintain public facilities, including highways, rail beds, waterways and airports; engage in neighborhood-renewal projects, both physical and social. Some would elect military service, others the peace Corps. Except for the latter two alternatives and others like them, they could live anywhere they pleased. They would not wear uniforms. They would be employed and supervised by people already employed locally in public-agency careers.

Refutation (cont.)
Payment

Volunteers would be paid only a subsistence wage, because they would receive the benefits of job training (not necessarily confined to one task) as well as assistance toward post-secondary education if they were so motivated and qualified. If cheap mass housing for some groups of volunteers were needed, supervised participants in the program could rebuild decayed dwellings in metropolitan areas.

Additional confirmation
Alternative version
  private employment

All that might work. But perhaps an even more attractive version of universal national youth service might include private industrial and commercial enterprise as well. A private employer would volunteer to select a stated number of volunteers. He would have their labor at the universally applied subsistence wage; in return he would offer guaranteed job training as well as the exact equivalent of what the Federal government would have to pay for assistance toward post-secondary education. The inclusion of volunteer private employers would greatly amplify job-training opportunities for the youth volunteers, and would greatly lessen the costs of the program in public funds.

Direct benefits
  a. a meaningful role
  b. job training
  c. earned educational assistance
  d. greater motivation and success
  e. careers

The direct benefits of such a universal national-youth-service program would be significant. Every young man and woman would face a meaningful role in society after high school. Everyone would receive job training, and the right to earn assistance toward post-secondary education. Those going on to post-secondary education would have their education interrupted by a constructive work experience. There is evidence that they would thereby become more highly motivated and successful students, particularly if their work experience related closely to subsequent vocational interests. Many participants might locate careers by means of their national service assignments.

  f. union jobs retained
  g. cheap labor
Indirect benefits
  a. sense of usefulness
  b. service and earning capacity
Conclusion
  Qualification

No union jobs need be lost, because skilled workers would be needed to give job training. Many public services would be performed by cheap labor, but there would be no youth army. And the intangible, indirect benefits would be the greatest of all. Young people could regard themselves as more useful and needed. They could serve this country for a two-year period as volunteers, and *earn* job training and/or assistance toward post-secondary education. There is more self-esteem and motivation in earned than in unearned benefits. Universal national youth service may be no panacea. But in my opinion the idea merits serious and imaginative consideration.

Introduction

Whatever else the introduction does, it must indicate the subject of the essay and do so in a way that engages the reader. Very seldom does the essay begin with a statement of the thesis: that would be rather abrupt. Usually the writer builds to the thesis, through details that prepare for it. Here is another use of inductive order.

How much preparation is necessary? Again, the answer depends on how much information on the subject the readers are assumed to possess.

More preparation is usually necessary for the general audience. Muller uses two paragraphs to build to his thesis:

> So I ask myself why cannot we put it all together and ask our young people to volunteer in peacetime to serve America?

The details that build to it concern American youth—their problems, their potentialities, their ideals—and the present needs of American society. These details in fact constitute the background or narrative, which Muller has used as an introduction. A much more elaborate essay probably would have introduced the subject at length, stating not only what the essay is about but also what purpose Muller has in mind. It would then have made a transition to the narrative. Journalistic essays like Muller's are less formal and more economical.

The occasion of the essay determines how broad a statement of the issues the introduction needs to provide and how formal the presentation need be. The preface to a book on biomedical issues, written to a professional audience chiefly, begins with a very general formal statement that would be out of place in an essay like Muller's:

> Man is an animal linked to inanimate matter; but human life transcends its earthly origin. Knowledge of the physiochemical determinants of life is of course essential for the understanding of man's nature. In their present state, however, the exact sciences fail to account for the phenomena which are of most direct relevance to the human condition.
>
> René Dubos, *Man Adapting*

The preface becomes increasingly specific about the issues of the book. The writer of the following introductory paragraph by contrast identifies himself and his interests, and at the same time states a problem which he will deal with in the book:

> Nearly twenty years ago, as part of my self-education for writing *The Rise of the West: A History of the Human Community,* I was reading about the Spanish conquest of Mexico. As everyone knows, Hernando Cortez, starting off with fewer than six hundred men, conquered the Aztec empire, whose subjects numbered millions. How could such a tiny handful prevail? How indeed? All the familiar explanations seemed inadequate. If Montezuma and his friends first thought the Spanish were gods, experience soon showed otherwise. If horses and gunpowder were amazing and terrible on first encounter, armed clashes soon revealed the limitations of horseflesh and of the very primitive guns the Spaniards had at their disposal. Cortez's skill in finding allies among the Indian peoples of Mexico and rallying them against the Aztecs was certainly important, but his Indian allies committed themselves to the Spanish side only when they had reason to think Cortez would win.
>
> William H. McNeill, *Plagues and Peoples*

One purpose of the introduction, it must not be forgotten, is to capture the attention of readers and dispose them to give the ideas of the essay a fair hearing. Too forceful an introduction may put them on the defensive. Opening rhetorical questions—"Have you considered the possibility of mandatory national service?"—may invite an unexpected rejoinder. If the writer begins with experiences and problems familiar to readers, and leads gradually to the thesis, interest will be awakened gently and will be fixed.

Finally, a brief comment on tone, an important consideration in writing introductions. Achieving the right tone can be difficult, and failure to do so accounts for many false starts in writing. Knowing what we want to say, we may not be able to find the right tone or "voice" to say it in. The way we speak to readers in our introductory paragraphs determines how we will speak to them throughout the essay. The tone can change, of course, but it is difficult to manage a change from the impersonal factual voice we hear in Dubos to the personal one we hear in McNeill.

No prescriptions can be given on this matter. We did say earlier that too informal or chatty a tone will possibly lose as many readers as will too formal a one. This much can be said: you will do well to address readers as you would people in small groups. Some of these people you will know well, and some you probably will not know at all—and you must write with the awareness that though many will know something about the subject not all will. All readers probably will appreciate a reminder of the essential facts and an explanation of their importance.

Background of the case

The background or narrative provides the essential facts, as we noted. What facts are considered essential depends on the point at issue. As we saw, the background in Muller forms the introduction. Economy is a virtue in such narratives, because the thesis or confirming arguments should not be delayed unnecessarily. Those that tell everything and do not select the essential facts lose the reader's attention and interest quickly.

One important kind of narrative is the review of prior work on the subject and various conclusions reached about it; this kind of narrative often introduces technical and scholarly essays. It can be extensive and elaborate, particularly when the writer seeks to give a history of the issue or subject. Muller might have reviewed the history of service corps of the past; he refers in the course of the essay to the Peace Corps, and he might have referred to the Civilian Conservation Corps (CCC) and similar organizations during the 1930s. Details on their history would serve for comparison in a longer argument; indeed, Muller anticipates objections to his plan arising from dislike of the military trappings of earlier "youth armies."

The narrative can be combined with the confirmation and refutation, as well as with the introduction. For the reader may need facts about other aspects of the plan or controversy, and these are sometimes better distributed throughout the essay.

Division of proofs

If the argument is complicated, it may help the reader to outline the proofs to be used. Muller does not do so in his short essay; he might have summarized briefly the main points in favor of a youth service program. We find this kind of outline sometimes at the start of textbook discussions, and we noted it earlier in the prosecutor's charge against a defendant following a review of the facts of the case.

The thesis statement is often part of the division, sometimes coming at the end of it. Muller states his at the end of the third paragraph, as the capstone of the narrative. However, occasionally there are good reasons to delay the thesis statement until late in the essay. If the audience is unsympathetic or hostile, beginning with controversial or repugnant ideas may lose their attention, and even if they do continue reading, they may not be disposed to give the ideas a serious hearing.

If the writer decides to build toward the thesis, he or she needs to keep the subject before the reader and perhaps anticipate what the thesis will be. Of course, there may be good reason not to give the reader this indication. Jonathan Swift, in his satirical essay "A Modest Proposal," delays the thesis until he has reviewed at length the dire condition of the poor in Ireland at the time the essay was written, in the first half of the eighteenth century. He begins the essay with a description of what the traveler would see in Ireland:

> It is a melancholy object to those who walk through this great town, or travel in the country, when they see the streets, the roads, and cabin-doors crowded with beggars of the female sex, followed by three, four, or six children, all in rags, and importuning every passenger for alms.

Swift is ostensibly addressing British officials and landowners whom he considered responsible for the immense poverty and suffering of the Irish. No remedies having succeeded, the self-assured speaker builds to a modest proposal that he is certain will relieve starvation and create other benefits:

> I am assured by our merchants that a boy or a girl before twelve years old is no salable commodity; and even when they come to this age they will not yield above three pounds or three pounds and half-a-crown at most, on the exchange; which cannot turn to account either to the parents or kingdom, the charge of nutriment and rags having been at least four times that value.
>
> I shall now, therefore, humbly propose my own thoughts, which I hope will not be liable to the least objection.

> I have been assured by a very knowing American of my acquaintance in London, that a young healthy child, well nursed, is, at a year old, a most delicious, nourishing, and wholesome food, whether stewed, roasted, baked, or boiled; and I make no doubt that it will equally serve in a fricassee or a ragout.

The shock we experience in hearing this proposal depends on Swift's having postponed it to late in the essay.

Confirmation

There are many ways in which confirming arguments can be presented. Three orders of argument have been most favored in the past. The first presents the strongest arguments at the beginning and the weakest at the end. The second does the reverse, and begins with the weakest and builds to the strongest. The third begins and ends with strong arguments, the weaker arguments sandwiched between them.

The first order is sometimes effective with audiences who have no interest in the subject at the start, and therefore cannot sustain attention throughout a long presentation of details and supporting arguments. The second or climactic order intensifies interest as the argument builds to the strongest. The third takes advantage of the special emphasis possible at the beginning and end of discourses—and of sentences and paragraphs, too. This order depends most on the audience's familiarity with the issues and facts.

Where the audience is unfamiliar with them, climactic order is probably best, and indeed is an order well suited to a general audience. Muller favors this order, building his arguments in the order of their increasing appeal or attractiveness. We will analyze this order in more detail shortly.

Edward P. J. Corbett gives valuable advice on this matter:

> Where our arguments are of relatively equal strength, it might be best to present first those arguments that are likely to have suggested themselves to our readers. If we gain concurrence for the familiar arguments, we condition our readers to receive the unfamiliar. We have confirmed what they suspected and then have added what they did not know before.[1]

Refutation

Refutation usually takes up objections after the confirming arguments have been presented. In some arguments the refutation is combined with the confirmation, the confirming arguments doing double duty in giving

[1] *Classical Rhetoric for the Modern Student* (New York: Oxford University Press, 1971), p. 322.

evidence for the thesis and also answering objections to it. We see this form of refutation in Muller—first, the refutation combined with the main confirming arguments, then the introduction of additional confirming arguments leading into a brief conclusion.

Muller begins the refutation immediately following his statement of the thesis:

> I recognize that at first mention, universal national youth service may sound too much like compulsory military service or the Hitler youth or the Komsomol. I do not believe it has to be like that at all.

He states that such service will not be compulsory—in response to a major anticipated objection that it will be much like the compulsory paramilitary youth corps of Nazi Germany and Soviet Russia. More than that, he argues, it will not require a vast bureaucracy or large sums to work.

He then moves to a new argument through an effective transition: such a noncompulsory corps will have its own "compelling incentives." These are guaranteed job training and federal assistance for post-secondary education later. And benefits will accrue from these: an end to the bureaucratic procedures concerned with educational aid, and an end to tuition tax credits.

These arguments are confirmations of his thesis, and at the same time part of refutation. For he is answering the related objection that such a national youth service will cost too much and will require a large administrative apparatus.

The second objection is presented in the form of a question:

> But what, you say, would huge numbers of high school graduates do as volunteers in national service?

In his answer Muller outlines the various jobs that volunteers could perform, and he stresses the benefits of these jobs to the country. He then answers the question of how the youth are to be housed and paid, and after this turns to the "even more attractive" alternative of "private industrial and commercial employment." In the concluding paragraphs Muller gives additional confirming arguments, stating the direct and indirect benefits of such a program in answer to possible objections that may be raised against it.

The objections he anticipates and answers might have been introduced after the benefits had been stated, or they might have been introduced and answered before. Muller's combining of the refutation with the confirming arguments has the advantage of avoiding repetition, though he does reiterate his main points in his concluding discussion of the indirect benefits. One disadvantage of saving the refutation for later in the essay is that it may raise doubts in the minds of the audience after the confirming arguments have been presented. One advantage of dividing it from the confirmation and putting it at the end is that the opposing arguments are given recognition.

Where the refutation appears is a decision the writer must make in light of the audience, the familiarity of the facts and ideas, and the available time or space for their development.

Conclusion

The conclusion can be used to review the main confirming arguments or to direct the audience to new considerations and points that need further investigation. But it need not be long; indeed, a concise one is less likely to labor the obvious or repeat ideas unnecessarily. Muller uses his conclusion to restate his thesis briefly.

Though the conclusion marks a winding down, the emotional temperature of the essay must not drop so markedly that anticlimax results. And the tone must not shift markedly. Ending an informal discussion with a formal summary and nothing else will seem abrupt.

Additional supporting arguments

In the first chapter we discussed some methods of paragraph development in essays. These methods can also provide supporting arguments or reasons. We will look at some other methods now, beginning with similarity and difference—the counterpart in argument of comparison and contrast.

Similarity and difference

We are familiar with similarity from our earlier discussion of analogy. It is, in fact, a simple analogy or comparison meant to increase the probability of an argument. Such an argument may point out that what is true in one situation must be true in another exactly like it. If it is wrong for persons to sit in judgment on causes in which they have a personal interest, James Madison argues in one of the *Federalist* papers, it is equally wrong for legislatures to do so:

> And what are the different classes of legislators but advocates and parties to the causes which they determine?

The comparison may be made as briefly as John Stuart Mill does in this defense of freedom of speech:

If all mankind minus one, were of one opinion, and only one person were of the contrary opinion, mankind would be no more justified in silencing that one person, than he, if he had the power, would be justified in silencing mankind.

On Liberty

Difference is the use of a simple contrast for the same purpose. The author of the following uses the difference between natural and man-made radiation and chemicals to argue her thesis that we have not considered the effects of technology on the environment:

The rapidity of change and the speed with which new situations are created follow the impetuous and heedless pace of man rather than the deliberate pace of nature. Radiation is no longer merely the background radiation of rocks, the bombardment of cosmic rays, the ultraviolet of the sun that have existed before there was any life on earth; radiation is now the unnatural creation of man's tampering with the atom. The chemicals to which life is asked to make its adjustment are no longer merely the calcium and silica and copper and all the rest of the minerals washed out of the rocks and carried in rivers to the sea; they are the synthetic creations of man's inventive mind, brewed in his laboratories, and having no counterparts in nature.

Rachel Carson, *Silent Spring*

Degree

An argument from "degree" involves "less" and "more," "better" and "worse." It is also used to increase the probability of the argument. Rachel Carson employs such an argument in this statement on chemical pollution:

To adjust to these chemicals would require time on the scale that is nature's; it would require not merely the years of a man's life but the life of generations. And even this, were it by some miracle possible, would be futile, for the new chemicals come from our laboratories in an endless stream; almost five hundred annually find their way into actual use in the United States alone.

Silent Spring

Even if we could adjust to the chemicals now in existence, Carson is saying, it would be even more difficult to adjust to new ones produced every year—and we are not now adjusting to chemicals around us. We have here more than a simple comparison between present and future: the increase in the amount of chemical pollution makes the argument one of degree.

Antecedent and consequent

Another kind of supporting argument traces one or more desirable or undesirable consequences from an event that may occur or has occurred:

> If all children were vaccinated against polio, the continuing low incidence of the disease would decrease almost to zero. Since most American children are vaccinated against polio, the continuing low incidence seems assured.

The relation between antecedent and consequent is again one of probability, not certainty. We cannot guarantee that the very low incidence will continue because of vaccination.

Contraries and contradictions

Contraries are opposite terms that belong to the same class—for example, idealistic and realistic, two opposing attitudes. Here is a statement on an issue in medicine that uses these terms as contraries:

> The idealist will say that when human personality is at stake, no compromise is tolerable. To accept inadequate examining rooms or crowded waiting rooms is dehumanizing to the patient. Yet the realist will say that when human life is at stake, compromise of ideals is essential. It is precisely because the stakes are so high that a compromise is acceptable.
>
> Robert M. Veatch, *Case Studies in Medical Ethics*

Contrary statements cannot both be true: doctors who insist on always treating patients with dignity will never accept dehumanizing conditions, and doctors who insist on saving lives may sacrifice the dignity of their patients. But proving one of the contrary statements false does not thereby prove the other true. If, because of an uncrowded waiting room, I prove the doctor is not a realist, I have not proved him or her an idealist. The doctor may simply be unpopular and therefore not have many patients. The falseness of a statement says nothing about whether its contrary is true or false.

By contrast, contradictory statements present opposites only one of which can be true, as in terms like idealistic and unidealistic, realistic and unrealistic, just and unjust. If people are shown to be idealistic in all situations, they are shown by implication to be incapable of the opposite behavior. To prove the falseness of a statement containing a contradictory term is to assert the truth of its opposite. Indeed, a simple and effective resource in argument is to show that a particular belief is contradicted by experience:

> The strongest argument for the un-materialistic character of American life is the fact that we tolerate conditions that are, from a materialistic point of view,

intolerable. What the foreigner finds most objectionable in American life is its lack of basic comfort. No nation with any sense of material well-being would endure the food we eat, the cramped apartments we live in, the noise, the traffic, the crowded subways and buses. American life, in large cities, at any rate, is a perpetual assault on the senses and the nerves; it is out of asceticism, out of unworldliness, precisely, that we bear it.

Mary McCarthy, "America the Beautiful"

Past fact and future fact

Past fact and future fact argue that what was possible in the past is possible in the future. We must, therefore, establish that the event did occur in the past. Volunteer service corps were successful in the 1930s, Muller might argue; therefore, they probably have a chance of succeeding in the future. If we can prove that something happened in the past for a definite reason, we can also predict it will happen again under the same circumstances. Thalidomide, which had been insufficiently tested before use, caused birth defects when it was prescribed to pregnant women in the 1960s; similar tragedies will probably occur in the future if drugs are not sufficiently tested before they are used by the public.

Possible and impossible

There are many forms of arguments based on the possibility and impossibility of an action. For example, we may argue that if it is possible to treat some patients with respect and dignity, then it is possible to treat all patients in the same way. Or we may argue that since it is impossible to prevent the spread of nuclear weapons, it is impossible to prevent the spread of other catastrophic weapons like poison gas. Here is an example:

> If you can send a rocket round the moon, you can take out Moscow or, alternatively, New York. You can take out (I apologize for using this inhuman jargon) any town anywhere on earth. Nothing can stop you. It is as simple as that. Simpler than neolithic warfare used to be.

C. P. Snow, "The Moon Landing"

Law and precedent

A writer on occasion may appeal to actual laws to support a policy he is defending, or he may cite precedents for the policy, including laws that have the weight of precedent. In arguing that patients in mental hospitals have a right to psychiatric treatment, instead of remaining confined and untreated, the following writer cites both precedents for such treatment and actual laws that govern similar situations—alcoholism and drug addiction:

> Similarly, we have found that the statute in the District of Columbia recognizing alcoholism as a disease and promising treatment to those afflicted prevents the government from punishing alcoholics as criminals. Other examples are readily at hand. New York State allows a narcotic addict to accept an indeterminate commitment for treatment as an alternative to punishment as a criminal. If an addict has elected commitment, and after several years has received no treatment or rehabilitation, it seems doubtful that his continued commitment can be justified—certainly not after the maximum prison sentence he might have received would have expired.
>
> Judge David L. Bazelon, *"The Right to Treatment: The Court's Role"*

This appeal is like general appeals to authority—to previous writers on the subject, for example. On controversial issues, we gain support for our viewpoint when we show that informed writers have taken the same stand on evidence they gathered and justified. We shall consider the problem of finding reliable sources of evidence in our final chapter.

Dilemma

A dilemma is a powerful form of argument that presents us with two alternatives, both of them unsatisfactory. Its purpose is to force us to accept a third alternative favored by the writer. Here is a formal statement of a popular dilemma used by opponents of the Equal Rights Amendment.

> If ERA deprives women of rights they now enjoy, it is bad legislation, and if it merely affirms rights they already enjoy, it is needless legislation. ERA will either deprive women of rights they now enjoy, or it will merely affirm rights they already enjoy. Therefore ERA is either bad or needless and should not be enacted.

The alternative favored is that we continue to rely on the protection of the Fourteenth Amendment, which allegedly gives the protection sought without nullifying rights women now enjoy.

Here is an argument by an opponent of ERA that expresses this dilemma. It was made to a Senate subcommittee, in a formal hearing, in 1970:

> I feel the passage of this legislation is unnecessary since women are covered by the provisions of the Fourteenth Amendment guaranteeing all persons equal treatment under law. As if, indeed, any legal act of and by itself can guarantee anything. But more to the point, unless this proposal includes the Hayden retention proviso, it will repeal the thousands of laws, rules, regulations, directives, opinions, which now protect women from insidious and destructive

working conditions visited upon them largely because of their biological composition and background.

And the speaker added later in his testimony:

> I remember the postulation "When the mores are adequate, laws are unnecessary; and when the mores are inadequate, laws are useless."

Two strategies may be used to deal with a dilemma. We may "go between the horns" (the disjuncts or alternatives) and show that a satisfactory alternative other than that the writer favors exists; or we may "grasp the dilemma" by its "horns" and show that one of the alternatives is false. Thus, we would be going between the horns of the dilemma posed above if, agreeing that the situation is as the speaker describes, we proposed a modification of the ERA so that it gives the required protections and at the same time guarantees existing rights. And we would be grasping one of the horns of the dilemma if, disagreeing with one of the alternatives, we asserted that the nullification of these rights would be beneficial.

Both strategies have been adopted by various supporters of ERA during the 1970s. Here is one example, a statement of a witness before the same congressional subcommittee, arguing that the denial of existing legal rights would benefit women:

> Thus we contend that today, special so-called protective legislation for women has become restrictive, burdensome, and discriminatory. We support passage of the equal rights amendment to eliminate such laws for women only. These laws will prohibit women from being bartenders but allow them to be barmaids, to serve the drinks they cannot mix, and at a lower pay. In some States women cannot work overtime in factories but laundry, hotel and restaurant workers, agricultural and domestic laborers are often exempt from the hours limitation. At the other end of the scale 27 States (out of 39 with maximum hours laws) exempt some or all women in administrative, executive and professional positions from hours limitation. We emphasize the restrictions imposed on women by this legislation because some continue to oppose the equal rights amendment in order to continue such legislation.
>
> Myra Ruth Harmon

Ways of reaching agreement

The desire to reach agreement with the audience is an important concern of writers on communications, including Kenneth Burke, Chaim Perelman and Carl Rogers. What follows is based on their ideas about what Burke calls "identification."

This word refers to the ways we achieve agreement with our audience and persuade them to accept a common ground, to adopt provisionally a new perspective or way of looking at the world. Of course, some people seek total identification with the audience, thereby leaving no room for criticism or doubt: that is the aim of a demagogue. But we need not think of identification as being so absolute. We may not be able to change the way our readers think or feel about the world, but we may be able to get them to identify with the way we think and feel. At least for the time we have their attention we would like to have their good will and sympathy, so that discussion remains open.

Thus Burke writes: "You persuade a man only insofar as you can talk his language by speech, gesture, tonality, order, image, attitude, idea, *identifying* your ways with his."[2] This is the aim of a speaker who begins by praising our city and its people, turning what seem faults or ugliness into virtues. Smoke and grime, the speaker tells us, are scars of honor—the marks of an industrious and independent working people. A city whose streets and buildings are new and clean has "realized its dream of growth." A city whose streets are old and neighborhoods in decay faces "the challenge ahead," and can look forward to a period of progress and growth in new directions.

It is honest praise we wish rather to emphasize in explaining how we try to secure good will and agreement. We sometimes employ praise in ordinary arguments when we want to secure and maintain the good will of friends. And we do much more. We choose words that will establish a wide though very general agreement. These words may even be broad in meaning, and we fix these meanings more exactly as we proceed—in an honest effort to win support for an urban project let us say, defining the change we have in mind, perhaps privately financed urban renewal, or new job training programs financed from local taxes. Our purpose, remember, is to gain assent and good will and maintain these at each stage of the argument. This building of agreement is, in fact, the real structure of our argument—what is sometimes called the rhetorical structure, in contrast to the logical one.

With an audience that has a stake in the issue and therefore may be hostile to our proposal, we are sometimes faced with fixed views or positions that we want to question and, if we can, change and reconcile with our own. That is, we want the audience to consider alternatives. Let us examine some ways of doing this.

If praise works at the start of an argument, it probably won't take us far once we come to concrete proposals. We may, then, begin with a form of refutation: we may take the set position of our opponent and show that what worked in the past is not working in the present. To remain with our urban project, we can argue that circumstances and conditions have changed, federal urban renewal had worked well in the

[2]Kenneth Burke, *The Rhetoric of Motives* (Berkeley: University of California Press, 1969), p. 55.

past but is not working well now. We can continue by arguing that if we encouraged private investment there would be a gain in local financing and an increase in local tax revenues. The use of local tax monies for public services tends to make people responsible for what happens in their community and gives them control over how money is spent. Or we may use an argument from degree to show that the urban problem has increased to the point where old solutions do not work anymore. Or we may try to show that they did not in the past (neighborhoods built without sufficient local involvement deteriorate rapidly), or that earlier standards are no longer acceptable today. Well-built houses and adequate sanitation may once have been the important measures of a desirable community; today we look for more—adequate living space and preservation of the environment as well.

A powerful means of argument is to show that contrary policies are worth considering. To cite a different issue, there may be good reason to outlaw marijuana, but legalizing it may discourage use of hard drugs like morphine and heroin. Opponents may retort that legalization can promote a climate favorable to hard drugs. Contraries, it will be recalled, cannot both be true, and both may be false. Since they both may be false, agreement can be sought by looking to other possible solutions.

Another powerful means is to show the unexpected consequences of a policy. To cite another current issue, if federal aid is given to prop up a sagging industry, then a precedent is established that may prove injurious when other industries demand equal treatment. Those who support such aid may argue that failure to grant aid can lead to the collapse of related industries. Again agreement may be sought in alternatives to outright grants of money.

Still another powerful method related to those just described is to point to a contradiction in thinking. Thus, George Bernard Shaw makes the argument that children have rights as inviolable as those of their parents. He then anticipates an objection which he answers by retorting:

> Experienced parents, when children's rights are preached to them, very naturally ask whether children are to be allowed to do what they like. The best reply is to ask whether adults are to be allowed to do what they like. The two cases are the same. The adult who is nasty is not allowed to do what he likes: neither can the child who likes to be nasty. There is no difference in principle between the rights of a child and those of an adult: the difference in their cases is one of circumstance.
>
> • Preface to *Misalliance*

Shaw's retort is a powerful one, not only because it shows that it would be a contradiction to deny children their rights if adults maintain their own, but also because it insinuates that it is in the best interests of adults not to deny the child.

But the retort raises a problem: it is effective as a retort but not as a basis for conciliation—for identification between author, adult, and child on the matter of rights.

Establishing a common ground, as we said at the beginning of this section, is an essential job for the writer who wants to persuade the reader and not just win an argument. To secure that persuasion, we must be certain that we really want to do so. This problem in communication has been given attention by the psychologist Carl Rogers, who argues that the stronger our feelings are in an argument, the less opportunity there is for real communication. In fact, there may be no real communication at all. And that is the problem with retorts as powerful as Shaw's.

As a solution, Rogers recommends that, in arguing, we make an effort

> to see the expressed idea and attitude from the other person's point of view, to sense how it feels to him, to achieve his frame of reference in regard to the thing he is talking about.
>
> *"Communication: Its Blocking and Its Facilitation"*

We can do this best by first lowering the emotional temperature of the argument, and then write as if we could *listen* to people whose good will and understanding we genuinely wanted. Rogers makes this suggestion:

> It would simply mean that before presenting your own point of view, it would be necessary for you to really achieve the other speaker's frame of reference— to understand his thoughts and feelings so well that you could summarize them for him.

It is, of course, much easier to follow this advice when we are talking to people face to face than when we are writing. But if we genuinely wish to conciliate our audience, then we can do so, Rogers suggests, by addressing the audience not as an adversary but as a friendly opponent in ideas only. We can win the good will of our opponents by stating their ideas accurately and fully, by showing through the tone of our presentation that we respect them as intellectual opponents and that we take their ideas seriously, and by giving recognition to the background and problems that explain ideas different from our own. Usually, in seeking agreement, we come to see our beliefs or stands on particular issues from new points of view, and we may change or modify them to an extent greater than we may have anticipated at the start of the argument.

These comments remind us that the debate between adversaries, as between opposing lawyers in a courtroom, provides an important and useful model for the argumentative essay, but debates between adversaries are just one kind of argument that engages people. The form of argument we described at the beginning of this chapter is one we can adapt to many writing situations. Adversary arguments are essential in law, in legislatures, and in other fields, and will continue to be so. At the same time, conciliation can play a greater role than may be realized, particularly in legislative and political arguments. Senators and presidential candidates are political adversaries, and we expect to find high emotion and sharp differences between them. Seldom does one senator or candidate try to state an opponent's arguments fully or seriously, or perhaps even try to understand them. We know that quite the opposite is happening as we listen to them debate, or when, in reading a letter to the editor or a political columnist we come upon statements like the following in a discussion of academic freedom:

> University presidents have to have spines of steel and the guts of billygoats. Their hard task is to fend off yahoos and rednecks at one extreme and doctrinaire super-libs at the other. They cannot afford to forget that they preside over public institutions financed by public funds.

James J. Kilpatrick, *Akron Beacon Journal*, 7 June, 1981

Whatever may be the truth about the people Kilpatrick is characterizing—and it is unlikely that any of them fit the characterization—nothing is gained in the argument except increased divisiveness and emotion. The decision we make about what we really are seeking in an argument is therefore crucial.

Exercises

1. For one of the following controversial issues, assume that you wish to seek the good will of people opposed to your viewpoint. To win their good will and get them to consider your ideas seriously, you need to establish a common interest. For example, if you are against reimposing the draft, you might try first to persuade your opponents that you share with them a belief in a strong national defense, though you disagree with them on how to achieve it. You would need to find another common interest in an argument with pacifists. Indicate what common interests might be appealed to in establishing good will and conciliation:

   a. registration of firearms

   b. repealing the 55-mile-an-hour speed limit

   c. taxing automobiles on the basis of their gas consumption

   d. enacting the Equal Rights Amendment

2. Examine an issue of *Vital Speeches*, and identify ways in which various speakers seek to conciliate their audience, to establish a common interest with them, or instead seek to alienate them.

Writing Assignment

Write an argumentative essay on one of the topics given above, and begin by identifying your audience (its makeup and special interests) and establishing a common interest with them in the issue under discussion. Gradually develop your argument toward the more serious or crucial differences you believe exist between you and this audience, and discuss how these might be bridged or resolved.

The appeal to emotion and character

Defense of character is another important means of achieving identification. The defense may be against a charge of dishonesty or lack of integrity. The charge may have been a direct one, as in the indictment that Socrates had corrupted the youth of Athens through ideas he had made current—an indictment which Socrates answers in his defense or apology to the jury at his trial. Or the charge may have been indirect. A recent and notable defense against this indirect kind occurs in Martin Luther King, Jr.'s letter from Birmingham jail, written on April 16, 1963, during his imprisonment on charges of fomenting civil disturbances:

> I think I should indicate why I am here in Birmingham, since you have been influenced by the view which argues against "outsiders coming in." I have the honor of serving as president of the Southern Christian Leadership Conference, an organization operating in every Southern state with headquarters in Atlanta, Georgia. . . . I am here because I have basic organizational ties here. But more basically, I am in Birmingham because injustice is here. Just as the prophets of the eighth century B.C. left their villages and carried their "thus saith the Lord" far beyond the boundaries of their home towns, and just as the Apostle Paul left his village of Tarsus and carried the gospel of Jesus Christ to the far corners of the Graeco-Roman world, so am I compelled to carry the gospel of freedom beyond my home town.

Appeals to emotion are also means of achieving identification, and have sometimes been attacked on the ground that they displace rational argument. Consider this passage from King's letter, directed particularly to Birmingham clergymen who were calling for an end to black demonstrations:

> Perhaps it is easy for those who have never felt the stinging darts of segregation to say, "Wait." But when you have seen vicious mobs lynch your mothers and fathers at will and drown your sisters and brothers at whim; when you have seen hate-filled policemen curse, kick, and even kill your black brothers and sisters; when you see the vast majority of your twenty million Negro brothers smothering in an airtight cage of poverty in the midst of an affluent society; when you suddenly find your tongue twisted and your speech stam-

mering as you seek to explain to your six-year-old daughter why she can't go to the public amusement park that has just been advertised on television, and see tears welling up in her eyes when she is told that Funtown is closed to colored children, and see ominous clouds of inferiority begin to form in her little mental sky, and see her beginning to distort her little personality by developing an unconscious bitterness toward white people; when you have to concoct an answer for a five-year-old son asking: "Daddy, why do white people treat colored people so mean?"; when you take a cross country drive and find it necessary to sleep night after night in the uncomfortable corners of your automobile because no motel will accept you; when you are humiliated day in and day out by nagging signs reading "white" men and "colored"; when your first name becomes "nigger," your middle name becomes "boy" (however old you are) and your last name becomes "John," and your wife and mother are never given the respected title "Mrs."; when you are harried by day and haunted by night by the fact that you are a Negro, living constantly at tiptoe stance, never quite knowing what to expect next, and plagued with inner fears and outer resentments; when you are forever fighting a degenerating sense of "nobodiness";—then you will understand why we find it difficult to wait.

How we respond to such an appeal depends on what justification we believe King has for it. The question is not whether emotion displaces rational argument but instead whether emotion takes the place of evidence. Reason and emotion are not opposites; sound arguments may contain as much emotion as unsound ones.

The statement of particular circumstances serves as the justification for King's defense of character. Similarly, the statement of wrongs just quoted is King's justification for his appeal to emotion. He is saying that these wrongs justify the pain and outrage he expresses in the statement. Indeed, it would be impossible to discuss so painful an issue without expressing outrage; a plain recitation of wrongs undoubtedly would seem unnatural and unconvincing. Appeals to emotion thus are appeals to experience itself.

Appeals to emotion, then, will not seem out of place when we have presented the facts and stated the basis that justifies them. At the end of a chapter in which he has reviewed the horrors of Soviet prisons in the time of Stalin, Solzhenitsyn summarizes some of the terrifying things done to prisoners. And with reference to the people who performed them, he writes:

> But let us be generous. We will not shoot them. We will not pour salt water into them, nor bury them in bedbugs, nor bridle them into a "swan dive," nor keep them on sleepless "stand-up" for a week, nor kick them with jackboots, nor beat them with rubber truncheons, nor squeeze their skulls in iron rings, nor push them into a cell so that they lie atop one another like pieces of baggage—we will not do any of the things they did! But for the sake of our

country and our children we have the duty to *seek them all out and bring them all to trial!* Not to put them on trial so much as their crimes. And to compel each one of them to announce loudly: "Yes, I was an executioner and a murderer."

And he concludes:

We have to condemn publicly the very *idea* that some people have the right to repress others. In keeping silent about evil, in burying it so deep within us that no sign of it appears on the surface, we are *implanting* it, and it will rise up a thousandfold in the future.

The Gulag Archipelago, I

Few readers can fail to be moved by this appeal, but it is moving precisely because Solzhenitsyn has shown that the emotion he expresses is emotion justified by the need to express horror and outrage, and not remain silent. For to remain silent will guarantee the rise of such repression again. That same kind of demonstration is what gives the writings of King and other writers in America their power.

Writing Assignments

1. Advertising appeals to various emotions and to the character and judgment of the consumer. Identify the various appeals you notice in the advertisement on the opposite page, and discuss their effectiveness.

2. Each of the following contains a defense by the speaker or writer for his conduct, actions, or ideas. Identify in one of them the appeals to character or emotion made in the defense, and the stated or implied justifications given for these:

   a. Plato, *Apology* [the statement of Socrates to the Athenian jury]

   b. Bartolomeo Vanzetti, his last speech to the Massachusetts court

   c. Henry David Thoreau, *Civil Disobedience*

   d. Richard M. Nixon, television speech announcing his resignation as President

   e. Shakespeare, *Richard the Third*, act 1, scene 1, the opening soliloquy of Richard

   f. Shakespeare, *Othello*, act 1, scene 3, Othello's defense of his marriage to Desdemona

In our family business there's three things you don't mind spending your money on. Copper tubing. Fast cars. And a fine pair of warm, dry boots. And that third one is just as important as the first two. When you're crouching down in some gully with your feet in ice-cold ditch water, never moving a muscle for hours, whilst them damn Treasury agents snoop around with their dogs barking and sniffing, well, that's the time you're glad you didn't cut corners on your boots. These boots we bought are fine boots, well made, need no breaking in. But to us, that don't mean so much compared to the way they're waterproof and warm.

The Timberland Company, Newmarket, NH 03857

Timberland®
A whole line of fine leather boots
that cost plenty, and should.

Enthymemic arguments again

We return, finally, to enthymemic arguments, in which one of the premises or the conclusion is left unstated. The following argument does not state its major premise:

> The United Nations is ineffective in resolving the Middle East crisis because it lacks military power.

The unstated premise is the following:

> World organizations that lack military power are ineffective in resolving regional crises.

Like the argument above, enthymemes are stated informally, not according to the rigorous pattern required of syllogisms.

Enthymemic arguments are probably the most common form of deductive arguments. One of their advantages is that unstated premises tend to create assent, for we are likely to accept them as generally understood and agreed to. As used by many speakers and writers, they not only presume agreement over one of the premises or the conclusion but also seek to assure it. They have considerable rhetorical force, therefore, as in the statement of President Franklin D. Roosevelt in 1939:

> When peace has been broken anywhere, the peace of all countries everywhere is in danger.

Aphorisms, that is, short and pithy statements of a principle, are forceful in leaving a premise or reason to inference.

> The tree of liberty must be refreshed from time to time with the blood of patriots and tyrants.
>
> Thomas Jefferson

The reason for the omission of a premise, we saw, is that it may be so clearly implied that its statement is unnecessary. But we saw too, that the premise may be omitted to hide it. Sometimes we need to identify a hidden premise or assumption to make clear what is wrong with an argument. Here is an example:

> I have been troubled in our debates by the implication that because a particular mental power or faculty can't do everything, it is therefore somehow suspect or inferior. Even if we accept the implicit equation of "reason" with "mere logic," and admit that "mere logic" can't make me a good or wise man, it still remains true that logical thought is one of the noblest achievements of man. If "mere logic" can't make me wise or good, neither can "mere" emotional commitment—as the history of the various *isms* of this century makes clear. Similarly, if "mere" logic or cold scientific method cannot make a scientist, it is equally true that there was never an effective scientist or scholar, in any

discipline, who had not mastered the logic of that discipline. Even if logic deserves the adjective *mere*, it is still an obviously essential element in all effective human action, whether painting a picture, testing a hypothesis, or raising a child; although it can't do everything, nothing at all can be done without it.

Wayne C. Booth, *"Reason and Emotion in Education"*

Many refutations are concerned with exposing hidden and mistaken assumptions such as Booth deals with. In a fair argument, controversial premises need to be identified and defended. If they are left to inference, the argument may be effective at the time it is made, but it will cease to be convincing when a controversial premise is exposed and shown to be undefended if not false.

Exercise

Archie Bunker, in the television show "All in the Family" and "Archie's Place," is given to what have been called "Bunkerisms"—comical misuses of words, confusions over names, and the like. Here is a Bunkerism containing an enthymemic argument. Identify the unstated assumptions or premises, and describe the argument Archie is making:

> You think he's a nice boy after he did what he did? Comin' in here, makin' suppository remarks about our country. And callin' me prejudiced, while I was singin' "God Bless America," a song written by a well-known and respected Jewish guy, Milton Berlin.

Prewriting

Materials for debate: should we curb "junk foods" in schools? (U.S. News & World Report, September 24, 1979)

Paired statements on the issue of "junk foods" in school follow. They are provided as background on the issue, and as identification of the major issues and arguments as viewed by two people in 1979—Carol Tucker Foreman, Assistant Secretary of Agriculture for Food and Consumer Services in the Carter administration, and James E. Mack, President and General Counsel, National Confectioners Association.

Before developing your opinion on the issue, you need to inform yourself on the background, issues, and arguments. These may constitute the narrative of an argumentative essay, perhaps in the form of a comparison of answers given by Foreman and Mack to questions posed to them in a news magazine interview. Here are four topics on which both state opinions:

the definition of "junk food"
control exerted by the Federal government
control exercised by others (for example, parents and children)
effectiveness of controls

And here are two ways in which a comparison might be organized:

Foreman
    definition of "junk food"
    government control
    control exercised by others
    effectiveness of controls
Mack
    definition of "junk food"
    government control
    control exercised by others
    effectiveness of controls

The advantage of this kind of comparison is that it would show the general thinking of each on the whole subject of junk foods. The relationship of ideas can best be pointed out through this approach. Additional statements in the interview can also be related to them.

A second approach is to compare their opinions one by one:

Definition of "junk food"
    Foreman
    Mack
Government control
    Foreman
    Mack
Control exercised by others
    Foreman
    Mack
Effectiveness of controls
    Foreman
    Mack

The advantage of this approach is that differences in assumptions and views emerge clearly.

In developing your own position on the issue, you might first identify the points of agreement you share with Foreman and Mack. You can then focus on the chief points of disagreement as a way of sharpening your position. Your refutation can be reserved for your specific response to Foreman and Mack, or you might combine your refutation with your confirmation—the statement of your position.

In writing an argumentative essay on the issue, choose a specific audience and organize your essay in a way that will best persuade them.

PRO AND CON: CURB "JUNK FOODS" IN SCHOOLS?

YES—"Restrict foods that have limited nutritional value"

Interview with
Carol Tucker Foreman
Assistant Secretary of
Agriculture for Food and
Consumer Services in 1979

Q Ms. Foreman, why do you favor banning so-called junk foods in the schools?

A We're not proposing a ban. We merely want to restrict, until after the end of the lunch period each day, the sale of certain foods that have limited nutritional value.

Q What sort of foods will be restricted?

A Soda pop, chewing gum, some candies and flavored ices.

Q That's not a very long list—

A In following the intent of Congress, we have been trying to identify those foods that make virtually no nutritional contribution to the diet. Consequently, our proposal restricts only those foods which have virtually no nutrients.

Some foods that are commonly thought to be junk turn out to have, in fact, some nutrients. Many nutritionists are concerned about high-salt, high-sugar and high-fat foods—as am I—but even those items may have a lot of a particular nutrient.

For this particular proposal, we would need more science before we could regulate sugar, fat or salt levels. Students still will be able, anytime during the day, to purchase hamburgers and potato chips, also fruits and vegetables and soups and nuts and sandwiches, if the school chooses to offer those.

Q Why shouldn't local school authorities decide what's best for their students?

A Perhaps they should, but Congress felt that local school officials were not taking action, so it passed a law directing the Department of Agriculture to get involved. Congress wanted to make sure that federal taxpayers are getting their money's worth from the 3 billion dollars spent each year on school feeding programs.

Interestingly, local school officials who have written to us favor the federal government's involvement.

Q How do parents feel about it?

A Parents who attended public hearings on our proposal were overwhelmingly in favor of going even further. When we were out on the road listening to people, we found that some parents were surprised that these foods were sold in the schools at all. Nobody had ever asked them whether they would object to those foods being sold there. The foods just showed up one day. Many parents are not happy to have the school undercut good nutritional habits that parents try to instill in the home.

Q Has there been any opposition from students?

A At our hearings, opinion was split about 50-50. Obviously, a lot of students are not particularly enthusiastic about such restrictions. Yet, I was taken aback when student-body representatives from a number of schools said they fully supported this sort of thing.

Q Won't some youngsters bring junk foods from home?

A Obviously some will, and some may go off the school grounds to purchase them.

We are not trying to solve the problems of the world—only to enhance the value of the school-lunch program in response to a directive from Congress. If students wish to eat these kinds of foods, the government can't stop them. We do want to discourage their substitution for the school lunch.

Q Is there danger that students will skip lunch just to fill up on junk foods afterward?

A We have no intention of sending an armed guard to force children into eating the school lunch. We're trying to create an atmosphere as favorable as possible for the consumption of a well-rounded diet and for good nutrition education.

Q How will this ban be enforced?

A It will be fairly simple. A lot of these foods are not sold in vending machines but over counters. The snack bar would not offer any restricted foods until the end of the lunch period each day. You might have certain vending machines that have fruits, vegetables and nuts open all the time, and others open only after lunch.

The federal government has, over the years, conducted fairly regular audits in the schools to make sure that their lunches conformed to minimum nutritional requirements. This has never required a large regulatory force—and I certainly don't anticipate one now.

Q Won't fund-raising efforts for extracurricular activities that involve the sale of food be hurt by this proposal?

A Fund-raising activities are not dependent upon the sale of the items that we're talking about. At hearings in Nashville, Tenn., for example, we heard from one group which sold candy one year and raised about $400. They sold candles the next year and raised a couple thousand dollars. If it is necessary to sell restricted food items, students are free to do that after the lunch period.

Q Couldn't candy bars be fortified or enriched to meet the government's nutritional requirements?

A Fortification is a fairly difficult process. It requires more than just sprinkling a few powdered vitamins over the candy. It requires substantial reformulation of the product. Since the sale of candy in schools represents only a tiny fraction of overall sales, I doubt that candy companies will want to go to all that expense for such a small market.

Q Does this law go far enough in restricting foods of dubious value?

A Certainly many people don't think the law or the regulation goes far enough. Many food-advocacy groups may suggest to Congress that the law be expanded.

Of course, there is nothing to prevent local school authorities from restricting the sale of such things as potato chips, corn chips, cookies and things like that. And some of them have gone beyond what we have proposed.

NO—"Everything we eat need not have a scientific, medical, nutritional reason"

Interview with
James E. Mack
President and General
Counsel, National
Confectioners Association

Q Mr. Mack, why do you oppose the banning of so-called junk foods from schools?

A First, the term *junk foods* is a misnomer when applied to confections. We sell our products for enjoyment, but many of them possess very substantial nutritional value. They contain milk, nuts, fruits, eggs and chocolate.

What we object to is the federal government in Washington telling parents and school authorities what foods may or may not be sold in their own schools. These are not federal schools. They're county schools, state schools. If local authorities are competent enough to run every other aspect of the schools, then they are best equipped to make decisions on food sales—as they have had the authority to do for many years. We think it's an insult to parents and local school authorities to assume they're incompetent to make their own decisions.

Q Do you object to local school officials banning these foods?

A If a particular school district decides that it wants to make available certain foods and not others, or to regulate when or where they may be sold, that's their prerogative, and we recognize and respect it. But if a local school board or state agency does not want to take action on this, why should the federal government dictate to it?

Q But if the federal government is spending billions to provide nutritious school lunches, doesn't it have the right to make sure that students are not filling up on snacks?

A You're proceeding on the false premise that it's the so-called competitive foods—foods that are not part of the regular school-lunch menu—that are primarily responsible for the plate waste in the lunchrooms. If youngsters are served nutritious, appealing, appetizing meals, they will consume them. The folks who run the school cafeterias should give more attention to providing such meals. The problem lies largely with what the children are served for lunch, rather than with the competitive foods.

In 1977, the U.S. General Accounting Office made a comprehensive study of this school-lunch plate-waste issue, and cited several reasons why it thought plate waste occurred. But competitive foods were not even mentioned.

Q Can children really be trusted to decide what's good for them to eat?

A There's no reason why a child should not have a soft drink or a candy bar. One of the main arguments we've heard is that if such foods are made available, children will consume them to excess. Well, a survey does not bear that out.

But it is important for the schools and parents to teach children good eating habits. You don't consume several candy bars at one time. You consume one. School authorities should teach moderation rather than try to prohibit the sale of these items.

Q What about the tooth-decay problem from eating candy?

A Tooth decay is caused by a combination of factors. Fermentable carbohydrates—of which sugar is only one—when allowed to remain in the mouth after eating, are one of a number of factors contributing to tooth decay. Others include heredity, overall diet, mouth formation, the position of the teeth in relation to one another and lack of oral hygiene.

But much can be done to counteract tooth decay by oral hygiene and fluoridation. If those advocating curtailment of school sales were as interested in encouraging children to brush their teeth and in getting water fluoridated as they are in trying to take candy away from them, they would accomplish much more.

Q Why doesn't the food industry offer children juices, fruits, vegetables and nuts, instead of potato chips and colas?

A It isn't necessarily "instead of." We feel they should be offered both kinds of foods. People consume things for different reasons. Eating is one of the enjoyments of life. Some things may be consumed solely for enjoyment and refreshment. Everything we eat need not have a scientific, medical, nutritional reason. However, as a practical matter, many confections do make substantial nutritional contributions.

Take fruit juices, for example. We feel that sugar is a fine food, but if you're concerned about the percentage of sugar consumption, fruit juices are one of the highest of all foods in sugar content—even unsweetened natural fruit juices.

Q Yet many parents seem to favor a tougher ban than the government is proposing—

A Unfortunately, there are some parents who want to abdicate their responsibility. There are also some folks who believe in the superior state and in complete national control.

Q Are there other reasons why these products should be sold in schools?

A If competitive foods are available at schools, it helps keep children on the premises. Confections are a very popular item, and if they are not available on the school grounds, the children may leave school in search of them. That creates a traffic hazard. Furthermore, while the children are away from school they may tend to turn to some other things instead of candy. They may be subject to other temptations.

When you keep competitive foods for sale on the school premises, you keep control. When you throw candy out of the schools, you don't solve anything. You just throw the issue out on the street.

Materials for debate: arguments for and against drafting women

The materials given here on drafting women include a summary of and quotations from arguments by two people who argued for and against registration in legal briefs—Donald L. Weinberg, and Wade H. McCree, Jr., Solicitor General of the United States. These summaries by no means exhaust the arguments presented for and against registration recently, but they do offer enough material for you to begin your thinking about the issue. They appeared in *U.S. News & World Report,* April 6, 1981.

Our suggestions for developing and organizing an essay on junk foods are pertinent to this topic, and we will not repeat them. We will add only that, in comparing these arguments, ask yourself whether the point at issue is the same for Weinberg and McCree, and what the point at issue is for you.

Again, select an audience for your essay and choose arguments and an organization that you think will best persuade them. You may wish to address this essay to your composition class after discussing the issue with them.

Emotion will probably rise higher on this issue than on that of junk food, in the course of this discussion, and your essay therefore gives you an opportunity to practice the art of conciliation. In adapting your presentation to the special concerns and beliefs of your audience, remember that admitting the seriousness of the argument you oppose and stating it fully and fairly are not indications of insincerity but rather of a desire to seek honest agreement. Indeed, you may discover a change in your position and thinking as you seek to understand and state the views you are arguing against.

THE CASE FOR REGISTERING WOMEN

There is no legal justification for males-only registration.

"All young men, fit or unfit, but no women, however fit to serve, are compelled to register." A program that "places in jeopardy basic personal liberties and ultimately life itself" has no legal basis for excluding one sex.

The Supreme Court previously has struck down "governmental decisions to subject men alone to a burden from which women are automatically exempt" except when such discrimination serves "important governmental objectives." The case in point: The Court's 1976 ruling invalidating an Oklahoma law that allowed women to buy beer at age 18 but barred men from doing so until age 21.

Here, federal authorities have not proved that a men-only registration process is needed to achieve a valid U.S. goal: Raising adequate armed forces.

Congress abused its authority to set policy for the military by omitting women from draft registration.

On military issues such as the draft, are not courts bound to accept "a policy decision by Congress, whether wise or unwise?" asked Chief Justice Warren Burger. No, replied Weinberg. Though courts typically do not interfere with internal military concerns, this issue affects civilians.

Donald L. Weinberg [attorney arguing against male-only registration] charged that when Congress wrote the draft law in 1948 it acted "in an atmosphere permeated by male chauvinism." Burger retorted, "Since when is it the function of the courts to inquire into atmospheres?"

Associate Justice Potter Stewart said that the Philadelphia men were "putting the cart before the horse" by demanding that Congress justify its decision to exclude women. "An act of Congress is presumed valid, and it's up to you to prove that it is not," he told Weinberg.

Judges are empowered to strike down military policies that are biased against women, Weinberg argued. In 1973, the Supreme Court declared unconstitutional laws that gave military men housing and health allowances for their spouses but limited such aid for spouses of military women.

Many women already serve as volunteers.

"Both the military and Congress have made concerted efforts over the last decade to increase the role of women in the armed forces."

Now, 8.4 percent of the nation's 2 million armed services personnel are female, and the proportion is going up. It is irrational to continue to exclude women from draft registration if U.S. policy is to give them expanded military duties.

Weinberg told the Justices that keeping women out of draft eligibility would be "excluding from the pool to whom we can turn in an emergency . . . the very skills we have sought to bring into the armed forces."

Even though federal rules bar women from combat, most military jobs are classified as noncombat.

Subjecting women to the draft would increase military flexibility. In an emergency, women would be among those best qualified for noncombat jobs, "and their availability would free more combat-trained soldiers for quicker redeployment to battle."

Women draftees would be qualified for tens of thousands of military jobs. In fact, a Defense Department official told Congress last year that if a mobilization were necessary, military leaders would like 80,000 out of a total of 650,000 inducted to be women.

Excluding women from registration "perpetuates . . . ancient sexual stereotypes."

The courts have held that laws based on outmoded views of the roles of men and women must be condemned—in part because they may be "self-fulfilling prophecies." In this case, the old "idea that men are meant for war and women solely for the home and hearth" should be discarded.

Added representatives of 11 women's-rights groups who filed a brief supporting the challenge to men-only registration: "The exclusion of women . . . is based solely on archaic notions of women's proper place in society that in the past prompted 'protective' labor laws and the exclusion of women from juries and the legal profession. Until women assume their equal share of societal obligations, they will retain their inferior status."

THE CASE AGAINST WOMEN'S REGISTRATION

Congress traditionally has decided U.S. military policy.

Excluding women from registration must be upheld because of "the power expressly granted to Congress by the Constitution . . . to raise an army." Because of that provision, this case differs from other kinds of sex-bias suits. Here, it is inappropriate for a court "to substitute its judgment for that of Congress. . . . Congress knew exactly what it was doing when it refused to require the registration of women."

Five congressmen who filed a brief warned that if women are forced to register, courts would be asked to decide related questions such as whether men and women must be drafted in equal numbers.

Since women are ineligible for combat assignments, they need not be required to register for the draft.

History shows that most draftees are sent into combat. In addition, "in recent years, more than sufficient numbers of women have been volunteering to staff those noncombat positions for which they are eligible." Even in the event of a mobilization, enough women would sign up to avoid the need for a draft.

Forcing women to register would cost taxpayers about 8.5 million dollars but would accomplish nothing.

The Senate Armed Services Committee concluded that "processing and training would be needlessly burdened by women recruits who could not be used in combat."

Furthermore, an influx of women would lessen military flexibility. When combat troops are to be rotated into noncombat jobs after assignments in the field, many of those positions would already have been filled by women. "The nation's ability to respond with maximum speed and efficiency would be compromised." What the military needs most are persons of "maximum flexibility," such as male nurses who can be shifted to combat if necessary.

It is possible that the armed forces at some point will decide that women should be allowed to fill combat positions. If that happens, the draft-registration law can be amended.

Sex discrimination in the armed forces can be constitutional, even though other forms of bias are not.

Associate Justice William Brennan asked Wade H. McCree, Solicitor General of the U.S., "Could Congress decide to register only Negroes?" McCree replied, "That would not be legitimate." Brennan then asked, "Could Congress include or exclude people based on religion?" McCree said, "That would not be legitimate, either." Brennan concluded the exchange by remarking that in McCree's view, "gender" seemed to be the only appropriate form of bias in the military.

A 1975 Supreme Court case was cited by McCree as an example of valid sex bias. In that ruling, the Justices upheld a law that provided that male naval officers be discharged after twice failing to be promoted within 10 years but allowed female officers a 13-year period before being forced out. The Court said Congress had the power to enact different standards for male and female military officers if there was a rational reason for doing so.

Forcing women into the military would harm society.

In a brief filed in support of the Justice Department's position, 16 women argued that Congress properly found that the drafting of women "would place unprecedented strains on family life." Noting that only women can bear children, they argue that "even slight uncertainty as to when and how she will be required to fulfill a draft obligation can seriously affect a woman's plans."

The women contend also that "the potential absence of a mother from a home is . . . more likely to be disruptive than the potential absence of a father." Many women fear sexual abuse and invasions of personal privacy if they are forced into the military, and they generally regard military service "as repugnant and inappropriate to the female gender," the women asserted.

Chapter Six

The Uses of Language

Language is used for different purposes—to give information and explain things and ideas, to give directions, to perform certain acts, as in a marriage ceremony, to express and arouse emotions, and to persuade. Logic helps us understand these functions and to see their implications. For example, we have seen that not all statements are propositions. We cannot say whether the *wish* to shun violence is true or false, but we can make a judgment about the truth of a proposition that says "all people seek to avoid violence." Much failure in communication—particularly in argument—results from a misunderstanding of the nature of statements and of the words they contain.

Our concern in this chapter will be precisely with words and statements as instruments of communication. We will consider some important uses of language in exposition and argument, and also some abuses of language generally, including various kinds of ambiguity. We will also consider the way diction affects good exposition and argument, with particular emphasis on its persuasiveness. In the next chapter we will consider some of these topics with respect to fallacies in argument.

Let us begin our discussion of the uses of language by examining the way definitions work.

The uses of definition

Definitions have various uses in exposition and argument. They give us the current meaning of words, and tell us how they were used in the past. Dictionary definitions are of this sort. Some definitions are more extended, and describe the features of a thing or idea in detail. Indeed, essays like Rosnow's on gossip and books like Plato's *Republic* may be devoted almost entirely to such an extended definition. Definition is also important in clarifying meanings and avoiding ambiguity. This use of definition is common in argumentative essays.

Etymological definitions

Etymological definitions trace the original meanings of words. One of their purposes is to show how the original meaning illuminates current use. We had an example of etymological definition in Rosnow (p. 27):

> Derived from the Old English godsibb, for God-parent, it came to mean the women friends of the child's mother who were present at the birth and passed the long hours of waiting in small talk. This origin may also explain the sexist stereotype that brands gossiping as a feminine pastime.

Since words change in meaning over time, and often lose original or older meanings and sometimes even take on entirely opposite ones, it is an error to assume that a word that is used today must have the meanings it once did. The word *sinister* originally referred to the left side, and *sinistral* still refers to left-handedness. It would be absurd and mistaken to describe someone as sinister when we meant that the person was left-handed. Similarly, in argument we could misunderstand the purpose of an etymological definition, mistaking it for a denotative one, and we could easily create this misunderstanding in definitions of our own.

Denotative definitions

A denotative definition, to review some essentials briefly, names a thing, setting it off from all others like it. Since all things belong to classes, a common means of denoting is to distinguish a thing by its class and specific difference:

CLASS

star: Any of the heavenly bodies

SPECIFIC DIFFERENCE

visible from earth on clear nights as apparently fixed points of light.

Standard College Dictionary

The definition can, of course, be technical:

> [Astronomy] One of a class of self-luminous celestial bodies, exclusive of comets, meteors, and nebulae, but including the sun.

The essential defining quality of the class "celestial bodies" is that they are "self-luminous." The moon therefore cannot be included in this class, nor can planets like Saturn though they are luminous to our sight.

Misunderstanding can arise if we are led to expect one kind of definition and find another. In that case, we assume that some important bit of information has been deliberately left out. Skillful writers, however, will not lead us to expect the wrong kind of definition. Yet, they may not provide a complete definition of a word, for we define only as much as we need to. We know how much definition is necessary from our estimate of the audience—of what it knows, or needs to know, to understand a point being made. A highly specific definition like the astronomical one would be inappropriate for a child.

A writer may also choose to define a word broadly or narrowly. The purpose of the definition, as well as the audience, determines how broad or narrow it is. Thus in a popular article on farm equipment we might define a tractor as belonging to the broad class *vehicle* or to the more limited "a powerful, motor-driven vehicle," or we might choose to narrow it a bit further as a "farm implement." If we were describing a new kind of tractor in a technical article describing automotive equipment, many of these defining details could be omitted.

One purpose of a definition in argument, it must be remembered, is to clear up mistaken ideas. We may give the various meanings of "obscene" to clarify statements about allegedly obscene books or movies. The mistake may be a small one, requiring some information about an object— not a total account of it. The definition is considered adequate if this purpose is achieved.

Connotative definitions

In contrast to a denotative definition, a connotative definition states the feelings, impressions, and ideas commonly associated with a word:

> Anyone who shines prominently in a calling or profession; a sports *star*. To shine brightly as a star; be prominent or brilliant.
>
> *Standard College Dictionary*

Some connotative definitions also give personal associations not shared by everyone. Connotative meanings may create misunderstanding in metaphorical statements like the following:

He was the Samson of his generation.

The context probably would clarify the meaning of *Samson* that is intended—whether his strength, his succumbing to temptation, or his exceptional fortitude in the face of pain—but not enough context may be given to help us decide. In general, denotative meanings are easier to control than connotative ones, because it is easier to say what features a thing or idea possesses than to convey its associations.

Special types of definitions

When an existing word has strong connotations which may intrude on the desired sense and hence be misleading, or when a new concept or object is discovered, a new word may be created or an old word may be redefined in a narrow sense. However, when we are confronted with a new phenomenon, as in the case of the quasars (immensely bright and probably very distant celestial objects, discovered in the early 1960s), we often invent a new word. The invented term is usually provisional because the nature of the phenomenon is still to be discovered. And the definition we give this new term is also provisional. Such a definition is called *stipulative*.

The purpose of stipulative definitions is not to fix meanings, as denotative definitions do. Rather the new term and its definition are used for the purpose of discussion and investigation, and are understood to be temporary. As more is learned about the phenomenon, new terms may be proposed and later may be retained. In recent years, the word *stagflation*, formed by combining the prefix from *stagnation* with the root and affix of *inflation*, has been proposed to describe a period of rising costs accompanied by low economic productivity and high unemployment. It is too early to tell whether *stagflation* will become the standard term for this phenomenon. Its retention depends in part on its descriptive accuracy and in part on its attractiveness as a word.

Theoretical definitions, often confused with stipulative ones, claim to provide adequate, comprehensive explanations, not just provisional or highly tentative descriptions. An example is Justice William Brennan's statement that a literary work is obscene if, to "the average person, applying community standards, the dominant theme of the material taken as a whole appeals to the prurient interest." The stipulative definition of quasar, "quasi-stellar source of light," is not theoretical because it does not offer an explanation of this still puzzling phenomenon. It may turn out that quasars are ordinary stars with unrecognized and unexplained properties.

In debating, we should clarify whether such definitions are theoretical or merely stipulative. Unless we are speaking to a special audience that would immediately recognize the kind of definition being offered, we will do best to state exactly what we intend the definition to do, as for example, "Let me stipulate a term to describe this period of high inflation combined with unemployment and low productivity. . . ." Of course, all definitions are subject to revision, including theoretical ones, and we would do well to indicate their limits and perhaps the questions that the theory leaves unanswered.

Stipulative definitions may also be distinguished from a third kind. These are *precising* definitions that seek to give more exact meanings to words or phrases. Here no new meaning is proposed; instead the definition shows that the more exact meaning is implicit in the word if understood correctly. Legal decisions are often concerned with making established terms more precise in meaning and application, as in current redefinitions of *obscene* and *pornographic.* Here is a discussion of the character of civil disobedience that also contains a more precise definition of the phrase:

> It is at this point that we must recognize a distinction in principle between revolutionary violence and nonviolent civil disobedience, even though situations may arise which make it difficult *in practice* to draw the precise line. Although a democrat may condemn any kind of revolutionary violence, no matter how nobly motivated, he may condone, within certain narrowly prescribed limits, some forms of civil disobedience. . . . A situation may arise in which a democrat believes that a municipal or state law violates the fundamental law of the land. . . . Even when such laws are upheld by the courts of highest instance, even in cases where federal laws have been held constitutionally valid, a democratic dissenter may, without inconsistency to his principles, disobey them provided he is prepared to accept the consequences. His justification lies in his hope that his act, and the acts of others, will serve as moral challenge and educational reinfluence on the attitudes of the majority.
>
> Sidney Hook, The Paradoxes of Power

Willingness to accept the consequences is the precise difference Hook emphasizes. But he warns that this definition must be qualified:

> Of course no one can lay down in advance at what precise point civil disobedience, especially mass civil disobedience, by disorganizing essential services, may lead to the destruction of the entire democratic process. This is something which cannot be settled by principled formulations. But any democrat who advocates or undertakes a policy of civil disobedience must take note of considerations of this order and, as a democrat, must always stop short this side of the line.

Exercises

1. Determine the denotative and connotative definitions of each of the following words, using an unabridged dictionary:
   a. weasel
   b. badger

c. nag

d. donkey

2. Be ready to discuss what light the etymology of the following words sheds on their current meanings:

a. humorous

b. silly

c. nice

d. libertine

e. profile

f. reptile

3. Find a stipulative, a theoretical, and a precising definition—or a definition that combines the last two of these—in one of your text-books. Explain how the definition serves the purposes of exposition.

Writing Assignments

1. Write your own definition of a slang word that you are familiar with. Assume that you are writing this definition for those who do not know the word and need help in communicating with its users. Give the denotative and connotative meanings, and possibly an etymological definition if you know the origin of the word.

2. After consulting the *Oxford English Dictionary* and a current una-bridged dictionary on the meaning of a controversial word like *ob-scene*, write a precising definition of your own—an explanation of how the word should be used, and why.

The abuses of language

Much time is spent in ordinary conversation clarifying the meaning of words. The writer does not have the advantage of the instant challenge and correction that occurs in conversation, and therefore must be alert to the possible confusion a poor choice of words can create. To recognize this problem, a writer must be sensitive to the ways in which words convey meanings. We shall consider those ways in this and the following sections. In the next chapter we shall consider how abuses of language can affect arguments.

Ambiguous terms

When we find a term ambiguous, we are in doubt about which of two (or more) meanings may be intended by the writer. To discover the correct one, we must choose between these meanings. For example, in the statement "He is an exceptional person in more ways than I would care to say," the speaker's reluctance to name the ways makes us wonder whether the person is "exceptional" in the sense of brilliant or talented, or "exceptional" in the sense of dull or untalented—to suggest just a few of the many meanings this popular euphemism can have. The speaker would be employing a euphemism if the word was used to soften a blunt fact.

The context of the statement sets us right most of the time. If the speaker has been critical of the person in previous statements, we soon clear up the ambiguity. But context is not always a help, particularly when the statement opens the discussion. We may then have to ask, "Exceptional in what sense? Brilliant? Talented?" Much of the routine exchange between speakers in ordinary conversations is for the purpose of this kind of clarification.

In writing, we do not have the advantage of the give and take of conversation, and therefore we have to be careful to provide a context for words capable of ambiguity. We must be particularly careful with emotionally loaded words or statements that might be understood ironically or sarcastically, as in "He has a great future behind him," or even more ambiguously, in "She must really have been fun to go out with!"

Equivocal terms

The terms of a statement may also be equivocal if they shift in meaning during a discussion. The shift is often too subtle to detect immediately, and we find ourselves agreeing uneasily to what seems a good argument but is really unsound. This kind of confusion is possible because many words like "freedom" and "liberty" contain a wide range of meanings rather than single, fixed ones. We see how easily the meanings of a term— in this instance "discipline"—can shift in the following statement of the Italian dictator Benito Mussolini defending the fascist regime he established in 1922:

> The discipline that I have imposed is not a forced discipline; it is not born from preconceived ideas, does not obey the selfish interests of groups and of classes. Our discipline has one vision and one end—the welfare and the good name of the Italian nation. The discipline that I have imposed is enlightened discipline.
>
> *My Autobiography*

In an equivocal statement or argument, terms shift in meaning; in ambiguous ones, we simply do not know which of two (or more) possible meanings of a term is intended, and we must choose one. But the effect of both is the same: readers are confused and thrown mentally off balance, sometimes without being able to discover what is wrong. And if they cannot discover what is wrong, then they may conclude dangerously that the statement or argument is after all clear and cogent. This is the aim of the demagogue—to gain assent through confusion.

There is also another objection to ambiguous and equivocal terms. Because of the uncertainty of such terms, we may find ourselves arguing about semantics—the meanings of words—rather than about substance—the genuine subject of our discussion or dispute. In such cases, we are unable to come to grips with the issues that divide us.

Vague terms

Vague terms create somewhat different problems in arguments, though their effect is the same as ambiguity and equivocation—confusion and perplexity. With an ambiguous term we are in doubt about which of several meanings to accept; with a vague one, we know what meaning is intended, but we do not see that meaning distinctly.

This is because vague terms are frequently relative terms that depend on degree—terms like "intelligent" or "smart" or "fat" or "tiny," that may be clear to the people who use them because they know what things they *point* to, but are unclear to others. Thus the statement that "dogs are smarter than cats" is vague because we are not given either the measure or degree of intelligence intended by the comparison. Indeed, comparative terms present a constant danger of vagueness in exposition and argument.

Though people often *want* to be ambiguous and equivocal in their statements, they perhaps less often want to be vague. The problem of vagueness lies more often in the failure to clearly indicate the context of a term, including the attitudes or beliefs that condition its use. Because we too often assume that our readers share our attitudes and beliefs, and also our knowledge and sense of context, we do not think of telling our audience enough about these, and thereby create uncertainty. Much conversation and debate involve considerable talking at cross-purposes for this reason. This is why speakers routinely take several steps back in the course of a debate to redefine terms and clarify their context.

We are given a particularly cogent example of the difficulty that can arise by a writer on business management, in a comment on relative terms in the vocabulary of company managers:

It is no secret that people who become managerial and executive people work hard. Studies show inevitably that "highly motivated" people become managers. Necessarily, less highly motivated people *don't* become managers. Thus, most managers are going to see a lot of "lazy" people at lower levels in the organization. Very seldom do we hear managers complaining that *their bosses* are lazy. Laziness, to some degree, is relative.

Larry Steinmetz, *"Laziness: Is It Real?"*

Obviously, deeply ingrained attitudes stand behind a term like *lazy,* and attitudes are not always known to the people who hold them. So are the social attitudes prevailing in the world of the writer, as well as special circumstances that condition the way a word is defined. For example, Steinmetz points out that the term *alcoholic* is sometimes defined by the causes of alcoholism, and sometimes by its effects:

> What is an alcoholic? Some people will say a person is an alcoholic if they have a drink every day. . . . Others say one doesn't have a problem with alcohol unless his drinking behavior has a negative impact on his ability to do the job or on family relationships. But many is the salesman who can attest to the fact that non-drinking behavior has caused the loss of sales. In this case, non-drinking had a negative impact on job performance.

Of course, ambiguity and vagueness can be deliberately created to deceive an opponent. If the aim of a writer or a speaker in a debate is simply to "win" the argument, without conciliating the opponent, or coming to mutual agreement on the issue, then the tactic will be effective if it succeeds. But if the writer's or speaker's aim is to conciliate and reach agreement, it will have quite the opposite effect. Conciliation is, indeed, one very important reason for taking care with the definition and exposition of terms and ideas in argument. If there is any suspicion that the audience or opponent will not understand what is meant, then it is wise to define or explain what may seem obvious to the speaker or writer but may not be to others. Unless we intend to be ironic and surprise our audience with delayed meanings, we communicate best by seeking immediate understanding of the terms we use.

Exercise

Discuss whether the following statements can be considered ambiguous, equivocal, or vague:

a. While I recognize that everybody is equal before the law, I also recognize that not everybody can be treated equally and that applies to senators and congressmen and government officials—not because of the person but because of the office.

A Justice Department official during Watergate

b. Article 1, Section 2. Any person who commits an act which the law declares to be punishable or which is deserving of punishment according to the idea of a penal law and healthy popular feeling, shall be punished. If there is no penal law directly covering an act it shall be punished under that law the basic idea of which fits it best.

Law passed in Germany, June 28, 1935

c. Everybody in this society is a policeman. We all police ourselves. When we free ourselves, the real cops take over.

A Yippie Manifesto

Accent and nuance

The meaning of a statement can also change depending on the accent or stress given to particular words. We are familiar with the special accent given to certain ideas and feelings in advertisement with the size of lettering and the sharp emphasis of short phrases. Thus, an ad for a men's cologne presents these phrases in bold letters:

Bold, Honest, Heroic.
A genuine fragrance of the American West.
Colorado Sage.

Statements can also exhibit slight variations or shades of meaning— nuances that are often hard to pin down. There is a subtle difference between a particular perfume or cologne and all others, we may be told in another ad, and of course only the true expert will recognize that difference. The "subtle difference," we are told in an ad for another product, "for the man who really cares."

In spoken statements, the inflection given a word may convey a nuance of meaning that communicates important attitudes. We may not be able to say exactly what that meaning is, but we are certain that we understand the attitude. We look for these nuances or shades of meaning in the slight emphasis or twist that may be given the word in a written sentence. Since vocal inflection is not present in writing, we read the sentence as we would hear it spoken, and we pay close attention to the context.

We can best illustrate the role nuance plays in argument with President Lyndon B. Johnson's address to Congress, on March 15, 1965, on the right to vote:

Allow men and women to register and vote whatever the color of their skin. Extend the rights of citizenship to every citizen of this land. There is no constitutional issue here. The command of the Constitution is plain. There is no moral issue. It is wrong—deadly wrong—to deny any of your fellow Americans the right to vote in this country. There is no issue of States rights or National rights. There is only the struggle for human rights.

President Johnson has here played on the subtle nuances in the word "rights," developing these nuances through his qualifying words, "States," "National," and "human." Most people, whether they are in favor of the President's statement or not, would probably agree on the general definition of *right* as "a power or privilege to which one is justly entitled." By developing the nuances of this word, President Johnson has implied that the struggle for human rights must take precedence over the conflict between the rights of the States and those of the federal government. At this point there may be considerable differences of opinion.

In contrast to nuance, accent is achieved through particular stress on key words, as we have said, and through repetition and the placement of words in prominent positions in the sentence. Thus, the placement of "States rights," "National rights," and "human rights" at the end of their respective sentences gives weight to these ideas: the beginning and end of sentences are the prominent positions. It is also possible to achieve emphasis through balanced phrases in sentences—that is, through similar ideas that are given equal weight in similar constructions:

> We dare not forget today that we are the heirs of that first revolution. Let the word go forth *from this time and place, to friend and foe alike,* that the torch has been passed to a new generation of Americans—*born in this century, tempered by war, disciplined by a hard and bitter peace, proud of our ancient heritage*—and unwilling to witness or permit the slow undoing of those human rights to which this nation has always been committed, and to which we are committed today at home and around the world.
>
> President John F. Kennedy, *Inaugural Address* (italics added)

One final point about accent and nuance. The meaning of a sentence can depend on the placement of a single word:

> The union members say only they are willing to bargain.
> The union members only say they are willing to bargain.
> The union members say they are willing to bargain only.
> Only the union members say they are willing to bargain.

The first sentence says that, according to the union members, only they and not others are willing to bargain. The second sentence suggests that the members do not mean what they say. The third sentence says that the members want to bargain for now, and perhaps reserve decisions or agreements until a later time; the fourth sentence, that only the members have been heard from—their employers have not said whether they will come to the bargaining table.

In ordinary conversation a word like "only" may be used without concern for subtle differences in meaning. In writing we must be especially alert to the range of possible meanings.

Exercises

1. Distinguish between accent and nuance in the following transcription of a spoken sentence. The speaker is a parking lot attendant:

> We had a lady come in about six months ago. She wanted her car in the same spot. I said, "Sorry lady, can't put it in a certain spot." She said, "I want it in *that* spot." She came back and I had it in *that* spot. She said, "Thank you." I said, "Okay, lady." She came back again and we was filled up. She wanted *that* spot again, and I said, "No, I'm filled, lady. I can't get you *that* spot. I can't get you any spot."
>
> Studs Terkel, *Working*

2. Examine the headlines in a newspaper or news magazine, and write down examples of accent and nuance you find in them. Discuss how they shape meaning.

Figurative language in exposition and argument

In literature, figurative language often calls attention to itself and our enjoyment often arises from the use of figures of speech. In exposition and argument, this kind of language use may serve another purpose—to make ideas clear, vivid, and concrete. In the following description of the brain, metaphors help us see and understand qualities that are difficult to understand in technical language:

> As for the brain, it is all mystery and memory and electricity. It is enough to know of its high-topping presence, a gray cloud, substantial only in the bony box of the skull and otherwise melting into a blob of ghost-colored paste that can be wiped up with a sponge. The very idea of it, teeming with a billion unrealized thoughts, countless circuits breaking and unbreaking, flashing tiny fires of idea on and off, is too much.
>
> Richard Selzer, *Mortal Lessons*

More importantly, figurative language conveys what we do not find in a technical description of the brain—Selzer's feelings. It is the connotative value of the words, on which figurative language depends, that makes it possible to express these feelings.

Let us review the most common figures of speech. *Simile* is an explicit comparison of unlike terms using the words "as" and "like" as signals: a person in love is *like* an object on fire. *Metaphor* treats an entity as if it were something else: the flame of love. At one point, we find three metaphors joined in Selzer's description of the brain as "a blob of ghost-colored paste." Earlier, he had called the brain "a gray cloud." A deliberate exaggeration is called *hyperbole*: "He's all heart." *Synecdoche* iden-

tifies a part with the whole: "She worked to put bread on the table."
Metonymy uses a quality or object associated with a thing to stand for
it: "City hall rejected the union's offer." *Personification* gives living or
human qualities to something abstract or inanimate: "The ship fought
the storm and survived."

Figurative language plays an important role in exposition and argument
through its ability to make ideas striking and colorful. As a rule, it serves
in these forms of discourse to make ideas concrete as good illustrations
do. In both functions, figurative language is perhaps most effective when
it does so without calling attention to itself, as it often does in imaginative
literature, and without distracting the reader from the content of ideas.
Compare the following metaphorical description of a woman entering an
office, in a contemporary American novel, with the description of a baby's
brain in a contemporary essay on science:

> Then I heard the racket outside in the reception room, and opened my eyes.
> Somebody had slammed a door. Then I caught the whir of a passage and
> Sadie Burke swung into my ken, making a great curve through my open door,
> and, all in one motion, slamming it behind her and charging on in my direc-
> tion. She stood in front of my desk and fought for air enough to say what she
> had to say.
>
> Robert Penn Warren, *All the King's Men*

> The period immediately after birth is probably the most promising. The baby
> is born with a huge head for his size, with a brain weighing one-quarter of its
> adult weight, but during his first six months of life his brain weight will
> double. The glial cells will multiply, the neurons will branch out in a wealth
> of dendrites, and the little spines on the dendrites will sprout magically to
> receive connections from other cells. It is a time of explosive growth—and yet
> the human infant has the longest period of helplessness of any animal. His
> cortex takes longer to mature than any other creature's. Just because his cortex
> is so big and takes so long to develop, the environment has ample time and
> opportunities to shape it. We are only beginning to discover how it does so.
> Only in recent years have scientists begun to study and rate home environ-
> ments, for instance—to clock what parents do to infants, to classify the kinds
> of interactions that take place, to record the language that is spoken.
>
> Maya Pines, *The Brain Changers*

Both descriptions use figurative language for dramatic effect, but the
Pines' piece does so in a much more muted fashion. In the excerpt from
Warren's novel we are probably more aware of the use of such metaphorical phrases as "the whir of a passage" than we are of Pines' use of
metaphors in "neurons will branch out in a wealth of dendrites" or of
personification in "the environment has ample time and opportunities
to shape it." Indeed, we would in all likelihood be surprised to find in
a nonliterary work so dramatic and colorful a use as occurs in a later
sentence from the Warren passage:

That morning she had exploded out of the Boss's door, and had described a parabola into my office, with her black chopped-off hair wild and her face like a riddled plaster-of-Paris mask of Medusa except for the hot bituminous eyes, which were in full blaze with a bellows pumping the flame.

Were this action to appear in the narrative of a prosecutor's statement of a case, the sentence would contain much less colorful language. The degree of color and dramatic effect varies, however, from writer to writer and from age to age. The courtroom speeches of Clarence Darrow, the great defense lawyer, are full of highly dramatic, colorful writing, though never as vivid as the sentence just quoted.

It should be added that metaphorical language is often absorbed into ordinary language, particularly after long use, and probably is not recognized as metaphorical by most of us:

Television has *enlarged* the audience for sports while *lowering* the *level* of its understanding; at least this is the *operating* assumption of sports commentators, who direct at the audience an *interminable stream of tutelage* in the basics of the game, and of the promoters who *reshape* one game after another to conform to the *tastes* of an audience supposedly incapable of *grasping* their *finer points.*

Christopher Lasch, *The Culture of Narcissism* (italics added)

"Buried" metaphors can convey meanings or nuances not intended, and for this reason sentences are often phrased as literally as possible in legal arguments and the like where exactness of meaning is essential.

In the give and take of ordinary arguments, we need often to clarify statements we make in the plainest language we can find. In writing arguments, and in expository writing too, we need to take the greatest care in examining the words we use not just for the possible nuances discussed earlier but for unintended meanings arising from metaphor.

Exercises

1. Identify the hidden or obvious metaphors in the following passage. Discuss whether substitutions can be made for them without changing the meaning of the sentences:

   The hero was born of time: his gestation required at least a generation. As the saying went, he had "stood the test of time." A maker of tradition, he was himself made by tradition. He grew over the generations as people found new virtues in him and attributed to him new exploits. Receding into the misty past he became more, and not less, heroic. It was not necessary that his face or figure have a sharp, well-delineated outline, nor that his life be footnoted. Of course there could not have been any photographs of him, and often there was not even a likeness. Men of the last century were more heroic than those of today; men of antiquity were still more heroic; and those of pre-history became demigods. The hero was always somehow ranked among the ancients.

Daniel J. Boorstin, *The Image*

2. Write three sentences that contain no figures of speech—no similes, metaphors, personifications, or the like. Then rewrite the sentences, using some or all of these figures to make the ideas vivid.

3. In the following excerpts, translate the metaphors and other figures into literal language. Then write down what is lost in the paraphrase:

a. Yesterday, we split the atom. We assaulted that colossal citadel of power, the tiny unit of the substance of the universe. And because of this, the great dream and the great nightmare of centuries of human thought have taken flesh and walk beside us all, day and night.

Doris Lessing, *The Small Personal Voice*

b. The lenses we wear are ground to the prescription of our textbooks and teachers. Even while we are undergraduates a certain image of the nature of man is fitted to our eyes. We grow accustomed to the image and when we become practitioners or teachers we may still take it for granted.

Gordon W. Allport, "*Psychological Models for Guidance*"

c. Science fiction once prophesied, in its apparently wild flights of fancy, many of the aerial feats that have come to pass.

Nancy Hale, "*The Two-Way Imagination*"

d. Science provides the understanding of the universe in which we live. Mathematics provides the dies by which science is molded.

Morris Kline, "*The Meaning of Mathematics*"

e. When as kids we came to an orchard wall that seemed too high to climb, we took off our caps and tossed them over the wall, and then we had no choice but to follow them. I had tossed my cap over the wall of life, and I knew I must follow it, wherever it had fallen.

Frank O'Connor, *An Only Child*

f. We do not ride on the railroad; it rides upon us.

Henry David Thoreau, *Walden*

g. Intelligence is often more completely educated than desire; our outward behavior has an appearance of being grown up which our inner vanities and hopes, our dim but powerful cravings, often belie.

Walter Lippmann, *A Preface to Morals*

Simple and pretentious diction

Writing that avoids figurative language entirely often seems bland and colorless, as in the literature coming from government bureaus and courts of law. The need for meticulous explanation and legal exactness explains this lack of color. Here is part of a 1968 Supreme Court ruling on destroying Selective Service cards:

> The information supplied on the certificates facilitates communication between registrants and local boards, simplifying the system and benefiting all concerned. To begin with, each certificate bears the address of the registrant's local board, an item unlikely to be committed to memory. Further, each card bears the registrant's Selective Service number, and a registrant who has his number readily available so that he can communicate it to his local board when he supplies or requests information can make simpler the board's task in locating his file. Finally, a registrant's inquiry, particularly through a local board other than his own, concerning his eligibility status is frequently answerable simply on the basis of his classification certificate; whereas, if the certificate were not reasonably available and the registrant were uncertain of his classification, the task of answering his questions would be considerably complicated.
>
> *United States* v. *O'Brien*

Formal statements such as this may require an impersonal tone, but it need not be pompous; careful elaboration on each point and the use of words like "certificates" for *card*, "facilitates" for *aids* or *helps* makes the writing stuffy. The dependence on the passive voice in official and public statements of all sorts heightens this effect:

Notification is required of change of address.

Even legal decisions, however, do not have to resemble a stuffed bird. They can be lively, as shown in this dissenting opinion by the late Justice William O. Douglas concerning freedom of speech and the press:

> Debate and argument even in the courtroom are not always calm and dispassionate. Emotions sway speakers and audiences alike. Intemperate speech is a distinctive characteristic of man. Hotheads blow off and release destructive energy in the process. They shout and rave, exaggerating weaknesses, magnifying error, viewing with alarm. So it has been from the beginning; and so it will be throughout time. The Framers of the Constitution knew human nature as well as we do. They too had lived in dangerous days; they too knew the suffocating influence of orthodoxy and standardized thought. They weighed the compulsions for restrained speech and thought against the abuses of liberty. They chose liberty.
>
> *Beauharnais* v. *Illinois*

The ideas here are no less abstract, but the occasional use of colloquial expressions and concrete examples eases the formality considerably.

Dependence on technical or jargon words and abstract nouns increases the formal effect and often buries meaning, particularly when prepositional phrases are strung together:

> Throughout the entire evolution of conspicuous expenditure, whether of goods or of services or human life, runs the obvious implication that in order to effectually mend the consumer's good fame it must be an expenditure of superfluities. In order to be reputable it must be wasteful. No merit would accrue from the consumption of the bare necessaries of life, except by comparison with the abjectly poor who fall short even of the subsistence minimum; and no standard of expenditure could result from such a comparison, except the most prosaic and unattractive level of decency. A standard of life would still be possible which should admit of invidious comparison in other respects than that of opulence; as, for instance, a comparison in various directions in the manifestation of moral, physical, intellectual, or aesthetic force.
>
> Thorstein Veblen, *The Theory of the Leisure Class*

Veblen is saying that in modern society reputation is based not on what we consume out of necessity but on what we waste; we could base the comparison on how the poor live, but not much credit would come from this. And there are measures of consumption besides opulence.

Many readers find prose like Veblen's very hard going, not because Veblen is ambiguous or vague, but rather because he writes at a high level of abstraction and is precise in stating each abstract relationship. Indeed, the effect is one of overprecision and overqualification. But even more seriously, the sense of someone speaking is absent. Veblen departs widely from the rhythms of spoken sentences, and there is not a single colloquial expression to lighten the discussion. Notice also how the repetition of the same sounds deadens some of the sentences:

> . . . . a comparison in *various directions* in the *man*ifestation of moral, physical, intellectual, or aesthetic force.

Unintended rhyme can be highly distracting in expository prose.

At the opposite extreme from this highly formal writing, a chatty style can seem just as patronizing:

> Ever thought of why people put on the dog so much? I'll bet you have many times. I know I have. Let's see if we agree on the reasons.

The reader is here taken into the writer's confidence immediately, much as customers are taken into the confidence of oily pitchmen. Such prose conveys an impression of all-knowingness and infallibility. Newspaper gossip columns provide too many examples to require quotation.

The examples given show that dependence on one kind of sentence structure—dependence on the passive voice or on a string of words that sound alike—work against clear and effective prose. And overprecision and overqualification as in Veblen must be controlled if the writing is to be kept from sounding stuffy.

Jargon and technical words

Every special field, from engineering to the social sciences and the humanities, uses special terms that convey technical meanings. Sometimes ordinary words like *manual* and *search* are given special meanings, as in this discussion of computer information banks:

> In the context of the search stage, manual systems are those in which intellectual decisions relating to all aspects of a search have to be made at the time of search of a request, and the examination of the index entries is also done by hand.
>
> Michael Keen, *"Search Strategy Evaluation in Manual and Automated Systems"*

Notice that the word *manual* refers both to work done by hand and also to decisions made at the time of the search: the person seeking information from the computer decides at the time of the search what questions to ask.

The advantage of such special terms or jargon words is that they provide a shorthand or code for those in the special field. Often a special term is created to cover a number of operations; a shorthand word like *manual* makes discussion more concise. Brevity also explains the popularity of acronyms—abbreviations like NATO and UNESCO. The student of sociology or psychology or nuclear physics must master a special vocabulary and a special style, sometimes highly compressed, and sometimes extremely complex and formal in grammar and sentence structure:

> The interaction of the Ojibwa reservation subculture and its environment can be brought into finer focus by examination of several interdependent role patterns in Deerpoint. Each such general role pattern can be conceived, in turn, as a cluster of specific roles.
>
> Bernard J. James, *"Social-Psychological Dimensions of Ojibwa Acculturation"*

Notice how much knowledge of special terms readers of these passages must possess to understand not just the essential ideas but the attitudes being expressed. These ideas can be turned into plain English, but in the opinion of the writers with a loss of exactness of meaning and concision. For this reason, there has been resistance to the demand that technical language be discarded in favor of plain English. Recently some insurance companies have begun to provide translations into plain English of the policies they issue; the translation is not, however, a substitute for the policy which must meet legal standards of precise language. It is true that a gain in general comprehension is often achieved at the expense of precision, but it is also true that sentences like Veblen's are difficult to understand because of their cumbersome structure and strings of modifiers.

In writing for a general audience, you should remember that jargon words from special fields will often create confusion and may make writing seem pompous and clumsy. George Orwell's advice on this matter is worth quoting: "Never use a foreign phrase, a scientific word, or a jargon word if you can think of an everyday English equivalent." But borrowings from science and other fields have made this advice too simple. We need to consider the meaning of words as well as the occasion of their use. For example, the word *retrieval* has special meaning in computer science: it refers to the complex operations by which computers produce or recover stored information. To use the related word *retrieve* to describe a routine search of a library catalog, when the perfectly adequate phrase "look up" is available, is to make our statement sound pretentious and even comic. In a personal letter, *peer group* would be inaccurate and inexact if we mean only "friends," for the phrase has broader meanings in the social sciences from which it is derived. For a similar context, the word *correlation* would be out of place and indeed would be an error if used instead of "conclusion" or "resemblance."

But it is not always true that the simpler word is the better: we need words like *correlation* to describe mutual relationships. The remedy is to be aware of the appropriate context as well as the exact meaning. There is no better way to avoid needless jargon than to consult the dictionary often.

We turn in the next chapter to fallacies of arguments, many of them containing errors in the use of language that we considered briefly here.

Exercises

1. Make a list of ten to fifteen jargon words in a chapter in one of your textbooks. For ten of these words check your dictionary for the exact meaning. Write down these meanings and also their equivalents in ordinary language if you find any.

2. Using the subject catalog of your library, make a list of ten dictionaries or handbooks devoted to technical language in specialized fields. To start, check to see whether a dictionary exists for users of Citizen Band radios, audio equipment, and shortwave transmitters. Also include one or two dictionaries that contain a listing of common acronyms and abbreviations.

Writing Assignment

Evaluate the language of the following passage. State whether the ideas could be expressed in simpler language without a loss of exactness, and comment on the effectiveness of the sentences and phrasing:

> In human interaction it is also possible to identify, at least in principle, these two kinds of control. Let us call them *outcome control* and *cue control* to distinguish between the direct manipulation of rewards and punishments and the provision of information that gears into pre-established environment-behavior contingencies. Outcome control seems to be the necessary precursor to cue control, except for those cases in which innate reflexive behavior is elicited by appropriate stimulation. Presumably, however, such innate contingencies between stimuli and reactions do not play an important role in human social behavior. Although outcome control seems to underlie cue control in most cases, the former requires some command over reinforcement resources, whereas the latter requires appropriate information and the ability to put it to use.
>
> Edward E. Jones and Harold B. Gerard, "Dyadic Interaction"

Chapter Seven

Fallacies

In earlier chapters we concentrated on sound arguments, using unsound ones merely to illustrate the methods required to evaluate ways of arguing. In this chapter we will turn our attention to false reasoning or fallacy, as it is commonly called in logic.

The study of fallacies is important, for through it we can sharpen our understanding of legitimate methods of reasoning while learning to recognize the techniques of false arguments. Recognizing fallacious arguments can sometimes be a problem since they often resemble legitimate ones and the distinction between the two can be very subtle. Although a fallacy is an error in reasoning, its psychological or emotional appeal may be—indeed, often is—so strong that its faulty logic is obscured and we are moved by its persuasive power. Beyond that, some fallacies use methods of persuasion that in some contexts, under limited circumstances, are legitimate. For example, it is perfectly correct to use or quote authorities as support for an argument in the area of their expertise, but the opinions of the same authorities are wholly beside the point in subjects about which they have no special knowledge.

We have just glanced at a kind of faulty argument that uses irrelevant evidence. There are a number of fallacies of relevance, the best known of which is perhaps the *ad hominem* attack. All fallacies of relevance have one characteristic in common: the evidence used to support an argument, whether it is a premise or a fact, has no logical bearing on the point at issue. There are other kinds of fallacies as well. One of the most common of these results from the faulty use of language and is known as fallacies of ambiguity. An amusing example of faulty language is the advice, offered no doubt with the best intentions, that "if you don't go to other people's funerals, they won't come to yours."

Fallacies have been grouped together in different ways by different logicians. But, most logicians agree on dividing fallacies into two broad categories: formal fallacies, which result from the incorrect use of the forms of inference that we studied in Chapter Four, such as the fallacy of the undistributed middle; and informal fallacies, which result from a careless or distorted use of subject matter or language, such as those we have just considered and that we will examine in greater detail in this chapter.

But before going on to the rest of the chapter, just look at the cartoon reproduced below. It sums up the subject we are about to examine.

The meaning of relevance

A fallacious argument presents evidence that is not pertinent to the conclusion. We have no reason to believe that the facts given, or the premises, can be taken as evidence for it, that is, are "relevant." Thus, if we are arguing whether a city income tax should be enacted, it is fallacious

" 'Buzz off' in no way constitutes valid rebuttal."

to argue that it should not because the one who has proposed the tax has previously been convicted for tax fraud. We have not been told that the character of this person in any way affects the merits of the proposal. If we had been given a justifiable reason to think so, the argument would not seem to us fallacious, at least with respect to character.

Another way of claiming relevance is to say that we are warranted in considering the facts or data pertinent to the conclusion. We saw that in the Toulmin model a "warrant" states the basis for connecting the facts or data to the conclusion drawn from them. If necessary, the basis may itself be given backing. Thus the argument that a tax fraud conviction disqualifies a person for the office of mayor may be warranted by the statement that honesty and reliability go together. If that justification is challenged (as it well may be), backing can be sought in recent political history.

Arguments often concern the justification or warrant itself. In arguing that a new drug should be licensed for public use, a pharmaceutical company may state that licensing is warranted because repeated testing on animals proves the safety of the drug for human beings. Though the tests may be accepted for one class of drugs, it may be rejected for another class—or for products of a wholly different sort. Those who argue that tests on laboratory animals are insufficient to prove that saccharine is dangerous to humans are rejecting a warrant they might accept in other circumstances. They are saying, in other words, that the relevance of the evidence has not been established and the conclusion is therefore unwarranted. The argument is claimed to be fallacious on this ground. In short, reasoning considered to be sound in one set of circumstances may be considered fallacious in another.

It is such fallacies of relevance that we will consider first, followed by the fallacies of ambiguity. We will then go on to several other types of false argument and conclude our discussion with three fallacies of induction: hasty generalization, false analogy, and false cause.

Exercise

Each of the following arguments states a reason for considering the data or evidence presented for the conclusion to be relevant to it. We have italicized the conclusion in each argument. Identify the justification for it in each argument. Do you think the conclusions are warranted by the reasons given for them? Explain your answers.

a. Before the days of universal pasteurization, streptococcal sore throats, including scarlet fever, were rather frequently a result of milk infection, sometimes resulting from contamination of the milk by infected dairy employees, sometimes actually from a streptococcal infection of the cows.

Since all food and drink passes the tonsils on its downward journey, it is only to be expected that *those organisms which tend to infect that region may be spread as readily in milk as by the droplet method*

—Sir MacFarlane Burnet and David O. White, *Natural History of Infectious Disease*

b. [After being sentenced to hang for inciting a slave rebellion, John Brown said the following at his trial in 1859] In the first place, I deny everything but what I have all along admitted, of a design on my part to free slaves. I intended certainly to have made a clean thing of that matter, as I did last winter when I went into Missouri, and there took slaves without the snapping of a gun on either side, moving them through the country, and finally leaving them in Canada. I designed to have done the same thing again on a larger scale. That was all I intended to do. I never did intend murder or treason, or the destruction of property, or to excite or incite the slaves to rebellion, or to make insurrection. I have another objection, and that is that it is unjust that I should suffer such a penalty. Had I interfered in the manner, which I admit, and which I admit has been fairly proved—for I admire the truthfulness and candor of the greater portion of the witnesses who have testified in this case—had I so interfered in behalf of any of the rich, the powerful, the intelligent, the so-called great, or in behalf of any of their friends, either father, mother, brother, sister, wife, or children, or any of that class, and suffered and sacrificed what I have in this interference, it would have been all right, and every man in this court would have deemed it an act worthy of reward rather than punishment. This Court acknowledges, too, as I suppose, the validity of the law of God. I see a book kissed, which I suppose to be the Bible, or at least the New Testament, which teaches me that all things whatsoever I would that men should do to me, I should do even so to them. It teaches me further to remember them that are in bonds, as bound with them. I endeavored to act up to that instruction. I say I am yet too young to understand that God is any respecter of persons. I believe that *to have interfered as I have done, as I have always freely admitted I have done in behalf of His despised poor, is no wrong, but right.* Now, if it is deemed necessary that I should forfeit my life for the furtherance of the ends of justice, and mingle my blood further with the blood of my children and with the blood of millions in this slave country whose rights are disregarded by wicked, cruel, and unjust enactments, I say let it be done.

c. *In our time it is broadly true that political writing is bad writing.* Where it is not true, it will generally be found that the writer is some kind of rebel, expressing his private opinions and not a "party line." Orthodoxy, of whatever color, seems to demand a lifeless, imitative style. The political dialects to be found in pamphlets, leading articles, manifestoes, White Papers and the speeches of undersecretaries do, of course, vary from party to party, but they are all alike in that one almost never finds in them a fresh, vivid, homemade turn of speech. When one watches some tired hack on the platform mechanically repeating the familiar phrases—*bestial atrocities, iron heel, bloodstained tyranny, free peoples of the world, stand shoulder to shoulder*—one often has a curious feeling that one is not watching a live human being but some kind of dummy: a feeling which suddenly becomes stronger at moments when the light catches the speaker's spectacles and turns them into blank discs which seem to have no eyes behind them. And this is not altogether fanciful. A speaker who uses that kind of phraseology has gone some distance toward turning himself into a machine.

George Orwell, "Politics and the English Language"

Fallacies of relevance

Ad hominem *arguments*

When attorneys cross-examine hostile witnesses they often try to point out flaws of character as a way of making the witnesses' testimony less believable. Since the truthfulness of a witness is important in establishing evidence, any means of calling into question the integrity of the witness is relevant to the issues of the trial. For example, if a person has committed perjury in the past, there are good reasons to view his or her present testimony with some scepticism. This then is not a fallacious use of argumentative techniques.

But, if in a debate one attacks the character of an opponent instead of the issue he or she addressed, that is a false means of arguing, for the opponent's character is irrelevant. An abusive attack on a speaker or writer rather than on his or her position is an instance of an *ad hominem* argument. The phrase *ad hominem* is Latin for "to the man," or as it is often translated, "against the man." This kind of argument is irrelevant because whether a proposition or belief is true or false does not depend on the character of the person advocating that belief. For example, it does not matter what the character of a person supporting welfare is; the reasons he or she offers in defense of that support is what counts.

Ad hominem attacks are common in politics, chiefly because issues are difficult to understand and caricatures are easy. For example, in the New York primary race of 1981, a newspaper editorial endorsed the opponent of Mayor Edward I. Koch as the candidate of the Democratic party. The newspaper claimed that "this is not an anti-Koch editorial," yet instead of criticizing the mayor's policies, it said:

> Six months ago Ed Koch seemed destined for a three-party coronation for a second term as mayor. He had earned the Republican and Conservative Party

endorsements with his race politics and trickled-down economics, but even the Democrats, out of resignation, cynicism, fear, or exhaustion, seemed poised to crown their quisling without a fight.

Then Frank Barbaro stood up, alone, and said: No, this bully, this bigot, does not represent the party of Roosevelt and Lehman, of labor and immigrant poor.

The Village Voice, September 2–8, 1981

Attention has here shifted from Koch's policies, which were indeed controversial, to his character. Moreover, that character is presented in emotionally loaded terms, like "bully" or "bigot," and is subtly depicted as autocratic through the allusions to monarchy. At no point in the editorial is there any explanation of these terms and allusions, or for that matter of what is meant by the mayor's supposed "race politics" and "trickled-down economics." Nor is there much respect for the few "facts" mentioned in the article. As it happens, Koch had not received the endorsement of the Conservative party, and he was challenged in the Republican primary as well as the Democratic one. Finally, a statement is attributed to Koch's opponent, but not placed within quotation marks, thus implying an authoritative source for the slur of Koch's character.

The editorial not only maligns Koch's character, but also incidentally the character of members of the Democratic party. As we can see from our excerpt, *ad hominem* attacks on individuals can sometimes be extended to include groups of people. In the following excerpt from a speech delivered in 1900, Senator Ben Tillman of South Carolina leads up to a discussion of the disenfranchisement of black citizens by saying:

But it cannot be denied that the slaves of the South were a superior set of men and women to freedmen of today, and that the poison in their minds— the race hatred of the whites—is the result of the teachings of Northern fanatics. Ravishing a woman, white or black, was never known to occur in the South till after the Reconstruction era.

Here we have the numbing effect caused by fear and revulsion. Tillman has shifted attention away from the need for a reasoned explanation of the denial of voting rights for blacks to a wholesale defamation of the very victims of this denial. There is no consideration here of questions of justice, civil rights, or constitutional obligations. When, indeed, he does turn to the question of disenfranchisement, he merely asserts that blacks were gradually removed from state government after 1876:

We have had no fraud in our elections in South Carolina since 1884. There has been no organized Republican party in the State.

He asserts that blacks were later disenfranchised, stating how and to whose supposed benefit:

We did not disfranchise the Negroes until 1895. Then we had a constitutional convention convened which took the matter up calmly, deliberately, and avowedly with the purpose of disfranchising as many of them as we could under the Fourteenth and Fifteenth Amendments. We adopted the educational qualification as the only means left to us, and the Negro is as contented and as prosperous and as well protected in South Carolina today as in any State of the Union south of the Potomac. He is not meddling with politics, for he found that the more he meddled with them the worse off he got. As to his "rights"—I will not discuss them now. We of the South have never recognized the right of the Negro to govern white men, and we never will. We have never believed him to be equal to the white man, and we will not submit to his gratifying his lust on our wives and daughters without lynching him. I would to God the last one of them was in Africa, and that none of them had ever been brought to our shores.

Poisoning the well. After a speech such as Tillman's, black people could defend their rights only with great difficulty. For they could not ignore the libel of their character, and it is harder to prove that one's acts are generally virtuous than disprove specific charges of bad conduct. From a practical point of view, Tillman might just as well have said, "Don't listen to any blacks, they are all evil." This type of *ad hominem* attack is called "poisoning the well," and is a means of prejudicing the audience beforehand.

We can also see the technique of poisoning the well in a speech quoted by Richard Hofstadter in his *Anti-Intellectualism in American Life*. Attacking a proposal to allow the National Science Foundation to include social scientists, a Congressman said the following in testimony before a House subcommittee in 1946:

> Outside of myself, I think everyone else thinks he is a social scientist. I am sure that I am not, but I think everyone else seems to believe that he has some particular God-given right to decide what other people ought to do. . . . The average American does not want some expert running around prying into his life and his personal affairs and deciding for him how he should live, and if the impression becomes prevalent in the Congress that this legislation is going to establish some sort of an organization in which there would be a lot of short-haired women and long-haired men messing into everybody's personal affairs and lives, inquiring whether they love their wives or do not love them and so forth, you are not going to get your legislation.

As with the *ad hominem* attack on the individual, the argument here has shifted from the merits of the proposal to the character of social scientists and, by implication, their supporters in Congress. The speaker suggests here that social scientists are un-American and ready to intrude "into everybody's personal affairs and lives," thus clearly prejudicing his hearers before they have an opportunity to vote on the proposal.

Circumstantial* ad hominem *arguments. The other major type of *ad hominem* argument is directed at the circumstances of an opponent rather than at his or her personality or beliefs. This is a favorite device of Marxists, who argue that class interest determines political or social action. For example, they charged that Franklin D. Roosevelt developed relief programs for the poor during the Great Depression because these would keep his own economic class in power and prevent a working class revolution. When presenting this argument, Marxists did not grant that Roosevelt dealt with the immediately pressing needs of the poor and was thus acting from a sense of public responsibility toward all Americans, poor as well as rich. Instead Marxists dirtied his efforts by charging that he acted from self-interest.

As we have seen in the Tillman and *Village Voice* excepts, these kinds of attacks raise the emotional temperature of debate. *Ad hominem* arguments generate a lot of heat and very little light. It is their very strong appeals to emotion that make these arguments so effective and difficult to counter.

Ad populum *arguments*

When an appeal is made to the biases of the audience as a substitute for presenting facts and reasons, we describe such a fallacious appeal as an *ad populum* argument, or "argument to the people." As in the *ad hominem* argument, no facts are really presented. Instead the speaker or writer presumes certain facts or attitudes to be true and depends on known biases or prejudices. We saw an appeal to bias against social scientists in the statement of the Congressman just discussed. When patriotic emotions are involved, this fallacy is sometimes referred to as "flag-waving."

Ad populum arguments have the same effect as *ad hominem* ones: they "poison the well," as in Philip Wylie's attack on "rabid bureaucrats":

> These are the issue of the professors—these, and the educated moms who decorate our political bureaucracy. They are extremely well-meaning people, so long as the ship of state is looping along in the precise course of their own meaning, whether it is pensions for the aged, tree planting for the young, high excess profit taxes, a garden behind every home or a bathtub in it, a rose in every buttonhole.
>
> *A Generation of Vipers*

Important issues like pensions and excess profit taxes are trivialized or ridiculed in the course of this attack. In effect, Wylie is confirming attitudes he is sure his readers hold.

Appeal to force

When a threat is made to the audience, as in Nikita Khrushchev's famous statement "we will bury you," the fallacy is called the argument or "appeal to force." Like *ad populum* arguments, it avoids discussing the issue. The speaker or writer says in effect, "It does not matter which of us is right. What matters is that I am stronger." This is a fallacious argument because it relies on fear rather than reason as a method of persuasion.

Irrelevant appeals to authority

As we had seen earlier, the use of authorities in a discussion related to their areas of expertise is entirely proper. But when these authorities are quoted or used outside of their specialties, then their opinions are irrelevant or, at best, carry no more weight than that of any other "inexpert" individual. For example, it is certainly correct to quote Albert Einstein on the theory of relativity or on quantum mechanics; it is wholly irrelevant to cite him on a question of political belief. On matters of politics, Einstein's opinions are no better than John Smith's at the corner barbershop.

The fallacious appeal to authority is grounded in the feeling of respect or admiration most people have for the great. Because of these feelings, we can be intimidated, so it is supposed, into accepting an argument merely because some venerated person has backed it. A movie actor may be used, for example, in an advertisement that calls for pollution controls. But in all likelihood the actor knows nothing about the technical matters involved in such controls, and his skill as an actor has nothing whatever to do with the position he advocates.

The appeal is also fallacious when it claims truth for an argument on the ground of superior standing in life. Thus I may claim authority on the ground that I am older than the person I am debating, or am a father or a professor. Citing "unnamed sources" for unverified facts is yet another fallacy, much used in confidential articles and book and television exposés by what David Riesman has termed "inside dopesters"—people who claim to have secret sources of information on public figures.

But the appeal to authority has an important part to play in many kinds of discourse: in scholarship, in debate, in judicial and legislative deliberations, to name a few. Recognized authorities often provide the justification for accepting certain kinds of evidence and interpreting it in particular ways. In law courts, this justification may take the form of precedents that tell lawyers and judges how the law has been interpreted and applied in the past. Scholars cite previous research and interpretations to show the relevance of new evidence and conclusions to the subject they are concerned with. Debaters appeal to the relevant ideas of respected people from the past to indicate or illustrate consistency with earlier thought on a subject. In all these instances, though, authorities are quoted or referred to with great caution. When they are used, it is always as a supplement to other facts or reasons that serve as the primary support.

It is important to keep in mind that when an authority is cited, he or she must be an acknowledged expert in the subject under consideration and that what is quoted or referred to is pertinent to the discussion. Otherwise, we have committed the fallacy of an irrelevant appeal to authority.

Exercises

1. Examine the political ads and statements of candidates published in the *New York Times* or another newspaper in your library. To what extent did the character of a candidate become an issue in the most recent presidential election? You will do best to examine the paper in the month or two preceding the election. Distinguish *ad hominem* arguments from what you consider legitimate arguments or discussions concerning character. Look also for any appeals to authority. Were these relevant to the issues of the campaign?

2. Examine editorials and letters to the editor on an issue that is in dispute, then identify attempts to poison the well or other *ad hominem* arguments, as well as legitimate arguments in favor of one or another position. Discuss how these arguments shape or give direction to the debate.

Writing Assignments

1. Examine accounts of the presidential election of 1928 and 1960 in the *New York Times* to discover what role the religion of the candidates played in the campaigns. In a discussion of your findings, distinguish fallacious arguments in political statements, letters, and the like from legitimate ones. In your opinion, was the issue of religious belief legitimate in the campaign of 1928? Why?

2. Examine issues of the *London Times* published in the weeks before the parliamentary election of 1977 to find out what role *ad hominem* attacks and other appeals play in British political campaigns. You may want to compare British campaigns with what an American newspaper reveals about American ones.

Arguing from ignorance

The evidence we present for a conclusion not only must be pertinent, but it must exist. For to argue from an absence of evidence only is to argue from ignorance. This kind of argument is popular with people who believe the earth is being visited by flying saucers: "No one has proved they don't exist!" The same fallacious reasoning is found in the statement that smoking must not be as harmful as the Surgeon General claims since Congress has not banned the sale of tobacco. Notice that the argument is made in the absence of positive evidence of any sort—that flying saucers have been observed or that Congress believes tobacco is harmful.

Under some circumstances, evidence may be presented for or against a proposition, but no conclusion is drawn from it because it is thought to be indecisive. The question is thus left open. But the writer must say that the evidence presents no conclusion, and explain why it does not. Once facts have been set before the reader, the writer has the obligation to state what they mean; conclusions must not be left to inference. In a fair argument, the reader or opponent is given a full opportunity to test the premises or the evidence, and is given a complete understanding of the reasoning that led to a particular conclusion.

Begging the question

When the conclusion of an argument restates the premise, we say that it is begging the question. It is important to remember in this context that underlying all arguments is the question, "Is the conclusion true or false?" When the conclusion merely repeats the premise which is supposed to be its proof, it evades the question of truth. If the premise and conclusion were to be stated in exactly the same language, the circularity of reasoning would be obvious. But most often the conclusion restates the premise in different words:

> Why should the government warn the public about the dangers of smoking? Because harmful acts like smoking are a proper concern of government officials.

It is the change in wording in the second sentence that disguises the circular reasoning here.

A related form of question-begging occurs when we assume something as proved or accepted when it is not:

> Nobody really believes that high interest rates will bring down the rate of inflation!

We say that statements like the following are "loaded" in favor of what is being proposed or defended. It too assumes as proven the very proposition that needs to be proved.

> The citizen in the Fascist State is no longer a selfish individual who has the anti-social right of rebelling against any law of the Collectivity.
>
> Benito Mussolini, *My Autobiography*

Red herring

A "red herring" is a deliberate diversion, a masking of the real issue by introducing another one that is irrelevant to the point at issue but nevertheless of concern to those the writer is trying to persuade. The term comes from the practice of using a dried herring to divert dogs from the scent during a hunt. If the issue under debate is whether present defense spending is adequate, arguing that American involvement in Vietnam was wrong is a diversion from the point at issue. Of course, the right or wrong of our participation in the Vietnam War might be the issue in another argument. *Ad hominem* attacks and appeals to prejudice can serve as red herrings: a racial or religious minority may be attacked by a politician for present economic ills to divert attention from circumstances he does not want discussed.

Complex question

A complex question asks two or more questions when it seems to be asking only one. Consider the following asked during a debate over the wisdom of constructing nuclear power plants: "Should we build a nuclear power plant close to the city?" This question implies another much in dispute: "Should we build a nuclear power plant at all?" If we answer the first question in any way, our answer implies an affirmative response to the second, underlying question. In other words, if we answer, "No, we should not build a plant close to the city," we may be understood as saying that *we should build the plant*, if not close to the city, then at some other place.

The legitimate procedure is to divide the question properly. Before arguing whether a nuclear energy plant should be built close to a large city, we may first need to argue whether the plant will be safe if built, and perhaps also whether any nuclear energy plant can be safe. This kind of division occurs in the following statement that crime is not a single entity and must be looked at in different ways.

> A skid-row drunk lying in a gutter is crime. So is the killing of an unfaithful wife. A Cosa Nostra conspiracy to bribe public officials is crime. So is a strong-

arm robbery by a 15-year-old boy. The embezzlement of a corporation's funds by an executive is crime. So is the possession of marihuana cigarettes by a student. These crimes can no more be lumped together for purposes of analysis than can measles and schizophrenia, or lung cancer and a broken ankle. As with disease, so with crime: if causes are to be understood, if risks are to be taken, each kind must be looked at separately. Thinking of "crime" as a whole is futile.

> The President's Commission on Law Enforcement and Administration of
> Justice

Thus, the apparently simple question, "How can we reduce crime?" requires a complex answer. We need, first, to define what we mean by crime, and then to recognize that different types of crime call for different solutions. Without recognizing the underlying issues in a seemingly simple question, we run the risk of being led astray and responding inappropriately.

"Accident"

The popular saying that "the exception proves the rule" is sometimes taken to mean that every rule probably has an exception to it. In fact, a rule is a generalization drawn from a number of experiences or observations, and it is taken to cover not just these but all other experiences and observations that were not examined. It is, then, a form of inductive prediction. The generalization that oxygen is necessary for burning is true of all observed acts of burning, and we assume it to be true of all other acts we did not observe. If burning can be shown to occur in the absence of oxygen, we must qualify or restate the generalization.

The rules or laws that govern our lives present a different problem. These are not iron-clad like the laws of science. We recognize that special or "accidental" circumstances do exist where the rule is inapplicable. The legal prohibition against speeding, for example, allows for exceptional circumstances. The fallacy of "accident" comes into play when a general rule is applied without concern for exceptional circumstances.

Ronald Dworkin exposes what he sees as this fallacy in the argument presented to require newspeople to reveal their confidential sources when ordered to in a court of law. The argument is the following: news reporters have "no greater right to free speech than anyone else," and because they do not they are subject to the same obligations as other citizens, including the obligation to give testimony in criminal cases. Giving relevant testimony may, indeed, require the reporter to reveal the source of information given confidentially.

Dworkin agrees with the general principle that newspeople are under the same obligations as other citizens but argues that special circumstances exist that justify confidentiality:

> There are, however, reasons of policy that may justify special rules enhancing the ability of newsmen to investigate. If reporters' confidential sources are protected from disclosure, more people who fear exposure will talk to them, and the public may benefit. There is a particular need for confidentiality, for example, and a special public interest in hearing what informers may say, when the informer is an official reporting on corruption or official misconduct, or when the information is information about a crime.
>
> "The Rights of Myron Farber"

Of course, disagreement exists over what may be special circumstances. The issue Dworkin raises is now being debated nationwide. As in the Farber case, which concerned the issue of confidentiality and to which Dworkin is referring, court decisions are sometimes concerned with what constitute special rules or exemptions from general legal requirements. In arguing that a general rule or principle applies in a situation of concern to us, we need to ask whether special circumstances do exist and should be taken into account.

Exercise

Explain what is fallacious about the following statements:

a. There can be no doubt that millions of civilizations exist in the billions of galaxies of the universe. No evidence has yet been presented to show that life as we know it is impossible on other planets than earth.

b. If nothing is done about violence on television, we will not be able to reduce the violence children are exposed to in the programs they watch.

c. Inflation and unemployment get worse when fatcat millionaires, who have never punched a timeclock, come into Washington and put into effect harebrained economic schemes.

d. If we're not free to drive at what speed we want, then we're not a free people as Americans once were.

e. If the president of the United States says that solar energy will solve the energy crisis, his opinion is good enough for me.

f. It's obvious why doctors and their friends in the FDA oppose Laetrile as a treatment for cancer. There's no money in patients who get well!

g. America—love her or leave her!

Writing Assignments

1. Write down a list of official or understood rules that prevailed in your high school, and then list exceptions that were made to them with which you agreed. Then write down a list of rules that you believe should prevail in school without exception, and rules to which exemptions should be made because of special circumstances. Use the list to discuss good and bad ways to run a high school—perhaps what you would do as principal to reduce friction between students and teachers.

2. Discuss to what extent problems between teenagers and parents arise from conflicting ideas over "special exceptions" to rules of behavior. Illustrate from your own experience or observation.

Fallacies of ambiguity

Ambiguity, equivocation, and accent

Statements may be general in their meaning because of a wide application of a term or phrase. The 1957 Supreme Court ruling that a book alleged to be obscene is protected by the First Amendment if it has "redeeming social value" was meant to encompass many standards of social value in our society, not just those of a few groups. There is nothing inherently wrong with such general usage when there is no misunderstanding of what the terms mean, but misunderstanding can easily arise because of different interpretations given to words like *redeeming* or because of the ambiguity of words like *obscene*.

A statement is ambiguous when a word has more than one meaning and we cannot tell which is intended. Thus the word *obscene* can refer to a statement thought to offend *any* prevailing moral concept, or to offend any of the senses, or to incite lust. The words *indecent*, *disgusting*, and *lewd* are used to express these various meanings, and for some people all are synonymous with *obscene*. Hearing a book or movie branded as obscene, we find the statement ambiguous if we do not know which of the meanings is intended; perhaps all are, perhaps only one is. An argument commits the fallacy of ambiguity when it fails to clarify which of several possible meanings of a word it intends.

Related to the fallacy of ambiguity is the fallacy of equivocation. A statement or argument is equivocal when the meaning of a term changes or shifts in the course of it, as in the statement that whatever offends decent people offends the law. The equivocation becomes apparent when we discover that the writer of the sentence is saying that whatever *displeases* or *angers* decent people *violates* the law. Equivocal terms are

frequently used to disguise such differences in meaning. To prevent ambiguity or equivocation, a writer may insist that different meanings or
implications of a word be distinguished:

> Men speak of the freedom of belief and the freedom of property as if, in the
> Constitution, the word "freedom," as used in these two cases, had the same
> meaning. Because of that confusion we are in constant danger of giving to a
> man's possessions the same dignity, the same status, as we give to the man
> himself.
>
> Alexander Meikeljohn, "Political Freedom"

Finally, words and phrases can seem ambiguous if we are unsure what
accent to give them. The following statement has different meanings depending on the accent given to the italicized words:

> He never *admitted* to being part of the *conspiracy*.

The sentence could mean that although the person actually took part in
the conspiracy, he refused to admit it; or the sentence could mean that
though he was not part of the conspiracy, he did encourage and approve
it. Accented somewhat differently, the sentence could also mean that we
have no grounds for believing he was part of the conspiracy, since he
did not admit it. To prevent any possible misreading, a writer may qualify the statement carefully:

> He never admitted or implied that he was part of the conspiracy or
> that he encouraged or approved it in any way.

In arguments, propositions must be worded so that ambiguity does not
result through accent.

Composition and division

Sometimes we attribute to a group qualities possessed by each of its
members. We say that a committee is hard working, knowing that each
member is a hard worker. But what is true of each member may not be
true of the members collectively; they may not be hard working if they
do not work well together. When we reason from parts of a group to the
whole in this way, we have committed the "fallacy of composition." The
same error may occur when we reason from parts of a system or composite to the whole. It is fallacious to argue that because various ingredients of a stew are good to eat the stew must be also. Clearly, the stew
may be inedible or bad tasting if these ingredients do not mix well.

The reverse of this fallacy is called "division." Here the supposed
qualities of the group are attributed to each of its members. If the United
States is the richest nation on earth, it does not follow that each of its

citizens must be rich too. The belief that no American could be severely malnourished sometimes arises from this error in reasoning.

Ignoring the context of facts and statements

A frequent source of ambiguity or misunderstanding is the failure to provide the appropriate context for facts and statements, or ignoring the context altogether. Consider the following comment on George Washington:

> If George Washington were alive today, what a shining mark he would be for the whole camorra of uplifters, forward-lookers and professional patriots! He was the Rockefeller of his time, the richest man in the United States, a promoter of stock companies, a landgrabber, an exploiter of mines and timber. He was a bitter opponent of foreign entanglements, and denounced their evils in harsh, specific terms.
>
> H. L. Mencken, "Pater Patriae"

None of these "facts" are given to us with concern for their historical context. Washington could have been "the Rockefeller of his time" in the full meaning of what John D. Rockefeller was and did only if the economic and social conditions of Rockefeller's time also existed in Washington's. Words like "landgrabber" and "exploiter" have special meanings in the twentieth century and are applicable to Washington only with considerable qualification based on his special circumstances. Mencken neither qualifies his characterization or states these circumstances. And to know whether Washington would have protested "foreign entanglements" in the twentieth century, we would have to know what historical circumstances prompted his warning about them and what this phrase meant to him in his world.

By historical context we mean the web of circumstances that influence, perhaps govern, opinions and policies. There is also the context of language, the setting of words and phrases that affect the meaning of a phrase like "foreign entanglements." We need to examine that context carefully to be sure we understand as fully as we can what a writer of the past meant. Fallacious appeals to authority succeed by playing down or ignoring these contexts and circumstances. Causes may be stated falsely in the same way. We shall return to the matter of context in the final chapter.

Exercises

1. Deliberate ambiguity is often a source of humor or witty rejoinder. Identify the ambiguity in the following statements, and discuss its use:

    a. Familiarity breeds contempt—and children.

Mark Twain

    b. In uplifting, get underneath.

George Ade

    c. To be a leader of men one must turn one's back on men.

Havelock Ellis

    d. In the misfortune of our best friends, we find something which is not displeasing to us.

La Rochefoucauld

2. Explain how the accenting of certain words through italics shapes the meaning of the following:

> The fact that man knows right from wrong proves his *intellectual* superiority to the other creates; but the fact that he can *do* wrong proves his moral *inferiority* to any creature that *cannot*.

Mark Twain, *What Is Man?*

3. Describe the type of ambiguity that is involved in the two fallacies below:
   a. The policy of the New Deal under Franklin D. Roosevelt favored low interest bank rates. Democrats to a man and woman were thus in favor of a policy that fueled inflation in later years.
   b. Since doctors exert immense influence in their communities, the medical profession is very influential in the country as a whole.

Writing Assignments

1. Examine the definitions of one of the following words in the *Oxford English Dictionary,* and write a short paper discussing how some of the meanings distinguished there might become confused in the course of an argument:

   a. obscene

   b. liberty

2. Choose one of the two above topics and write a short argumentative essay on some aspect of it. Make sure that your terms are used unambiguously.

False dilemma

The so-called false dilemma, or either-or argument, presents two alternatives and states or implies that no other alternatives exist. Here is an example:

> Either we stop building nuclear power plants, or we suffer radiation poisoning from explosions or leaks. This is the only choice open to us.

And here is another:

> Either we build nuclear power plants, or we suffer brownouts. We have no other choice.

Such dilemmas can be shown to be false by proposing alternatives. We could continue building nuclear power plants, and at the same time improve controls over radiation leaks. We could avoid brownouts by stopping the building of nuclear power plants, conserving electricity, and supporting research into solar energy.

False dilemmas are reductive and make complex situations look simpler than they are. Thus we may be asked to consider a single cause for a problem that requires an analysis of a large set of varying conditions. We are simplifying a complex phenomenon like "crime" when we say "either we will have law and order or we will have a criminal society" instead of asking what kinds of crime exist and what may be some of the conditions that produce them. The same fallacious reasoning occurs when people say "either you agree with me and are therefore my friend, or you disagree with me and are therefore my enemy," as if one could not disagree with a friend. Catch phrases in politics encourage us to think in this reductive way about a vast range of problems.

Slanting

A true or plausible statement can be slanted by making it imply something that is not true. The statement may mislead us by leaving out essential facts or by adding details that imply an attitude or point of view that the writer wants us to accept. An ad may claim, for example, that a brand of face soap "cleanses with a magical ingredient whose remarkable chemical formula" is given; the ingredient, however, may be nothing more than ordinary soap. The ad has implied by its use of the adjectives "magical" and "remarkable" that the ingredient must be something more than other soaps contain. The very name of a product may slant thinking about it, such as names for cars like Cougar and Fury.

This last example raises a problem. Almost no name of a product is without emotional overtones, for names are chosen to influence buying. We grant the right of producers and advertisers to persuade us that the product is a desirable one, and we also grant their right to suggest pleasant associations. The decisive consideration is whether the ad lies to us about essential qualities we assume the product possesses, or leaves out information that would discourage purchase.

We are familiar with the ways news stories can be slanted. Consider the following introductory paragraphs to an informative article on radiation that appeared following the accident at Three Mile Island in April of 1979:

> Almost as soon as the accident at Three Mile Island occurred, Radiation Physicist Ernest Sternglass was at the scene, Geiger counter in hand, crying disaster to anyone who would listen. He predicted an increase of 5% to 20% in the incident of leukemia in children of the area within a year. A vehement foe of nuclear power, the University of Pittsburgh scientist exclaimed: "The reaction of the community should be to stand up and scream!"
>
> Sternglass's warning was exaggerated. But no one—not even radiation experts—can say for sure that he is totally wrong. Despite science's long experience with radiation and bitter knowledge of its risks, like the cancers inflicted on early radium workers, including Madame Curie, disturbingly little is known about how much radiation, or what length of exposure, is safe for humans.

Time, "How Much Is Too Much?", April 9, 1979

If "disturbingly little is known about radiation, or what length of exposure, is safe for humans," it is hard to understand how *Time* knows that Sternglass was exaggerating. The reader can deal with this contradiction in *Time*'s account directly, but it is harder to deal with attitudes conveyed through details and adjectives that seem descriptive in intent but suggest qualities difficult to pin down.

What does the statement that Sternglass appeared "Geiger counter in hand" imply? It would be a normal situation for a radiation physicist to carry a Geiger counter, but the phrasing somehow suggests the behavior of a fanatic. The word *vehement* can suggest intensity, but in the context here it implies shrillness. Wording such as this colors the reader's response and calls for a negative reaction. Indeed, the purpose of slanting is exactly to prejudice the reader either in favor of or against a particular person or position.

Fallacies of induction

Hasty generalization

Hasty generalization occurs when a rule or statement meant to apply to a group of people or things is based on exceptional or untypical cases. For example, it is fallacious to argue that Dobermans are vicious as a breed of dog when the only ones observed are those trained as watchdogs. Hasty conclusions are easily drawn about teenagers or women or old people as drivers on the basis of driving behavior that may not be typical. Indeed, as we saw earlier, deciding what is representative or a "fair sample" of a group is a difficult job. Often hasty generalizations are drawn because we have preconceptions of what certain people are like and we notice only those acts that meet these preconceptions—acts that may not be typical at all. Charles E. Silberman gives us this particularly graphic illustration of hasty generalization in his book on education in America:

> In lecturing the assembled students on the need for and virtue of absolute silence, an elementary school principal expostulates on the wonders of a school for the "deaf and dumb" he had recently visited. The silence was just wonderful, he tells the assembly; the children could all get their work done because of the total silence.
>
> *Crisis in the Classroom*

Exercises

1. Discuss how you would challenge the following hasty generalizations, or comparable ones, in the course of a debate:
   a. Teenagers are incurable optimists.
   b. Women are worse gossips than men.
   c. College professors are super liberals.
2. Find examples of hasty generalization in letters to newspapers and magazines, and explain why you consider them ill founded.

False cause

Some of us would say that turning the ignition key by itself makes our car run, and some of us would say that getting wet in a rainstorm makes us catch cold. Each is a mistake in reasoning, and both mistakes may arise from ignorance about the mechanical or physical processes involved, or from the assumption that one event is the "cause" of another simply because it precedes it in time.

This mistake, common in children who see a magical occurrence when the ignition key is turned on, is known as the fallacy of *post hoc, ergo propter hoc*. Here is an obvious example in an article on drug addiction and rock music:

> A young woman who graduated from high school in 1967 observed a decade later, "I was the last of the beer generation. All those songs were coming out, and the drugs were just starting to be used in my class. The kids who came right behind us were all into drugs. A lot of them—and I mean a *lot*—are dead now. Of course the music was responsible."
>
> Gene Lees, "*The Drug Connection*," *High Fidelity Magazine*

Notice that, in the statement of the young woman, rock music is cited as the cause of drug addiction in the generation of the 1960s by virtue of its connection in time. No other basis for the connection is given.

Even when we think we have discovered all the conditions that together make up the "cause" of something like the common cold, we realize there may have been present some conditions that are unknown to us. For this reason, it is customary to distinguish between necessary and sufficient conditions: conditions that must be present for the cold to occur, and conditions in whose presence the cold must occur.

Thus a scientist may tell us that the cold cannot occur without the presence of a virus (necessary condition), or that a virus in company with other conditions (lowered resistance, a drop in body temperature) is sufficient to produce cold symptoms. In neither statement does the scientist say that all the conditions needed to produce a cold are known.

In debate, writers often warn against too simple a statement of cause by insisting on this distinction between necessary and sufficient conditions. The following writer is discussing what makes a good teacher:

> Liberal education is necessary but not sufficient; teachers need professional education as well. This is not to deny that one may be a good teacher without professional preparation; some of the greatest teachers have never taken a single education course. Nor is it to suggest that people be denied the right to teach without having had such training.
>
> Charles E. Silberman, *Crisis in the Classroom*

Silberman is saying that liberal education and professional education are both necessary to good teaching, but they do not alone guarantee it; indeed, there are exceptional instances where good teaching occurs without professional education. He thus qualifies his original point, and uses the argument to imply that the notion that professional education is the "cause" of good teaching is false.

False analogy

We noted earlier that an analogy is weakened when a sufficient number of differences affect the main comparison. We say in such an instance that the logical force of the argument has been weakened, even though the emotional appeal of the analogy may be great.

Such is the case with the following analogy used by Clarence Darrow to argue that violence is inevitable during protracted labor strikes:

> Let some cataclysm occur and destroy all the particles of matter in the physical world, and they must readjust themselves. . . . The same is true of man.

In a war, a pestilence, a great strike, all these social relations are changed in a moment. The orbits of the individual atoms are changed. It means force, it means violence, it means a clashing of individuals, a clashing that caused the orbits to change and society is changed. There can be no disturbance of human relations, or of physical relations, that does not bring this conflict.

Attorney for the Damned

The central comparison is between atoms and strikers. At best, this analogy has emotional force only, for the disparity between the physical and social processes involved is too great to serve as evidence for the conclusion. Much depends on the causes of the conflict and on whether these causes are subject to human control. Two important differences in the analogy are obscured: strikes are not acts of nature but rather acts resulting from human decision. And cataclysms of nature are not subject to human control, whereas human conflicts may be. These differences weaken the analogy considerably. The test of a good analogy, to repeat, is that the points of similarity are directly relevant to the conclusion—and the points of dissimilarity are irrelevant.

Exercise.

Decide how strong the analogy is in the following, and how much evidence it provides for the conclusion:

a. "School is just like roulette or something. You can't just ask: 'Well, what's the point of it?' . . . The point of it is to do it, to get through and get into college. But you have to figure the system or you can't win, because the odds are all on the house's side."

A high school student quoted in Charles E. Silberman, *Crisis in the Classroom*

b. Observe, the merchant's function . . . is to provide for the nation. It is no more his function to get profit for himself out of that provision than it is a clergyman's function to get his stipend. The stipend is a due and necessary adjunct, but not the object, of his life, if he be a true clergyman, any more than his fee (or honorarium) is the object of life to a true physician. Neither is his fee the object of life to a true merchant. All three, if true men, have a work to be done irrespective of fee—to be done even at any cost, or for quite the contrary of fee; the pastor's function being to teach, the physician's to heal, and the merchant's, as I have said, to provide. That is to say, he has to understand to their very root the qualities of the thing he deals in, and the means of obtaining or producing it; and he has to apply all his sagacity and energy to the producing or obtaining it in perfect state, and distributing it at the cheapest possible price where it is most needed.

John Ruskin, *"The Roots of Honor"*

Analysis of an Argumentative Essay

The following defense of the Soviet Union by a commentator with the semiofficial Soviet news agency, Novosti, was published in the *New York Times* on June 16, 1977. We will analyze the logic of the essay paragraph by paragraph:

WHO IS RIGHT?

By Vadim Golovanov

MOSCOW—References to the alleged totalitarian character of the Soviet State and its so-called closed society still remain favorite subjects of Western political parlance. It is common to speak of "governments" in the capitalist world and "regimes" in the socialist world, of the "forces of public order" there and "secret police" here, of the "Free World" there and the "Iron Curtain" here.

With a persistence worthy of a better cause, the situation in the Soviet Union and other socialist countries is described as gloomy. Consider the argument about the free movement of people and information. This is a matter of great importance for normalized international relations and for better mutual understanding between peoples. Yet, the West insists that the Soviet Union tries to cut itself and its people off from broad international contacts.

Nothing can be farther from the truth. Now, during détente, which the Soviet Union has worked so hard to bring about, we are extending our external relations step-by-step in the field of scientific cooperation, in joint projects, and in various humanitarian and cultural fields.

Concerning the "free flow of information" and "Soviet censorship," it is easy to see by simply scanning our press that we raise no obstacles to the free flow of scientific, technical, international, sports and other information. But neither do we accept what is alien to the interests of our society and contrary to our traditions.

Soviet newspapers and magazines do not, for instance, seek sensational news, meddle in people's private affairs or use unsubstantiated reports.

Our country has laws forbidding war propaganda, inciting racial or national strife or humiliating the dignity of any people. Our newspapers would never publish insulting comments about the government leaders of other nations, mock them in cartoons and infect their readers with mistrust towards other peoples.

Freedom of information must serve to strengthen peace and friendship among peoples, and promote mutual understanding and economic, scientific, technological and cultural contacts between peoples. What is good for one country is not necessarily an ideal model for another. What amazed me in the United States, where I lived for quite a while, was that everything people see, hear, read or eat there is dictated by the media and publicity rather than by their own free choice. This system molds their tastes to suit the play of market forces. We do not like this system.

We do not deny that Western constitutions do proclaim democratic rights in the context of a capitalist society, but the problem of ensuring these rights and putting them into practice is still unsolved. For many in the West, these rights are nonexistent in the face of poverty and unemployment, lack of free education and medical care. Direct legal restrictions on the rights of people of different races and social segments, women and old people are directly contrary to professed constitutional principles.

One gets the impression that the heated issue of "human rights in the Soviet Union" serves as a social lightning rod for the West to deflect the resentment of its own population.

The opening references to the "alleged totalitarian character of the Soviet state" and "its so-called closed society" raises the expectation that Golovanov will deal with these charges. And the succeeding references to charges that the Soviet Union is a "regime" with a "secret police" confirms this expectation. But Golovanov does not deal with these charges, either in these opening paragraphs or in the remainder of the argument.

He diverts attention from the issues contained in these charges in a number of ways. One way he does so is to make a countercharge worth serious consideration: the West deals with the Soviet Union as a closed society in emotional language that raises the temperature of discussion. He returns later to this countercharge in arguing that Western rhetoric covers up discrimination and legal disabilities that violate Western constitutional guarantees.

Golovanov's counter charges clearly have merit, and deserve our consideration. But that consideration is in no way a substitute for discussing the point at issue—conditions of freedom in the Soviet Union. In a response, however, the Western writer would need to address Golovanov's charges.

A second way Golovanov diverts the issue is by centering discussion on international scientific ventures and cultural exchanges, to which he refers in asking us to consider the "free movement of people and information." Though there can be no question that these ventures and exchanges have occurred during détente, he does not address the real issue of whether freedom of movement and information is permitted all Soviet citizens under all circumstances, the usual meaning of the term "free society."

A third diversion or "red herring" is thrown in by pointing to the sensational and slanderous stories that appear in Western newspapers. The Soviet Union does not publish sensational stories and slanders, Golovanov tells us. But the free flow of information refers to political freedom and the right to criticize—*justly or unjustly*—political leaders; the Western charge is that the Soviet press is denied precisely this freedom, as Golovanov well knows. This is the meaning of the charge that human rights are suppressed in the Soviet Union. Golovanov sidesteps this issue.

When Golovanov says that Soviet censorship does not exist because the state raises "no obstacles to the free flow of scientific, technical, international, sports and other information," it is impossible to know whether that "other information" includes political criticism of Soviet leaders. And in asserting (quite contrary to the facts) that Soviet newspapers "would never publish insulting comments about the government leaders of other nations" or "mock them in cartoons," he does not say whether any critical comments or cartoons of an internal political nature are allowed. Golovanov implies that all stories critical of government leaders must be sensational, slanderous, meddling, unsubstantiated and insulting. At best, his defense skirts the central issues of political freedom by raising diversionary questions that rightly point to deplorable practices in some Western news media.

His statements, however, are equivocations: statements that can have several meanings and are deliberately misleading. Golovanov proceeds to define freedom of information not by its characteristics but by its effects or by some ideal goals. The implication is that if a piece of information weakens peace and friendship, it of necessity cannot be published in the Soviet Union. This is an *ad populum* argument, and is irrelevant to the issue, which is whether freedom of inquiry is served by *prior* restrictions on information. In debate, the Western writer would be entitled to ask that this question be addressed. The hasty generalization that American thinking and tastes are dictated by the media, in the service of "market forces," deserves challenge too.

In the concluding paragraphs, Golovanov insinuates that Western democracy is not necessarily true democracy, but he leaves his own conception of democracy undefined. He does not state whether democracy includes those rights he claims are denied in the West, and he fails to state whether these rights are enjoyed in the Soviet Union. He thus commits the fallacy of ambiguity.

In the brief concluding paragraph, Golovanov resorts to the fallacy of "counterquestion": instead of saying whether the Soviet Union denies human rights Golovanov implies that the West does. Indeed, that has been his strategy in the whole defense. In the whole essay he equivocates by using the word "free" in more than one sense, and failing to clarify all of these senses.

Prewriting

Our analysis of Golovanov suggests how various statements can be analyzed one by one. We have suggestions here for organizing an analysis of another essay on which strong disagreement exists about its logic. Some consider the reasoning in it sound, others have attacked it as fallacious. You will need to make your own judgment, not only about the chief argument, but also about the supporting ones. These contain many of the appeals and forms of reasoning discussed in this and earlier chapters.

The argument is particularly interesting because of the circumstances of its delivery. In 1902, the warden of Cook County Jail in Chicago invited the famous lawyer Clarence Darrow to speak to the prisoners. Darrow's speech shocked his friends, the prison officials, and some of the prisoners. When Darrow published his speech, he wrote a sarcastic introduction: "Realizing the force of the suggestion that the truth should not be spoken to all people, I have caused these remarks to be printed on rather good paper and in a somewhat expensive form. In this way the truth does not become cheap and vulgar, and is only placed before those whose intelligence and affluence will prevent their being influenced by it."

CRIME AND CRIMINALS

by Clarence Darrow

If I looked at jails and crimes and prisoners in the way the ordinary person does, I should not speak on this subject to you. The reason I talk to you on the question of crime, its cause and cure, is that I really do not in the least believe in crime. There is no such thing as a crime as the word is generally understood. I do not believe there is any sort of distinction between the real moral conditions of the people in and out of jail. One is just as good as the other. The people here can no more help being here than the people outside can avoid being outside. I do not believe that people are in jail because they deserve to be. They are in jail simply because they cannot avoid it on account of circumstances which are entirely beyond their control and for which they are in no way responsible.

I suppose a great many people on the outside would say I was doing you harm if they should hear what I say to you this afternoon, but you cannot be hurt a great deal anyway, so it will not matter. Good people outside would say that I was really teaching you things that were calculated to injure society, but it's worth while now and then to hear something different from what you ordinarily get from preachers and the like. These will tell you that you should be good and then you will get rich and be happy. Of course we know that people do not get rich by being good, and that is the reason why so many of you people try to get rich some other way, only you do not understand how to do it quite as well as the fellow outside.

There are people who think that everything in this world is an accident. But really there is no such thing as an accident. A great many folks admit that many of the people in jail ought to be there, and many who are outside ought to be in. I think none of them ought to be here. There ought to be no jails; and if it were not for the fact that the people on the outside are so grasping and heartless in their dealings with the people on the inside, there would be no such institution as jails.

I do not want you to believe that I think all you people here are angels. I do not think that. You are people of all kinds, all of you doing the best you can—and that is evidently not very well. You are people of all kinds and conditions and under all circumstances. In one sense everybody is equally good and equally bad. We all do the best we can under the circumstances. But as to the exact things for which you are sent here, some of you are guilty and did the particular act because you needed the money. Some of you did it because you are in the habit of doing it, and some of you because you are born to it, and it comes to be as natural as it does, for instance, for me to be good.

Most of you probably have nothing against me, and most of you would treat me the same as any other person would, probably better than some of the people on the outside would treat me, because you think I believe in you and they know I do not believe in them. While you would not have the least thing against me in the world, you might pick my pockets. I do not think all of you would, but I think some of you would. You would not have anything against me, but that's your profession, a few of you. Some of the rest of you, if my doors were unlocked, might come in if you saw anything you wanted—not out of any malice to me, but because that is your trade. There is no doubt there are quite a number of people in this jail who would pick my pockets. And still I know this—that when I get outside pretty nearly everybody picks my pocket. There may be some of you who would hold up a man on the street, if you did not happen to have something else to do, and needed the money; but when I want to light my house or my office the gas company holds me up. They charge me one dollar for something that is worth twenty-five cents. Still all these people are good people; they are pillars of society and support the churches, and they are respectable.

When I ride on the streetcars I am held up—I pay five cents for a ride that is worth two and a half cents, simply because a body of men have bribed the city council and the legislature, so that all the rest of us have to pay tribute to them.

If I do not want to fall into the clutches of the gas trust and choose to burn oil instead of gas, then good Mr. Rockefeller holds me up, and he uses a certain portion of his money to build universities and support churches which are engaged in telling us how to be good.

Some of you are here for obtaining property under false pretenses—yet I pick up a great Sunday paper and read the advertisements of a merchant prince—"Shirtwaists for 39 cents, marked down from $3.00."

When I read the advertisements in the paper I see they are all lies. When I want to get out and find a place to stand anywhere on the face of the earth, I find that it has all been taken up long ago before I came here, and before you came here, and somebody says, "Get off, swim into the lake, fly into the air; go anywhere, but get off." That is because these people have the police and they have the jails and the judges and the lawyers and the soldiers and all the rest of them to take care of the earth and drive everybody off that comes in their way.

A great many people will tell you that all this is true, but that it does not excuse you. These facts do not excuse some fellow who reaches into my pocket and takes out a five-dollar bill. The fact that the gas company bribes the members of the legislature from year to year, and fixes the law, so that all you people are compelled to be "fleeced" whenever you deal with them; the fact that the streetcar companies and the gas companies have control of the streets; and the fact that the landlords own all the earth—this, they say, has nothing to do with you.

Let us see whether there is any connection between the crimes of the respectable classes and your presence in the jail. Many of you people are in jail because you have really committed burglary; many of you, because you have stolen something. In the meaning of the law, you have taken some other person's property. Some of you have entered a store and carried off a pair of shoes because you did not have the price. Possibly some of you have committed murder. I cannot tell what all of you did. There are a great many people here who have done some of these things who really do not know themselves why they did them. I think I know why you did them—every one of you; you did these things because you were bound to do them. It looked to you at the time as if you had a chance to do them or not, as you saw fit; but still, after all, you had no choice. There may be people here who had some money in their pockets and who still went out and got some more money in a way society forbids. Now, you may not yourselves see exactly why it was you did this thing, but if you look at the question deeply enough and carefully enough you will see that there were circumstances that drove you to do exactly the thing which you did. You could not help it any more than we outside can help taking the positions that we take. The reformers who tell you to be good and you will be happy, and the people on the outside who have property to protect—they think that the only way to do it is by building jails and locking you up in cells on weekdays and praying for you Sundays.

I think that all of this has nothing whatever to do with right conduct. I think it is very easily seen what has to do with right conduct. Some so-called criminals—and I will use this word because it is handy, it means nothing to me—I speak of the criminals who get caught as distinguished from the criminals who catch them—some of these so-called criminals are in jail for their first offenses, but nine tenths of you are in jail because you did not have a good lawyer and, of course, you did not have a good lawyer because you did not have enough money to pay a good lawyer. There is no very great danger of a rich man going to jail.

Some of you may be here for the first time. If we would open the doors and let you out, and leave the laws as they are today, some of you would be back tomorrow. This is about as good a place as you can get anyway. There are many people here who are so in the habit of coming that they would not know where else to go. There are people who are born with the tendency to break into jail every chance they get, and they cannot avoid it. You cannot figure out your life and see why it was, but still there is a reason for it; and if we were all wise and knew all the facts, we could figure it out.

In the first place, there are a good many people who go to jail in the wintertime than in summer. Why is this? Is it because people are more wicked in winter? No, it is because the coal trust begins to get in its grip in the winter. A few gentlemen take possession of the coal, and unless the people will pay seven or eight dollars a ton for something that is worth three dollars, they will have to freeze. Then there is nothing to do but to break into jail, and so there are many more in jail in the winter than in summer. It costs more for gas in the winter because the nights are longer, and people go to jail to save gas bills. The jails are electric-lighted. You may not know it, but these economic laws are working all the time, whether we know it or do not know it.

There are more people who go to jail in hard times than in good times— few people, comparatively, go to jail except when they are hard up. They go to jail because they have no other place to go. They may not know why, but it is true all the same. People are not more wicked in hard times. That is not the reason. The fact is true all over the world that in hard times more people go to jail than in good times, and in winter more people go to jail than in summer. Of course it is pretty hard times for people who go to jail at any time. The people who go to jail are almost always poor people—people who have no other place to live, first and last. When times are hard, then you find large numbers of people who go to jail who would not otherwise be in jail.

Long ago, Mr. Buckle, who was a great philosopher and historian, collected facts, and he showed that the number of people who are arrested increased just as the price of food increased. When they put up the price of gas ten cents a thousand, I do not know who will go to jail, but I do know that a certain number of people will go. When the meat combine raises the price of beef, I do not know who is going to jail, but I know that a large number of people are bound to go. Whenever the Standard Oil Company raises the price of oil, I know that a certain number of girls who are seamstresses, and who work night after night long hours for somebody else, will be compelled to go out on the streets and ply another trade, and I know that Mr. Rockefeller and his associates are responsible and not the poor girls in the jails.

First and last, people are sent to jail because they are poor. Sometimes, as I say, you may not need money at the particular time, but you wish to have thrifty forehanded habits, and do not always wait until you are in absolute want. Some of you people are perhaps plying the trade, the profession, which is called burglary. No man in his right senses will go into a strange house in the dead of night and prowl around with a dark lantern through unfamiliar rooms and take chances of his life, if he has plenty of the good things of the world in his own home. You would not take any such chances as that. If a man had clothes in his clothes-press and beefsteak in his pantry and money in the bank, he would not navigate around nights in houses where he knows nothing about the premises whatever. It always requires experience and education for this profession, and people who fit themselves for it are no more to blame than I am for being a lawyer. A man would not hold up another man on the street if he had plenty of money in his own pocket. He might do it if he had one dollar or two dollars, but he wouldn't if he had as much money as Mr. Rockefeller has. Mr. Rockefeller has a great deal better hold-up game than that.

The more that is taken from the poor by the rich, who have the chance to take it, the more poor people there are who are compelled to resort to these means for a livelihood. They may not understand it, they may not think so at once, but after all they are driven into that line of employment.

There is a bill before the legislature of this state to punish kidnaping children with death. We have wise members of the legislature. They know the gas trust when they see it and they always see it—they can furnish light enough to be seen; and this legislature thinks it is going to stop kidnaping children by making a law punishing kidnapers of children with death. I don't believe in kidnaping children, but the legislature is all wrong. Kidnaping children is not a crime, it is a profession. It has been developed with the times. It has been developed with our modern industrial conditions. There are many ways of making money—many new ways that our ancestors knew nothing about. Our ancestors knew nothing about a billion-dollar trust; and here comes some poor fellow who has no other trade and he discovers the profession of kidnaping children.

The crime is born, not because people are bad; people don't kidnap other people's children because they want the children or because they are devilish, but because they see a chance to get some money out of it. You cannot cure this crime by passing a law punishing by death kidnapers of children. There is one way to cure it. There is one way to cure all these offenses, and that is to give the people a chance to live. There is no other way, and there never was any other way since the world began; and the world is so blind and stupid that it will not see. If every man and woman and child in the world had a chance to make a decent, fair, honest living, there would be no jails and no lawyers and no courts. There might be some persons here or there with some peculiar formation of their brain, like Rockefeller, who would do these things simply to be doing them; but they would be very, very few, and those should be sent to a hospital and treated, and not sent to jail; and they would entirely disappear in the second generation, or at least in the third generation.

I am not talking pure theory. I will just give you two or three illustrations.

The English people once punished criminals by sending them away. They would load them on a ship and export them to Australia. England was owned by lords and nobles and rich people. They owned the whole earth over there, and the other people had to stay in the streets. They could not get a decent living. They used to take their criminals and send them to Australia—I mean the class of criminals who got caught. When these criminals got over there, and nobody else had come, they had the whole continent to run over, and so they could raise sheep and furnish their own meat, which is easier than stealing it. These criminals then became decent, respectable people because they had a chance to live. They did not commit any crimes. They were just like the English people who sent them there, only better. And in the second generation the descendants of those criminals were as good and respectable a class of people as there were on the face of the earth, and then they began building churches and jails themselves.

A portion of this country was settled in the same way, landing prisoners down on the southern coast; but when they got here and had a whole continent to run over and plenty of chances to make a living, they became respectable citizens, making their own living just like any other citizen in the world. But finally the descendants of the English aristocracy who sent the people over to Australia found out they were getting rich, and so they went over to get possession of the earth as they always do, and they organized land syndicates and got control of the land and ores, and then they had just as many criminals in Australia as they did in England. It was not because the world had grown bad; it was because the earth had been taken away from the people.

Some of you people have lived in the country. It's prettier than it is here. And if you have ever lived on a farm you understand that if you put a lot of cattle in a field, when the pasture is short they will jump over the fence; but put them in a good field where there is plenty of pasture, and they will be law-abiding cattle to the end of time. The human animal is just like the rest of the animals, only a little more so. The same thing that governs in the one governs in the other.

Everybody makes his living along the lines of least resistance. A wise man who comes into a country early sees a great undeveloped land. For instance, our rich men twenty-five years ago saw that Chicago was small and knew a lot of people would come here and settle, and they readily saw that if they had all the land around here it would be worth a good deal, so they grabbed the land. You cannot be a landlord because somebody has got it all. You must find some other calling. In England and Ireland and Scotland less than five per cent own all the land there is, and the people are bound to stay there on any kind of terms the landlords give. They must live the best they can, so they develop all these various professions—burglary, picking pockets and the like.

Again, people find all sorts of ways of getting rich. These are diseases like everything else. You look at people getting rich, organizing trusts and making a million dollars, and somebody gets the disease and he starts out. He catches it just as a man catches the mumps or the measles; he is not to blame, it is in the air. You will find men speculating beyond their means, because the mania of money-getting is taking possession of them. It is simply a disease—nothing more, nothing less. You cannot avoid catching it; but the fellows who have control of the earth have the advantage of you. See what the law is: when these men get control of things, they make the laws. They do not make the laws to protect anybody; courts are not instruments of justice. When your case gets into court it will make little difference whether you are guilty or innocent, but it's better if you have a smart lawyer. And you cannot have a smart lawyer unless you have money. First and last it's a question of money. Those men who own the earth make the laws to protect what they have. They fix up a sort of fence or pen around what they have, and they fix the law so the fellow on the outside cannot get in. The laws are really organized for the protection of the men who rule the world. They were never organized or enforced to do justice. We have no system for doing justice, not the slightest in the world.

Let me illustrate: Take the poorest person in this room. If the community had provided a system of doing justice, the poorest person in this room would have as good a lawyer as the richest, would he not? When you went into court you would have just as long a trial and just as fair a trial as the richest person in Chicago. Your case would not be tried in fifteen or twenty minutes, whereas it would take fifteen days to get through with a rich man's case.

Then if you were rich and were beaten, your case would be taken to the Appellate Court. A poor man cannot take his case to the Appellate Court; he has not the price. And then to the Supreme Court. And if he were beaten there he might perhaps go to the United States Supreme Court. And he might die of old age before he got into jail. If you are poor, it's a quick job. You are almost known to be guilty, else you would not be there. Why should anyone be in the criminal court if he were not guilty? He would not be there if he could be anywhere else. The officials have no time to look after all these cases. The people who are on the outside, who are running banks and building churches and making jails, they have no time to examine 600 or 700 prisoners each year to see whether they are guilty or innocent. If the courts were organized to promote justice the people would elect somebody to defend all these criminals, somebody as smart as the prosecutor—and give him as many detectives and as many assistants to help, and pay as much money to defend you as to prosecute you. We have a very able man for state's attorney, and he has many assistants, detectives and policemen without end, and judges to hear the cases—everything handy.

Most all of our criminal code consists in offenses against property. People are sent to jail because they have committed a crime against property. It is of very little consequence whether one hundred people more or less go to jail who ought not to go—you must protect property, because in this world property is of more importance than anything else.

How is it done? These people who have property fix it so they can protect what they have. When somebody commits a crime it does not follow that he has done something that is morally wrong. The man on the outside who has committed no crime may have done something. For instance: to take all the coal in the United States and raise the price two dollars or three dollars when there is no need of it, and thus kill thousands of babies and send thousands of people to the poorhouse and tens of thousands to jail, as is done every year in the United States—this is a greater crime than all the people in our jails ever committed; but the law does not punish it. Why? Because the fellows who control the earth make the laws. If you and I had the making of the laws, the first thing we would do would be to punish the fellow who gets control of the earth. Nature put this coal in the ground for me as well as for them and nature made the prairies up here to raise wheat for me as well as for them, and then the great railroad companies came along and fenced it up.

Most all of the crimes for which we are punished are property crimes. There are a few personal crimes, like murder—but they are very few. The crimes committed are mostly those against property. If this punishment is right the criminals must have a lot of property. How much money is there in this crowd? And yet you are all here for crimes against property. The people up and down the Lake Shore have not committed crime; still they have so much property they don't know what to do with it. It is perfectly plain why these people have not committed crimes against property; they make the laws and therefore do not need to break them. And in order for you to get some property you are obliged to break the rules of the game. I don't know but what some of you may have had a very nice chance to get rich by carrying a hod for one dollar a day, twelve hours. Instead of taking that nice, easy profession, you are a burglar. If you had been given a chance to be a banker you would rather follow that. Some of you may have had a chance to work as a switchman on a railroad where you know, according to statistics, that you cannot live and keep all your limbs more than seven years, and you can get fifty dollars or seventy-five dollars a month for taking your lives in your hands; and instead of taking that lucrative position you chose to be a sneak thief, or something like that. Some of you made that sort of choice. I don't know which I would take if I was reduced to this choice. I have an easier choice.

I will guarantee to take from this jail, or any jail in the world, five hundred men who have been the worst criminals and lawbreakers who ever got into jail, and I will go down to our lowest streets and take five hundred of the most abandoned prostitutes, and go out somewhere where there is plenty of land, and will give them a chance to make a living, and they will be as good people as the average in the community.

There is a remedy for the sort of condition we see here. The world never finds it out, or when it does find it out it does not enforce it. You may pass a law punishing every person with death for burglary, and it will make no difference. Men will commit it just the same. In England there was a time when one hundred different offenses were punishable with death, and it made no difference. The English people strangely found out that so fast as they repealed the severe penalties and so fast as they did away with punishing men by death, crime decreased instead of increased; that the smaller the penalty the fewer the crimes.

Hanging men in our county jails does not prevent murder. It makes murderers.

And this has been the history of the world. It's easy to see how to do away with what we call crime. It is not so easy to do it. I will tell you how to do it. It can be done by giving the people a chance to live—by destroying special privileges. So long as big criminals can get the coal fields, so long as the big criminals have control of the city council and get the public streets for streetcars and gas rights—this is bound to send thousands of poor people to jail. So long as men are allowed to monopolize all the earth, and compel others to live on such terms as these men see fit to make, then you are bound to get into jail.

The only way in the world to abolish crime and criminals is to abolish the big ones and the little ones together. Make fair conditions of life. Give men a chance to live. Abolish the right of private ownership of land, abolish monopoly, make the world partners in production, partners in the good things of life. Nobody would steal if he could get something of his own some easier way. Nobody will commit burglary when he has a house full. No girl will go out on the streets when she has a comfortable place at home. The man who owns a sweatshop or a department store may not be to blame himself for the condition of his girls, but when he pays them five dollars, three dollars, and two dollars a week, I wonder where he thinks they will get the rest of their money to live. The only way to cure these conditions is by equality. There should be no jails. They do not accomplish what they pretend to accomplish. If you would wipe them out there would be no more criminals than now. They terrorize nobody. They are a blot upon any civilization, and a jail is an evidence of the lack of charity of the people on the outside who make the jails and fill them with the victims of their greed.

If you disagree with Darrow, you may want to write a rebuttal. If you agree with him, you may want to write a confirming argument. Or, you may want to rebut part of the argument and confirm another. Here are possible ways of doing these.

To begin, you need first to identify Darrow's chief assumptions. Notice that he makes a number of statements about human nature:

> We all do the best we can under the circumstances.
> Everybody makes his living along the lines of least resistance.

First consider where these ideas come from. Does Darrow establish them inductively and grant them a degree of probability, or are they absolute "truths" for which Darrow provides examples—examples which show why these truths should be accepted?

In answering this question, you are seeking to define the nature of the argument; that is, whether it is chiefly deductive or inductive, or both. This definition is a necessary step in deciding what response to make to the argument. If you disagree in whole or in part with the statements just quoted, and you want to rebut them, you must know on what basis Darrow supports them. For example, they may be based on religious, social, or political creeds that tell us what people are ideally. It is not necessary for an *ideal* to be supported by experience, and therefore it is not necessary for any examples of Darrow's view of human nature to actually exist. On the other hand, Darrow's view of human nature may have come from experience and observation. In this case, his view of human nature can be tested inductively. Indeed, both his beliefs and experiences may be the basis of his views, and you in turn can present counter-beliefs and experiences in rebuttal, if you so wish.

We have already suggested one way to organize a rebuttal. The chief argument deserves to be analyzed first, because its faults or strengths will bear on the subordinate arguments. You need then to decide on an order of consideration. We presented the fallacies discussed in this chapter in three major groups—fallacies of relevance, fallacies of ambiguity, and fallacies of induction. Since the subordinate arguments closest to the main argument are those in which the premises or details are held to be relevant to the conclusion, it seems logical to consider these first. But if you consider important terms in the argument ambiguous, it might be best to begin with these. The order of presentation on what thesis you want to develop concerning the argument you are criticizing.

If you agree with the argument and wish to confirm it, you can proceed by showing that its premises or assumptions are confirmed by other beliefs you hold, and indeed may be illustrated (or confirmed) by other examples drawn from the world you know. And you might show that the appeals made by the writer are fair ones, and that supporting arguments are sound.

If you agree with the writer on some matters and disagree with him on others, a different organization is possible. You might work from the matters on which you agree, state why you do, and then devote the greater part of your discussion to those you disagree with.

In developing your analysis, remember that arguments that are fallacious in one context may be legitimate in another. If you are showing that some or all of the arguments are fallacious, you might show how they could have been made legitimately.

Exercise

Identify the fault in reasoning pinpointed by the writers or evident in the writers' own statement:

a. Another piece of stupidity shows how much we are at the mercy of ignorant men pretending to be knowledgeable. During the International Geophysical Year, 1957-58, the Van Allen Belt was discovered. This is an area of magnetic phenomena. Immediately it was decided to explode a hydrogen bomb in the Belt to see whether an artificial aurora could be produced. . . . Every eminent scientist in the field of cosmology, radioastronomy or physics of the atmosphere protested at this irresponsible tampering with a system which we did not understand. And typical of the casual attitude toward this kind of thing, the Prime Minister of the day, answering protests in the House of Commons that called on him to intervene with the Americans, asked what all the fuss was about. After all, they hadn't known that the Van Allen Belt even existed a year before.

Lord Richie-Calder, *"Mortgaging the Old Homestead," Foreign Affairs,*
January 1970

b. We laugh at the haughty American nation because it makes the negro clean its boots and then proves the moral and physical inferiority of the negro by the fact that he is a shoeblack; but we ourselves throw the drudgery of creation on one sex, and then imply that no female of any womanliness or delicacy would initiate any effort in that direction.

Bernard Shaw, *Man and Superman*

c. We know of one man—a farmer in Vermont—who has figured out that whenever the oil companies want to force the price of oil up a notch they manufacture a shortage by running one of their supertankers onto the rocks. Each time he reads about an oil spill from a tanker somewhere in the world, he feels that his theory is being confirmed. Conditioned, perhaps, by the ineradicable uncertainty that really does underlie most large events, he and others are staring past the explanation of the energy crisis which stands in plain view, and taking refuge in a complexity that, for once, does not exist.

> Talk of the Town, *The New Yorker*, July 16, 1979

d. [From a letter of Nazi propaganda minister Josef Goebbels to a symphony conductor protesting government interference in the arts] It is your right to feel as an artist and to see things from an artist's point of view. But that need not mean that you regard the whole development in Germany in an unpolitical way. Politics too is an art, perhaps the highest and most comprehensive there is, and we who shape modern German policy feel ourselves in this to be artists who have been given the responsible task of forming, out of the raw material of the mass, the firm concrete structure of a people.

e. And furthermore, it is hypocrisy to talk about protecting women from lifting weights when technology as we know it is eliminating that muscular work from most jobs and when in fact the good jobs that are going to continue and not be eliminated from the machine are ones for which women might qualify equal with men and the special State protective laws only deny women the opportunity to move into these jobs.

> Betty Freidan, in testimony to a Congressional subcommittee on laws protecting women from lifting weights in factory work; May 5, 1970

f. Propagandists and politicians have blown up stories about segregation until the rest of the country believes it is a dirty word. The Southern white man has been ridiculed and pilloried before the world, until he is one of the underprivileged minorities of the earth.

> the editor of a South Carolina newspaper, quoted in John Hope Franklin and Isidore Starr, *The Negro in Twentieth Century America*

g. There comes a time when even speech loses its constitutional immunity. Speech innocuous one year may at another time fan such destructive flames that it must be halted in the interests of the safety of the Republic. That is the meaning of the clear and present danger test. When conditions are so critical that there will be no time to avoid the evil that the speech threatens, it is time to call a halt. Otherwise, free speech which is the strength of the Nation will be the cause of its destruction.

Yet free speech is the rule, not the exception. The restraint to be constitutional must be based on more than fear, on more than passionate opposition against the speech, on more than a revolted dislike for its contents.

> Justice William O. Douglas, *Dennis v. United States*, 1951

Chapter Eight

The Documented Paper

Defining a problem for research

We undertake research of a limited sort when we use the dictionary or consult an encyclopedia for answers to questions brought up in arguments with friends. Other questions and topics, such as those selected for research and term papers, require more extensive and complex investigations of source materials. Our concern in this chapter will be with the process of writing the documented paper.

We begin with an essential step in the process—defining the question or topic to be investigated as exactly as possible. Defining the question is not as simple as it may sound, for it is often the case that the question we think of asking is not the one posed or answered by the writers we consult. For example, if we wish to learn the "cause" and "cure" of cancer and therefore read accounts of cancer research to find out what the current theory is, we may be surprised to discover that cancer researchers are not looking for a single cause. Rather, they are seeking a number of causes, and their concern, we discover, is perhaps with prevention as much as with cure. Had we been aware of these concerns, we would have posed our initial question—What is the cause of cancer and how can it be cured?—in a different way.

Questions and topics arise for us everyday, in reading newspapers, watching television, talking with friends. An initial search of the library for materials may be difficult—perhaps because we have not posed the question in the terms writers on the subject have. A question relating to press censorship, for example, may be discussed in the context of "free-dom of speech" or "First Amendment rights," in books and articles. More than this, the terms in which a current issue is discussed may be consid-erably different from terms used in the past to discuss the same or a related issue. To cite a recent example, the term "supply-side econom-ics" has become prominent in public discussions of the national budget. Numerous explanations and discussions of this economic theory have appeared in newspapers and magazines since the inauguration of Presi-dent Reagan. To find the origin of the theory, and discussions in the past of related economic theories, we would need to discover those terms, such as "laissez-faire economics," in which these earlier theories were presented. If we confine ourselves to the exact terms of the current dis-cussion, then we will limit our investigation needlessly. A broader in-vestigation, taking past and present theories into account, may lead us to important insights and new and more significant questions.

Even when a question has been posed for us, as in an assignment from a magazine editor, we may find it necessary to restate it in light of our initial investigations, and perhaps to redefine the focus of our concern. To continue with our example, the question

What is new in supply-side economic theory?

might have to be rephrased,

Is supply-side economics a new theory?

Or we might ask,

What changes would be made in government spending and tax poli-cies if supply-side economics governed them?

How we phrase the question depends, then, not only on the language in which the idea or issue is discussed, but also on the focus of interest we wish to present in our writing. We must be clear in our minds about the purpose of the research to be done.

The purpose of our research may be no more than to satisfy our curi-osity about a puzzling statement in a newspaper story. We may also wish to do research so as to understand a new government policy, discover what research has previously been done on a subject, or get the facts on an issue we plan to debate. The amount and quality of our research will depend on our purpose. An encyclopedia account of laissez-faire eco-nomics may be adequate to an understanding of a newspaper story, but we would want to consult a variety of sources in preparing a report for local government officials concerned with the nature and impact of new federal economic policies. Secondary sources—articles and books writ-ten by scholars and observers—would be essential in preparing such a report, but we would seek also primary sources—firsthand accounts of new economic theories and policies by those who originate them. As we shall see, gathering material from primary sources is usually harder and more time consuming than going to reference books or newspaper and magazine articles, and for this reason we do so when we must.

Collecting information

Let us assume we have come across an allusion to the views on freedom of speech and press held by Justice William O. Douglas, and we decide to investigate it to complete a report. How much and what kind of information we collect depends on how much is needed to understand specific references in the statement.

The reference to Justice Douglas' views occurs in a discussion of the constitutional guarantee of free speech and press. Both Justice Hugo Black and Justice Douglas, the writer tells us,

> have confused the almost universal opposition to the doctrine of *prior restraint* on utterances, or censorship in *advance* of publication, with the view that individuals have a right to express their opinions, true or false, regardless of who or what is affected by their expression—a view which was almost universally rejected at the time [the Constitution was written], much as we may deplore that rejection. Freedom of speech and press in the light of existing practices meant the right to speak and publish without prior restraint or censorship or licensing. It did *not* mean the right to do so with impunity. It did *not* mean the right to legal protection against seditious or criminal libel. That the meaning of freedom was understood in this restricted sense at the time, I repeat, need not bind us and has not bound us.
>
> Sidney Hook, *The Paradoxes of Freedom*

Reference guides and indexes

If a general discussion or brief identification of Douglas' views on freedom of speech and press will provide the necessary background information, we need to locate the appropriate reference books, sometimes our best source for this kind of information. The basic guide to reference books by subject is *Guide to Reference Books*, published by the American Library Association. Although this book probably will not list works on William O. Douglas, it will list a book like the following that contains opinions of Supreme Court justices on censorship:

> Henry Steele Commager, et al., *Documents of American History*, 9th Edition

Let us assume that you consult this book and find some relevant opinions on censorship by Douglas. To broaden your view you may then wish to consult books on freedom of speech and press that contain discussions of Douglas, books on or by Douglas, and articles on various topics related to freedom of expression. Let us describe briefly how such articles may be found, then turn to books by Douglas himself.

Numerous articles have been published on Justice Douglas, in a variety of publications including newspapers like the *New York Times*. Here are some important indexes or compilations of fact that may prove of use:

New York Times Index: a listing of reports and articles in the *Times* by day and month, with a brief summary of the contents

Facts on File: a summary of national news by week, with reference to important information sources

Public Affairs Information Service Bulletin: listing of published material in periodicals, pamphlets, and books on current topics

Reader's Guide to Periodical Literature: listing of articles in popular magazines including *Saturday Review* and *Harper's Magazine*

Social Sciences Index: listing of articles in specialized journals in sociology, psychology, and related fields

Humanities Index: listing of articles in specialized journals in English, modern languages, philosophy, classics, history

Essay and General Literature Index: index by subject and author to essay collections

In searching these indexes, we will do best by beginning with the narrowest topic heading and, if this search produces no articles, going on to broader ones. Thus, a search under "Douglas, William O." may produce the articles we want, but if it does not, a search under the headings "Freedom of speech," "Freedom of press," "Censorship," "Obscenity," "Amendments, First" and the like may produce what we are looking for.

Exercises

1. Special bibliographies are often published in pamphlets, periodicals, and books. For example, a book on freedom of speech and press may contain a listing of important source materials on the subject at the end. Sometimes a list or bibliography appears at the end of each chapter. These bibliographies are listed in *Bibliographic Index*, published twice a year, with an annual cumulation in December. After reading directions for use of the index at the beginning of each volume, see whether any special bibliographies have been published on William O. Douglas or the Supreme Court since 1960.

2. *Bibliographic Index* supplies cross-references to the subject headings under which the bibliographies are listed. Find the subject

headings for each of the following, and indicate the number of books listed under each heading:

  a. freedom of speech

  b. U.S. Supreme Court

  c. First Amendment to the Constitution

  d. Shakespeare's *Hamlet*

  e. marijuana use in the U.S.

  f. college vs. professional football

3. Examine the following reference books, and write down a few of the special uses each would have in a study of the First Amendment to the Constitution. Cite particular entries and information:

  a. *Compton's Encyclopedia and Fact-Index*

  b. *The New Columbia Encyclopedia*

  c. *Documents of American History*, 9th edition

  d. *Essay and General Literature Index*

  e. *Social Sciences Index*

  f. *Books in Print*

  g. *Library of Congress Subject Catalog*

4. List the subject headings in your library card catalog that cover books about William O. Douglas. If your library has a divided catalog (an author-title catalog and subject catalog), use the latter.

5. Locate reference books in your library that would be useful in investigating one of the following topics. Write down these uses, and discuss them:

  a. expenditure for education of the handicapped in the U.S. in 1977

  b. gasoline consumption in the U.S. in 1978

  c. comparative size and economies of Los Angeles and New York City

  d. awards for scientific achievement in the U.S. in 1972

  e. the literary career of Kate Chopin

  f. public reaction to the assassination of Martin Luther King, Jr.

  g. size of grain sales to the Soviet Union between 1970 and 1974

  h. American casualties in the Vietnam War

  i. graduate programs in nuclear medicine, in the U.S. and Canada

  j. musical competitions and rules for entry

  k. Pulitzer Prize winners for poetry since 1970

  l. government regulations on disposal of hazardous chemical wastes

m. occurrence of tuberculosis in the U.S., 1960–1970

n. active volcanos and their effects

o. programs in Black Studies, Women's Studies, or Hispanic-American Studies, in U.S. and Canadian colleges and universities

Primary sources

Turning to kinds of information and their use, we need to distinguish two basic kinds—primary and secondary. We will illustrate the first from the writings of Justice Douglas before considering the second kind.

Primary sources include autobiographical writings, public statements, letters, birth and death records, bills of sale, contracts, taped interviews, and all other firsthand materials. In a study of an important governmental policy, firsthand materials would include documents involved in its formation, statements by its originators, and eyewitness accounts of how the policy was debated and given final shape—to name just a few. Secondary sources are interpretations of these various materials, statements, and accounts of people not directly involved, and by interpreters writing about them at a later time. The judicial opinions of Justice Douglas are primary sources; interpretations of them by writers on First Amendment decisions and their impact on press freedom are secondary source material. Contrary to what is sometimes assumed, primary material does not usually speak for itself. Birth and death records, contracts, even public statements and letters become meaningful in particular contexts. The context can be provided only by an interpreter who assembles various bits of primary material and synthesizes them. Thus the facts of Shakespeare's birth, parentage, and early years in his hometown of Stratford become meaningful when used by writers to trace the background of his life.

In searching for primary material on a topic, we need to seek out various kinds; for the more that we can assemble, the stronger the evidence for a particular belief will be. Evidence of various kinds can be compared and related, one piece helping to illuminate another.

Let us assume we wish to discover what Justice Douglas' exact opinions are on the matter of prior restraint and freedom of speech and press. A variety of primary sources exist including judicial opinions, various public statements, autobiographical writings, monographs (books, articles and scholarly papers devoted to a single subject), and the like. Here are a few of these:

a. In the June 30, 1971 verdict on the Pentagon Papers (*New York Times Co.* v. *United States*), Douglas issued a concurring opinion, in which he rejected "any prior restraint on expression," quoting from a previous decision involving the issue, and citing earlier precedents. This judicial opinion is particularly useful because Douglas reviews the recent history of the controversy.[1]

b. In his book *An Almanac of Liberty*, Douglas gives the earlier history of prior restraint, and in other pages gives historical information on freedom of speech and press in England and America, in the colonial period and later. Douglas expresses his opinion on prior restraint and other issues throughout the book:

> The same power that could suppress a "defamatory" paper today could suppress an "unorthodox" or unpopular one tomorrow. It was censorship that in an early day was used to stifle the efforts of patriots to inform the people of the duties of kings and the rights of subjects.[2]

Published in 1954, *An Almanac of Liberty* sheds important light on Douglas' thinking on the issue.

c. In his recent autobiography, Douglas traces the influence of events in his time and of court decisions, before and during his years on the Supreme Court, on his thinking about freedom of speech and press. As an informal discussion of these ideas, this memoir sheds important light on philosophical ideas and personal attitudes that we might not discover in a judicial opinion. Douglas, for example, concludes a paragraph discussing Court decisions on laws abridging speech with the following statement:

> Watergate was obscene to me, and very offensive. So were the passionate denunciations of Hugo Black and Earl Warren from the right. The twisting and distortion of the news by the Communist press and by some of our mass media were shocking to me. So were some laws pushed through Congress by powerful lobbies to line their own pockets. But one judge's standard of offensiveness is not a constitutional standard.[3]

A monograph by Douglas on the nature of liberty sheds light on his general philosophy. Knowing this philosophy, we are able to identify assumptions that underlie his concurring opinion in *New York Times Co.* v. *United States,* and in particular his rejection of prior restraint of expression. Knowing Douglas' philosophy, we can also test the accuracy of judgments made about his beliefs by interpreters like Sidney Hook. Here is a passage from the monograph that shows how Douglas applies his philosophy to common forms of censorship:

> Movies, like television, sometimes deal with political ideas, with social problems, with theological matters, with economic or educational questions. The

[1] Vern Countryman, ed., *The Douglas Opinions* (New York: Random House, 1977), p. 219.
[2] William O. Douglas, *An Almanac of Liberty* (Garden City, N.Y.: Doubleday, 1954), p. 149. See also pp. 37–41.
[3] William O. Douglas, *The Court Years, 1939–1975: The Autobiography of William O. Douglas* (New York: Random House, 1980), p. 105.

censor who, with the stroke of the pen, outlaws a movie or who, with scissors, deletes parts of a film decides what ideas are good and which ones are bad for society. The movie censor, like the censor of novels or poetry, also acts as arbiter of the arts and decides what is in good taste, what is vulgar, what is cheap. Freedom of expression through acting, through music, through the medium of the theatre, should be accorded the same constitutional dignity as freedom of expression through books, newspapers, or political tracts. The American theory is that the people need no office of oversight in any of these fields. Their applause or their rejection is the ultimate test, not a censor's notion of morality, ideology, or artistic worth.[4]

These various documents, taken together, are mutually illuminating and more revealing of Douglas' thinking on the issue of prior restraint than any one document would be. And other primary sources can shed additional light. We might cite, for example, the judicial opinions of other judges and Supreme Court justices to provide a wider context, a broader understanding of how issues of prior restraint and censorship were being defined during the years Douglas sat on the Supreme Court. The opinions of a jurist different in thinking and outlook from Douglas are particularly revealing, as are the various opinions of Justice John M. Harlan, who sometimes agreed with Douglas in decisions relating to obscenity, but often for different reasons. The opinions of a U.S. District Court Judge, Learned Hand, also provide important contrasting evidence.[5] And so do those of Justice Black, whose views were often identified with those of Douglas. Here is a portion from Black's concurring opinion in *Smith* v. *California* (1959), to which Hook is alluding in the statement quoted in the previous section:

> Certainly the First Amendment's language leaves no room for inference that abridgements of speech and press can be made just because they are slight. That Amendment provides, in simple words, that "Congress shall make no law . . . abridging the freedom of speech, or of the press." I read "no law abridging" to mean *no law abridging.* The First Amendment, which is the supreme law of the land, has thus fixed its own value on freedom of speech and press by putting these freedoms wholly "beyond the reach" of *federal* power to abridge. No other provision of the Constitution purports to dilute the scope of these unequivocal commands of the First Amendment. Consequently, I do not believe that any federal agencies, including Congress and this Court, have power or authority to subordinate speech and press to what

[4] William O. Douglas, *The Anatomy of Liberty: The Rights of Man Without Force* (New York: Trident Press, 1963), pp. 15–16.
[5] David L. Shapiro, ed., *The Evolution of a Judicial Philosophy: Selected Opinions and Papers of Justice John M. Harlan* (Cambridge: Harvard University Press, 1969), pp. 112–23; Hershel Shanks, ed., *The Art and Craft of Judging: The Decisions of Judge Learned Hand* (New York: Macmillan Company, 1968), pp. 29–37, 67–97.

they think are "more important interests." The contrary notion is, in my judgment, court-made not Constitution-made.[6]

The whole of Black's concurring opinion is reprinted toward the end of this chapter, in company with an opinion of Douglas, and we shall see what use one commentator makes of these statements in a critical examination of Black and Douglas.

Exercises

1. Choose one of the following topics for investigation of primary sources. Find in your college library as many different sources as you can, and write down the use that might be made of them in research on the topic:

   a. President Kennedy's attitude toward the space program

   b. President Johnson's attitude toward the Vietnam War

   c. President Nixon's decision to resign

   d. President Carter's attitude toward the press

   e. President Truman's firing of General Douglas MacArthur

2. In the following excerpt, identify facts that a reader unfamiliar with the subject would need to understand it completely. Then find reference books and primary sources that provide several of these facts:

   > Before the seventeenth century ended, the immunity claimed by [John] Lilburne had been broadly extended in England. It protected the person who was charged with a crime from testifying against himself at his trial. It also protected any witness from testifying to anything that might incriminate the witness in future proceedings.
   >
   > The idea spread to this country. The Puritans who came here knew of the detested oath, which Lilburne refused to take. They too had been its victims. *The Body of Liberties*, adopted in 1641 by Massachusetts, afforded protection against self-incrimination either through torture or through the oath (December 31). The highhanded practices of the Royal Governors who sought to compel citizens to accuse themselves of crimes also whipped up sentiment for the immunity. A majority of the Colonies, therefore, as part of their programs for independence, adopted bills of right, which included the immunity against self-incrimination. Later it was written into the Fifth Amendment and into most state constitutions.
   >
   > William O. Douglas, *An Almanac of Liberty*

[6]Irving Dilliard, ed., *One Man's Stand for Freedom: Mr. Justice Black and the Bill of Rights: A Collection of His Supreme Court Opinions* (New York: Knopf, 1963), p. 361.

Secondary sources

For many events of the past, both distant and recent, only secondary sources exist, or so few primary ones that we are dependent on very incomplete evidence. Where primary evidence exists, it usually has authority in establishing the basic facts, though as we have noted what we judge as "basic" depends on comparison and interpretation. There may also be disagreement over whether primary evidence cited is genuine evidence at all.

For example, eyewitness testimony can be notoriously unreliable or contradictory. Though numerous witnesses to President Kennedy's assassination have testified to what they saw and heard, and filmed evidence of the shooting exists, the facts are still in dispute almost twenty years after the event. Numerous investigations by people well skilled in sifting and interpreting forensic evidence have failed to dispel widespread public doubt about the conclusions reached by the Warren Commission. Just as circumstantial evidence is used in many criminal cases to bolster or support eyewitness accounts, so, in general, interpretation by those not present at an event—perhaps the reconstruction of events by people much later—plays an essential role even where primary materials are abundant.

Usually a number of facts converge—some established without any doubt about their authenticity, others established provisionally and considered probable only. Interpretation is needed to establish what these mean. No fact has meaning outside an interpretive context created by someone's understanding of what happened. The original historical context in which statements are made and events occur has to be reconstructed, and doing so is never an easy job.

That historical context may be reconstructed through the recorded statements of people of the past as well as through what is known about the climate of thought and social history of their time. And significant events of the time may be introduced to create a perspective. For example, Archibald Cox, who discussed the Supreme Court decision on the Pentagon Papers (classified government documents, chiefly concerned with military policy during the Vietnam War, that newspapers wished to publish), put the issue of prior restraint in the broader historical context beginning with the origin of the Bill of Rights in eighteenth-century thought:

> Belief in natural rights and natural law were deeply ingrained in the eighteenth-century American mind despite uncertainty whether their source was the King of Kings and Lord of all the earth, the immutable maxims of reason and justice, or the accumulated wisdom of English common law. The conviction that there were such natural rights made it easy to express them in a

Constitution, and then to accept the notion that a duly enacted statute in conflict with natural rights was not a binding law.[7]

And statements of eighteenth-century statesmen are quoted to illustrate how authoritative natural rights were taken to be, as we can see from the following words of James Madison:

> independent tribunals of justice will consider themselves in a peculiar manner the guardians of those rights; they will be an impenetrable bulwark against every assumption of power in the Legislative or Executive.[8]

And in discussing the opinion of Justices Black and Douglas that prior restraint of any kind would "make a shambles of the First Amendment," Cox puts this opinion in the context of recent history:

> One wonders whether they [Black and Douglas] would have ruled during World War II that a newspaper had a constitutional right to publish for Nazi eyes the knowledge that, because of the work of Bletchley [a British intelligence establishment], British authorities were reading the orders of the Nazi High Command.[9]

Secondary sources in general provide such interpretation and perspective. Sometimes these sources are in conflict, since they occasionally use different primary sources or facts and at times may disagree on their authenticity; moreover, they are often written from different points of view and assumptions. For these reasons, when we use several secondary sources, they must be compared carefully in light of both their own presuppositions and of the primary source itself. Cox's book, used as a source in a study of Justice Douglas and his opinion on the Pentagon Papers, should be compared with Douglas's opinion, the Pentagon Papers themselves, and, for a broader view, Sidney Hook's *The Paradoxes of Freedom* (from which we quoted earlier), which also considers the history of First Amendment rights and presuppositions in recent Supreme Court decisions.

Though many sources have a claim to authority on a subject, and we may depend on these mainly in the research we undertake, every book or article, no matter how authoritative, is subject to correction on the basis of later knowledge and thinking. No source can claim to be free of error.

It is difficult to judge the accuracy and cogency of even the most authoritative studies. Another difficulty is establishing the authority or reliability of sources we have found. We will turn to this problem next.

---

[7] Archibald Cox, *The Role of the Supreme Court in American Government* (New York: Oxford University Press, 1976), p. 31.
[8] Ibid., pp. 31–32.
[9] Ibid., p. 38.

Reliability

Before using material from the books turned up by our library research, we need to determine their reliability. As we just said, this is not an easy job. If we know something about the field we are working in, we may recognize at a glance the names of writers of wide experience and authority. If we continue with our research into Justice Douglas' views on prior restraint, books by former Supreme Court justices like Arthur J. Goldberg, and law professors and former Solicitor Generals like Archibald Cox, are likely to have an authority that other secondary sources would have difficulty matching.

If we are not familiar with the writers, we can check on their reliability in book reviews published in reputable newspapers, magazines, and scholarly journals. Most of these are listed in *Book Review Digest;* we can also consult other reference sources like the *New York Times Index* and guides that list the work experience and special qualifications of the writer. Usually reviews give brief information about the reviewer's qualifications, but we need to verify these qualifications. Usually the reputation of the newspaper or magazine is not a guarantee of reliability. We may, indeed, want to compare several reviews of the book to be used.

These precautions may seem excessive, but they are not. The experienced researcher works only with source materials whose authenticity and reliability can be verified. How difficult the problem is can be illustrated through a recent book on the workings of the Supreme Court, Bob Woodward and Scott Armstrong's *The Brethren.* For the student who wants to gain an understanding of the Court in the 1970s the book may seem indispensable. For, in contrast to the White House and Congress, little is known about the actual decision making and internal politics of the Court; few justices have written anything about these in recent years, and therefore books that describe the workings of the Court—even those whose reliability has been questioned—are given serious attention. In general, the increasing use of unnamed sources by journalists, resulting partly from the efforts by government officials to maintain secrecy and the practice by many high officials of giving interviews on condition that they not be named, has led to the publication of a large number of books that present little or no documentation, such as *The Brethren.* This situation makes verification difficult or impossible.

Consider the problem for the researcher wishing to rely on *The Brethren.* The following passage concerns alleged national security papers filed with the Supreme Court during the hearings on the Pentagon Papers in 1971:

> The papers that [Solicitor General Erwin] Griswold had filed with the Court remained under guard in the conference room.
> Douglas had none of Black's reluctance about reading the sealed record.

Unwilling to abide by the Chief's restrictions that all the material be kept in the conference room, protected by Pentagon security guards stationed outside, Douglas took the materials to his chamber and raised no objection when his clerks read the exhibits.

Douglas was totally unimpressed with what he found. His many trips to Vietnam, his own writing on the area (*North from Malaya*), and his close friendships with Vietnamese officials . . . had made him intimately familiar with Southeast Asia. With characteristic vanity, he told his colleagues that there was nothing in the materials he had not known or assumed.[10]

This little anecdote contains more than a statement of fact. We are given an interpretation of motive: "Douglas had none of Black's reluctance about reading the sealed record." And we are given an interpretation of basic character: "With characteristic vanity, he had told his colleagues that there was nothing in the materials he had not known or assumed." To some readers, previous details about Douglas in the book would give these interpretations enough support to make them credible, but the careful researcher will look for supporting documentation in the form of notes or sources. *The Brethren*, however, lacks this documentation, as Woodward and Armstrong explain in their introduction:

Most of the information in this book is based on interviews with more than two hundred people, including several Justices, more than 170 former law clerks, and several dozen former employees of the Court. Chief Justice Warren E. Burger declined to assist us in any way. Virtually all the interviews were conducted "on background," meaning that the identity of the source will be kept confidential.[11]

Woodward and Armstrong assure us that their sources were "persons of remarkable intelligence," with high recall about the cases heard by the Court. They took their "core documentation" from unpublished material including memoranda exchanged by the justices, diaries, drafts of opinions and the like—enough material to fill eight file drawers.[12]

However, none of this material is available to the researcher or any other readers of the book, at least not available at present. We therefore cannot know the source of information about what Douglas did and thought. The source may have been Douglas himself, or his clerks, or an observer, or someone to whom these events were reported, but we are not told.

The impossibility of verifying the information in *The Brethren* does not exclude it as a source of information about the Court. But any quotation from the book, or paraphrase of information, requires careful qual-

[10] Bob Woodward and Scott Armstrong, *The Brethren* (New York: Simon and Schuster, 1979), p. 145.
[11] Ibid., p. 3.
[12] Ibid., p. 4.

ification. The sources on which Woodward and Armstrong relied must be noted, and where possible comparisons must be made with existing documents. We are seeking here what reputable newspapers seek before they publish a story based on "background" sources—independent verification from second or third parties.

We need also to search for statements by present and past justices or any other persons quoted or referred to in the book to test its reliability. The *New York Times Index*, it might be noted, is a major source of information here. And so is the *Reader's Guide* and similar indexes: often rebuttals are published as articles in newspapers and magazines.

Exercises

1. Examine various indexes for a list of news stories, reviews, and articles relating to *The Brethren*, published in 1979. Use these to assess the reputation of the book among those qualified to judge its reliability.

2. Examine one of the following books to determine the sources on which it is based and the amount and kind of documentation it provides:

   a. Alexandr Solzhenitsyn, *The Gulag Archipelago*

   b. Bob Woodward and Carl Bernstein, *The Final Days*

   c. William Manchester, *American Caesar*

   d. Edward Jay Epstein, *Inquest: The Warren Commission and the Establishment of the Whole Truth*

   e. Erich von Däniken, *Chariots of the Gods*

   f. John Fuller, *Incident at Exeter*

   g. Nikita Khrushchev, *Khrushchev Remembers*

   h. Albert Speer, *Inside the Third Reich*

Writing Assignment

Discuss the problems that the book you examined presents to the researcher who wishes to use it as source material in an investigation of some kind. Discuss what kinds of support would be needed to confirm or supplement it.

Documentation

Direct quotation and paraphrase

The sources of all major ideas and references in a research or scholarly paper should be indicated in such a way that readers can easily find them if they wish to verify your quotation or paraphrase. This is usually done with footnotes. Only those ideas and references on which the discussion depends for its evidence need be footnoted, but this is at best a broad and loosely stated "rule" that calls for a judgment by the researcher. A reference to the views of President Nixon on the Pentagon Papers or the Watergate tapes, for example, need not be documented if they are introduced into a discussion of Douglas' legal philosophy as background or as an aside. But they would have to be documented if they provided important evidence of the White House policy at the time Douglas was stating his ideas.

Paraphrase is a complete rewording of a statement that retains the exact ideas or meaning of a passage, including special emphasis and tone. It is not a presentation of the original wording with a change of tense only:

> *Original passage:* While it is "obscenity and indecency" before us today, the experience of mankind—both ancient and modern—shows that this type of elastic phrase can, and most likely will, be synonymous with the political, and maybe with the religious unorthodoxy of tomorrow.
>
> Justice Hugo Black, *Smith v. California*

> *Unfair paraphrase:* The experience of history, both ancient and modern, shows that a flexible phrase like "obscenity and indecency" can and probably will mean the same as political and religious unorthodoxy in the future.
>
> *Fair paraphrase:* History proves that "elastic" terms like "obscenity and indecency" change in their application, so that unorthodox political and religious ideas may be called obscene and indecent in the future.

Notice that the word "elastic" was quoted rather than paraphrased because of its nuance and importance to the statement. "Flexible" (used in the unfair paraphrase) would, however, be a satisfactory substitute. The earlier paraphrase is unfair not only because it retains essential wording of the original but also because it makes Black sound more dogmatic than the original.

In taking notes from books and articles, it is essential to distinguish direct quotation carefully from paraphrase. All too often the two become confused, and direct quotations find their way into the completed paper as the writer's own words. It is important to proofread each note as it is written, particularly each direct quotation. It is also important to record as much of the original context as may be needed to understand the

246

quotation or paraphrase. To continue with our previous example, the statement of Black is part of an opinion on a Los Angeles city law which made it illegal to keep an obscene or indecent book on the premises of a bookstore; the Court was reviewing a municipal court's interpretation that the owner of the bookstore was liable to prosecution whether or not the person knew it was obscene. Black believed the law was unconstitutional as it stood, and disagreed with the majority opinion that censorship could be justified when "more important interests" than freedom of speech and press were at stake. For Black, the constitutional ban on any abridgment whatever of the First Amendment is absolute. This much of the context needs to be recorded in some form and indicated in the complete paper.

Ellipsis

In recording direct quotations, nonessential parts can be omitted and a row of periods substituted for the omitted words. Four periods are used to show the omission of one or more sentences:

> *Original passage:* In the 1930s and '40s, there came before the Supreme Court a series of cases involving attempts by municipalities to exact a license from Jehovah's Witnesses for the distribution of their religious literature. They are a religious sect who spread through pamphlets their religious beliefs and interpretations of the *Bible*. A city ordinance, which required a license to distribute literature, was applied against one of them, with a resultant fine for offering religious tracts without a license.
>
> William O. Douglas, An Almanac of Liberty

> *Passage with omission of complete sentence:* In the 1930s and '40s, there came before the Supreme Court a series of cases involving attempts by municipalities to exact a license from Jehovah's Witnesses for the distribution of their religious literature. . . . A city ordinance, which required a license to distribute literature, was applied against one of them, with a resultant fine for offering religious tracts without a license.

> *Sentence with omission of a clause:* A city ordinance . . . was applied against one of them, with a resultant fine for offering religious tracts without a license.

Notice that the omitted clause contains important but not essential information if it had been provided earlier in the passage. If not, it should be kept to identify the content of the ordinance.

In making omissions, we must be careful not to alter the meaning of the original or remove important qualifications. Here, is a statement of Sidney Hook on Black and Douglas discussed earlier:

> They have confused the almost universal opposition to the doctrine of *prior restraint* on utterances, or censorship in *advance* of publication, with the view that individuals have a right to express their opinions, true or false, regardless of who or what is affected by their expression—a view which was almost universally rejected at the time, much as we may deplore that rejection.

Here is the statement with omissions:

> They have confused the almost universal opposition to the doctrine of *prior restraint* on utterances, or censorship in *advance* of publication, with the view that individuals have a right to express their opinions . . . regardless of who or what is affected by their expression—a view which was almost universally rejected at the time. . . .

Though the omissions are shown correctly, the first ("true or false") alters the meaning of the statement, or at least removes an important qualification. The second removes a qualification so important to Hook that he repeats it a few sentences later:

> That the meaning of freedom was understood in this restricted sense at the time, I repeat, need not bind us and has not bound us.

Hook repeats it because he does not wish his statement about Black and Douglas to be taken as meaning that they are wrong *philosophically* as well as historically about prior restraint. He is saying *only* that Black and Douglas misconstrued what the authors of the Constitution believed on these matters. The omissions make the passage imply that they are wrong in general—which Hook is not saying.

As a rule, direct quotation should be reserved for statements whose special wording or nuance is essential to the discussion and cannot be easily paraphrased. A paper consisting of a string of quotations, with brief connecting statements, will lose its force; the essential quotations will not stand out. A few well-chosen quotations will make a greater impact. Significant quotations for which no appropriate place can be found in the text can be included in notes, but this resource should be used sparingly.

Exercise

Write out the following passage, omitting the italicized words. Punctuate the omission or ellipsis as shown in the text:

> Power-worship blurs political judgment because it leads, *almost unavoidably,* to the belief that present trends will continue. Whoever is winning at the moment will always seem to be invincible. *If the Japanese have conquered South Asia, then they will keep South Asia for ever; if the Germans have captured Tobruk, they will infallibly capture Cairo; if the Russians are in Berlin, it will not be long before they are in London: and so on.* This

habit of mind leads also to the belief that things will happen more quickly, completely, and catastrophically than they ever do in practice. The rise and fall of empires, the disappearance of cultures and religions, are expected to happen with earthquake suddenness, *and processes which have barely started are talked about as though they were already at an end.*

George Orwell, "Second Thoughts on James Burnham"

Discuss whether the omissions alter the meaning of the passage in any significant way.

Footnotes

The *MLA Handbook for Writers of Research Papers, Theses, and Dissertations* (New York, 1977), the standard guide to documentation in the humanities, prescribes simpler and shorter footnote style than was customary in earlier years. Of the Latin abbreviations once favored in scholarly papers, only *ibidem* or *ibid.* is still widely used. The term means that the reference given is to the work cited in the immediately preceding footnote. Even *ibid.* can be dropped and a short author or title citation given in its place. We illustrate from footnotes given earlier:

[1]William O. Douglas, *An Almanac of Liberty* (Garden City, N.Y.: Doubleday, 1954), p. 149.

[2]Ibid., p. 151; or Douglas, p. 151; or *Almanac,* p. 151.

When a second work by the same author is cited, the title—not the author's name—should be used to avoid confusion:

[3]William O. Douglas, *The Anatomy of Liberty: The Rights of Man Without Force* (New York: Trident Press, 1963), p. 15.

[4]*Almanac,* p. 153 (not Douglas, p. 153).

Where two authors with the same last name are cited, the information provided must be complete enough to distinguish them clearly:

[5]Paul Douglas, *Anatomy of Liberty* (Chicago: Wilson Press, 1957), p. 40.

[6]William O. Douglas, *The Anatomy of Liberty,* p. 20.

[7]Paul Douglas, *Anatomy of Liberty,* p. 45.

The title page of the book has authority for the details of author, editor, and title in the note. If the author of the main content of the book appears on the title page, then author's name precedes the title and the editor's name follows:

[8]James Madison, *The Complete Madison,* ed. Saul K. Padover (New York: Harper, 1953), p. 295.

If the author's name does not appear, the editor's name comes first:

> [9]Vern Countryman, ed., *The Douglas Opinions* (New York: Random House, 1977), p. 219.

Subtitles are always included, and are separated from the main title by colons, also according to what appears on the title page:

> [10]Irving Dilliard, ed., *One Man's Stand for Freedom: Mr. Justice Black and the Bill of Rights: A Collection of His Supreme Court Opinions* (New York: Knopf, 1963), p. 361.

Two or more authors are cited as they appear on the title page. When the number of authors is more than three, only the first author is listed as follows:

> [11]Elizabeth Smith et al., *The Bill of Rights* (Chicago: Wilson Press, 1972), p. 301.

A corporate author like the U.S. Government is listed in the same way as a personal author:

> [12]U.S. Bureau of the Census, *Statistical Abstract of the United States,* (Washington, D.C.: Government Printing Office, 1979), I, 235.

A book published as one volume of several with the same title is listed as follows:

> [13]Sculley Bradley, Richmond Croom Beatty, and E. Hudson Long, *The American Tradition in Literature,* rev. ed. (New York: Norton, 1962), II, p. 405.

A book published as one volume of a series with a different title is listed:

> [14]Will and Ariel Durant, *Rousseau and Revolution,* Vol. X of *The Story of Civilization* (New York: Simon and Schuster, 1967), p. 650.

An essay or story published in a collection is listed:

> [15]William Cohen, "Protection of the Individual Against Himself," in *The William O. Douglas Inquiry into the State of Individual Freedom,* ed. Harry S. Ashmore (Boulder, Colo.: Westview Press, 1979), pp. 27–35.

Articles and newspaper stories are listed as follows:

> [16]Frank A. Morrow, "Speech, Expression, and the Constitution," *Ethics,* 85, No. 3 (1975), 235–42.

> [17]James Reston, "The Art of Resigning," *New York Times,* 21 June 1981, Sec. E, p. 25.

[18]"Riding the Congressional Horse," Editorial, *New York Times*, 21 June 1981, Sec. E, p. 24.

Occasionally an article is published without attribution to a personal author:

[19]"First Amendment—Obscenity and Indecency," *Journal of Criminal Law*, 69, No. 4 (1978), 474–83.

A note at the beginning of this issue of the journal states that the casenotes in it were completed by members of the editorial staff, whose names are listed.

If a reprint is being used instead of the original edition, the original date of publication is given but not the original publisher:

[20]William O. Douglas, *The Right of the People* (1958; rpt. New York: Arena Books, 1972), p. 58.

The original publisher, Doubleday, is not included.

If an introduction or foreword by someone other than the author or editor is being cited, give that information as follows:

[21]Richard H. Rovere, Introd., *The Orwell Reader: Fiction, Essays, and Reportage*, by George Orwell (New York: Harcourt Brace Jovanovich, 1956), p. 101.

Material taken from the *Congressional Record* is given as follows:

Cong. Rec., 18 March 1959, pp. 805–16.

Reference to the U.S. Constitution is as follows:

U.S. Const., art. IV, sec. 2.

Reference to a Supreme Court decision is as follows:

Smith v. California, 361 U.S. 147 (1959), 157–59.

The following abbreviations appear in place of the usual information if it is absent in the book:

n.p. place of publication not given

n.p. publisher not given

n.d. date of publication not given

Thus:

No place of publication: (n.p.: Freedom Press, 1959), p. 10.

No publisher: (Chicago: n.p., 1959), p. 10.

No date: (Chicago: Freedom Press, n.d.), p. 10.

These are the most common references found in notes. For additional kinds and the form to be used, the *MLA Handbook* may be consulted. Where the paper contains references to a few sources only, page references can be included in the body of the paper, following the first full citation of the source in a note as given above. Thus, a paper containing references to two books of William O. Douglas might give the full citation in a note to the first reference, and subsequent references would be given in the text as follows:

> Douglas gives an account of the suppression of a publication called *The Saturday Press* by the state of Minnesota, and then draws this conclusion:
>
>> The same power that could suppress a "defamatory" paper today could suppress an "unorthodox" or unpopular one tomorrow. It was censorship that in an early day was used to stifle the efforts of patriots to inform the people of the duties of kings and the rights of subjects. (*Almanac*, p. 149).

If the quotation were not indented but printed as a continuation of the sentence, it would look like this:

> Douglas gives an account of the suppression of the suppression of *The Saturday Press*, and comments: "The same power that could suppress a 'defamatory' paper today could suppress an 'unorthodox' one tomorrow." (*Almanac*, p. 149).

Prose quotations of four lines or less are ordinarily incorporated in the text as shown, but on occasion they may be indented for emphasis.

A different method of documentation is now widely used in the sciences and social sciences: sources are arranged alphabetically in a bibliography at the end of the article or book, and are cited in the text by author and date only. Thus the following sources might be listed in a journal in the social sciences as follows:

> Douglas, William O. *An Almanac of Liberty*. Garden City, N.Y., Doubleday (1954).
>
> _____. *Anatomy of Liberty: The Rights of Man Without Force*, New York, Trident Press (1963).

A citation then appears in the text as follows:

> Douglas states: "The same power that could suppress a 'defamatory' paper today could suppress an 'unorthodox' or unpopular one tomorrow." (Douglas, 1954).

Bibliography

The documented paper should include at the end a list of materials that had been consulted. The form of the bibliography is the following for books and articles:

Bradley, Sculley, Richmond Croom Beatty, and E. Hudson Long. *The American Tradition in Literature.* Rev. ed. New York: Norton, 1962. Vol. II.

Countryman, Vern, ed. *The Douglas Opinions.* New York: Random House, 1977.

Douglas, William O. *An Almanac of Liberty.* Garden City, N.Y.: Doubleday, 1954.

——————————. *The Anatomy of Liberty: The Rights of Man Without Force.* New York: Trident Press, 1963.

Madison, James. *The Complete Madison.* Ed. Saul K. Padover. New York: Harper, 1953.

Morrow, Frank A. "Speech, Expression, and the Constitution." *Ethics,* 85, No. 3 (1975), 235–42.

Exercise

Compile a bibliography of books and articles that have primary source materials on court cases dealing with obscenity or freedom of speech and press that were heard by the Supreme Court since 1956. You will need to consult reference books, indexes, and your library subject catalog for names and materials. The obscenity opinions of Justices Black and Douglas that follow belong in your bibliography, along with other opinions of theirs. Books by lawyers who participated in these cases (for example, Charles E. Rembar, *The End of Obscenity*) may be considered primary. Be careful to record complete information for your bibliography.

Writing Assignment

Write a short documented paper drawing on the following source materials, and supplementing them with material drawn from your bibliography. Here are a few possible topics:

a. differences in reasoning about obscenity, in the opinions of Black or Douglas and one of their colleagues

b. similarities and differences between Black and Douglas in their reasoning about obscenity, with additional comparison with that of one of their colleagues

Provide enough background about the cases and opinions to help the uninformed reader understand the issues and reasoning. Footnote according to the models given earlier.

Some source material for a paper

Hugo L. Black in Smith v. California

The owner of a Los Angeles bookstore, Eleazar Smith, was convicted under a city law that forbade the possession of any obscene or indecent book anywhere that books were for sale. Smith appealed his conviction to the United States Supreme Court on the ground that the law had been interpreted to mean that a defendant could be held liable without knowledge that the book in possession was obscene. All nine justices ruled that Smith's conviction was invalid, holding that the law imposed too heavy a restriction on free speech. Justice Hugo L. Black, in his concurring statement, disagreed with a part of the decision that had been written for the Court by Justice William L. Brennan.

The appellant was sentenced to prison for possessing in his bookstore an "obscene" book in violation of a Los Angeles city ordinance. I concur in the judgment holding that ordinance unconstitutional, but not for the reasons given in the Court's opinion.

The Court invalidates the ordinance solely because it penalizes a bookseller for mere possession of an "obscene" book, even though he is unaware of its obscenity. The grounds on which the Court draws a constitutional distinction between a law that punishes possession of a book with knowledge of its "obscenity" and a law that punishes without such knowledge are not persuasive to me. Those grounds are that conviction of a bookseller for possession of an "obscene" book when he is unaware of its obscenity "will tend to restrict the books he sells to those he has inspected," and therefore "may tend to work a substantial restriction on freedom of speech." The fact is, of course, that prison sentences for possession of "obscene" books will seriously burden freedom of the press whether punishment is imposed with or without knowledge of the obscenity. The Court's opinion correctly points out how little extra burden will be imposed on prosecutors by requiring proof that a bookseller was aware of a book's contents when he possessed it. And if the Constitution's requirement of knowledge is so easily met, the result of this case is that one particular bookseller gains his freedom, but the way is left open for state censorship and punishment of all other booksellers by merely adding a few new words to old censorship laws. Our constitutional safeguards for speech and press therefore gain little. Their victory, if any, is a Pyrrhic one.

That it is apparently intended to leave the way open for both Federal and

State Governments to abridge speech and press (to the extent this Court approves) is also indicated by the following statements in the Court's opinion: " 'The door barring federal and state intrusion into this area [freedom of speech and press] cannot be left ajar; it must be kept tightly closed and opened only the slightest crack necessary to prevent encroachment upon more important interests.' . . . This ordinance opens that door too far."

This statement raises a number of questions for me. What are the "more important" interests for the protection of which constitutional freedom of speech and press must be given second place? What is the standard by which one can determine when abridgment of speech and press goes "too far" and when it is slight enough to be constitutionally allowable? Is this momentous decision to be left to a majority of this Court on a case-by-case basis? What express provision or provisions of the Constitution put freedom of speech and press in this precarious position of subordination and insecurity?

Certainly the First Amendment's language leaves no room for inference that abridgments of speech and press can be made just because they are slight. That Amendment provides, in simple words, that "Congress shall make no law . . . abridging the freedom of speech, or of the press." I read "no law abridging" to mean *no law abridging.* The First Amendment, which is the supreme law of the land, has thus fixed its own value on freedom of speech and press by putting these freedoms wholly "beyond the reach" of *federal* power to abridge. No other provision of the Constitution purports to dilute the scope of these unequivocal commands of the First Amendment. Consequently, I do not believe that any federal agencies, including Congress and this Court, have power or authority to subordinate speech and press to what they think are "more important interests." The contrary notion is, in my judgment, court-made not Constitution-made.

State intrusion or abridgment of freedom of speech and press raises a different question, since the First Amendment by its terms refers only to laws passed by Congress. But I adhere to our prior decisions holding that the Fourteenth Amendment made the First applicable to the States. It follows that I am for reversing this case because I believe that the Los Angeles ordinance sets up a censorship in violation of the First and Fourteenth Amendments.

If, as it seems, we are on the way to national censorship, I think it timely to suggest again that there are grave doubts in my mind as to the desirability or constitutionality of this Court's becoming a Supreme Board of Censors—reading books and viewing television performances to determine whether, if permitted, they might adversely affect the morals of the people throughout the many diversified local communities in this vast country. It is true that the ordinance here is on its face only applicable to "obscene or indecent writing." It is also true that this particular kind of censorship is considered by many to be "the obnoxious thing in its mildest and least repulsive form . . ." But "illegitimate and unconstitutional practices get their first footing in that way. . . . It is the duty of courts to be watchful for the constitutional rights of the citizen, and against any stealthy encroachments thereon." While it is "obscenity and indecency" before us today, the experience of mankind—both ancient and modern—shows that this type of elastic phrase can, and most likely will, by synonymous with the political, and maybe with the religious unorthodoxy of tomorrow.

Censorship is the deadly enemy of freedom and progress. The plain language of the Constitution forbids it. I protest against the judiciary giving it a foothold here.

William O. Douglas in Roth v. United States

In its decision, the Supreme Court affirmed the conviction of David S. Alberts for having obscene materials available for sale and the conviction of Samuel Roth for mailing such materials. Alberts had violated a California law and Roth a federal one. The Court stated that obscenity was "not within the area of constitutionally protected speech or press." It defined obscenity as dealing "with sex in a manner appealing to prurient interest" and being "utterly without redeeming social importance." Justice Douglas dissented from the majority opinion written for the Court by Justice William J. Brennan.

When we sustain these convictions, we make the legality of a publication turn on the purity of thought which a book or tract instills in the mind of the reader. I do not think we can approve that standard and be faithful to the command of the First Amendment, which by its terms is a restraint on Congress and which by the Fourteenth is a restraint on the States.

In the *Roth* case the trial judge charged the jury that the statutory words "obscene, lewd and lascivious" describe "that form of immorality which has relation to sexual impurity and has a tendency to excite lustful thoughts." He stated that the term "filthy" in the statute pertains "to that sort of treatment of sexual matters in such a vulgar and indecent way, so that it tends to arouse a feeling of disgust and revulsion." He went on to say that the material "must be calculated to corrupt and debauch the minds and morals" of "the average person in the community," not those of any particular class. "You judge the circulars, pictures and publications which have been put in evidence by present-day standards of the community. You may ask yourselves does it offend the common conscience of the community by present-day standards."

The trial judge who, sitting without a jury, heard the *Alberts* case and the appellate court that sustained the judgment of conviction, took California's definition of "obscenity" from *People* v. *Wepplo*. That case held that a book is obscene "if it has a substantial tendency to deprave or corrupt its readers by inciting lascivious thoughts or arousing lustful desire."

By these standards punishment is inflicted for thoughts provoked, not for overt acts nor antisocial conduct. This test cannot be squared with our decisions under the First Amendment. Even the ill-starred *Dennis* case conceded that speech to be punishable must have some relation to action which could be penalized by government. This issue cannot be avoided by saying that obscenity is not protected by the First Amendment. The question remains, what is the constitutional test of obscenity?

The tests by which these convictions were obtained require only the arousing of sexual thoughts. Yet the arousing of sexual thoughts and desires happens every day in normal life in dozens of ways. Nearly 30 years ago a questionnaire sent to college and normal school women graduates asked what things were most stimulating sexually. Of 409 replies, 9 said "music"; 18 said "pictures"; 29 said "dancing"; 40 said "drama"; 95 said "books"; and 218 said "man." Alpert, Judicial Censorship of Obscene Literature, 52 Harv. Law Rev. 40, 73.

The test of obscenity the Court endorses today gives the censor free range over a vast domain. To allow the State to step in and punish mere speech or publication that the judge or the jury thinks has an *undesirable* impact on the thoughts but that is not shown to be a part of unlawful action is drastically to curtail the First Amendment. As recently stated by two of our outstanding authorities on obscenity, "The danger of influencing a change in the current moral standards of the community, or of shocking or offending readers, or of stimulating sex thoughts or desires apart from objective conduct, can never justify the losses to society that result from interference with literary freedom." Lockhart & McClure, Literature, The Law of Obscenity, and the Constitution, 38 Minn. Law Rev. 295.

If we were certain that impurity of sexual thoughts impelled to action, we would be on less dangerous ground in punishing the distributors of this sex literature. But it is by no means clear that obscene literature, as so defined, is a significant factor in influencing substantial deviations from the community standards.

"There are a number of reasons for real and substantial doubts as to the soundness of that hypothesis. (1) Scientific studies of juvenile delinquency demonstrate that those who get into trouble, and are the greatest concern of the advocates of censorship, are far less inclined to read than those who do not become delinquent. The delinquents are generally the adventurous type, who have little use for reading and other non-active entertainment. Thus, even assuming that reading sometimes has an adverse effect upon moral conduct, the effect is not likely to be substantial, for those who are susceptible seldom read. (2) Sheldon and Eleanor Glueck, who are among the country's leading authorities on the treatment and causes of juvenile delinquency, have recently published the results of a ten year study of its causes. They exhaustively studied approximately 90 factors and influences that might lead to or explain juvenile delinquency, but the Gluecks gave no consideration to the type of reading material, if any, read by the delinquents. This is, of course, consistent with their finding that delinquents read very little. When those who know so much about the problem of delinquency among youth—the very group about whom the advocates of censorship are most concerned—conclude that what delinquents read has so little effect upon their conduct that it is not worth investigating in an exhaustive study of causes, there is good reason for serious doubt concerning the basic hypothesis on which obscenity censorship is defended. (3) The many other influences in society that stimulate sexual desire are so much more frequent in their influence, and so much more potent in their effect, that the influence of reading is likely, at most, to be relatively insignificant in the composite of forces that lead an individual into conduct deviating from the community sex standards. The Kinsey studies show the minor degree to which literature serves as a potent sexual stimulant. And the studies demonstrating that sex knowledge seldom results from reading indicates [sic] *the relative unimportance of literature in sex thoughts as compared with other factors in society."* Lockhart & McClure, *op. cit.*

The absence of dependable information on the effect of obscene literature on human conduct should make us wary. It should put us on the side of protecting society's interest in literature, except and unless it can be said that the particular publication has an impact on action that the government can control.

As noted, the trial judge in the *Roth* case charged the jury in the alternative that the federal obscenity statute outlaws literature dealing with sex which offends "the common conscience of the community." That standard is, in my view, more inimical still to freedom of expression.

The standard of what offends "the common conscience of the community" conflicts, in my judgment, with the command of the First Amendment that "Congress shall make no law . . . abridging the freedom of speech, or of the press." Certainly that standard would not be an acceptable one if religion, economics, politics or philosophy were involved. How does it become a constitutional standard when literature treating with sex is concerned?

Any test that turns on what is offensive to the community's standards is too loose, too capricious, too destructive of freedom of expression to be squared with the First Amendment. Under that test, juries can censor, suppress, and punish what they don't like, provided the matter relates to "sexual impurity" or has a tendency "to excite lustful thoughts." This is community censorship in one of its worst forms. It creates a regime where in the battle between the literati and the Philistines, the Philistines are certain to win. If experience in this field teaches anything, it is that "censorship of obscenity has almost always been both irrational and indiscriminate." Lockhart & McClure, *op. cit.* The test adopted here accentuates that trend.

I can understand (and at times even sympathize) with programs of civic groups and church groups to protect and defend the existing moral standards of the community. I can understand the motives of the Anthony Comstocks who would impose Victorian standards on the community. When speech alone is involved, I do not think that government, consistently with the First Amendment, can become the sponsor of any of these movements. I do not think that government, consistently with the First Amendment, can throw its weight behind one school or another. Government should be concerned with antisocial conduct, not with utterances. Thus, if the First Amendment guarantee of freedom of speech and press is to mean anything in this field, it must allow protests even against the moral code that the standard of the day sets for the community. In other words, literature should not be suppressed merely because it offends the moral code of the censor.

The legality of a publication in this country should never be allowed to turn either on the purity of thought which it instills in the mind of the reader or on the degree to which it offends the community conscience. By either test the role of the censor is exalted, and society's values in literary freedom are sacrificed.

The Court today suggests a third standard. It defines obscene material as that "which deals with sex in a manner appealing to prurient interest." Like the standards applied by the trial judges below, that standard does not require any nexus between the literature which is prohibited and action which the legislature can regulate or prohibit. Under the First Amendment, that standard is no more valid than those which the courts below adopted.

I do not think that the problem can be resolved by the Court's statement that "obscenity is not expression protected by the First Amendment." With the exception of *Beauharnais* v. *Illinois,* none of our cases has resolved problems of free speech and free press by placing any form of expression beyond the pale of the absolute prohibition of the First Amendment. Unlike the law of libel, wrongfully relied on in *Beauharnais,* there is no special historical evidence that literature dealing with sex was intended to be treated in a special manner by those who drafted the First Amendment. In fact, the first reported court decision in this country involving obscene literature was in 1821. Lockhart & McClure, *op. cit.* I reject too the implication that problems of freedom of speech and of the press are to be resolved by weighing against the values of free expression, the judgment of the Court that a particular form of that expression has "no redeeming social importance." The First Amendment, its prohibition in terms absolute, was designed to preclude courts as well as legislatures from weighing the values of speech against silence. The First Amendment puts free speech in the preferred position.

I would give the broad sweep of the First Amendment full support. I have the same confidence in the ability of our people to reject noxious literature as I have in their capacity to sort out the true from the false in theology, economics, politics, or any other field.

William O. Douglas in Byrne v. Karalexis

Serafim Karalexis, the owner of a movie theater in Massachusetts, was convicted of possessing an obscene film and intending to show it. When a federal court temporarily stopped the District Attorney, Garrett Byrne, from interfering with the showing of the film, he appealed to the Supreme Court to allow him to keep the film from being shown until the Court had ruled on his appeal. This case was not heard by the full Court, only three justices rendering opinions. Douglas dissented from the opinions of the other two.

. . . Some people think that "obscenity" is not protected by the Free Speech and Free Press Clauses of the First Amendment. They believe that both Congress and the States can set up regimes of censorship to weed out "obscenity" from literature, movies, and other publications so as to rid the press of what they, the judges, deem to be beyond the pale.

I have consistently dissented from that course but not because, as frequently charged, I relish "obscenity." I have dissented before and now because I think the First Amendment bars all kinds of censorship. To impose a regime of censors requires, in my view, a constitutional amendment. "Obscenity" is no exception. "Obscenity" certainly was not an established exception to free speech and free press when the Bill of Rights was adopted. It is a relatively new arrival on the American scene, propelled by dedicated zealots to cleanse all thought.

Prior to the Bill of Rights, state law, when it spoke of freedom of the press, meant only freedom from prior restraint. But an author or publisher could be held accountable for publishing what the statehouse thought was against "the public good." In other words, the First Amendment did not build on existing law; it broke with tradition, set a new standard, and exalted freedom of expression. There is no trace of a suggestion that "obscenity," however defined, was excepted.

That does not mean that "obscenity," is good or that it should be encouraged. It only means that we cannot be faithful to our constitutional mandate and allow any form or shadow of censorship over speech and press.

When our rewards go to people for thinking alike, it is no surprise that we become frightened at those who take exception to the current consensus. Then the hue and cry goes up for censors; and that is the start of an ominous trend. What can be done to literature under the banner of "obscenity" can be done to other parts of the spectrum of ideas when party or majoritarian demands mount and propagandists start declaiming the law.

The "obscenity" issue raises large questions. To what extent may government watch over one's shoulder as he reads?

Judge Jerome Frank said in *Roth* v. *Goldman:*

"I think that no sane man thinks socially dangerous the arousing of normal sexual desires. Consequently, if reading obscene books has merely that consequence, Congress, it would seem, can constitutionally no more suppress such books than it can prevent the mailing of many other objects, such as perfumes, for example, which notoriously produce that result. But the constitutional power to suppress obscene publications might well exist if there were ample reason to believe that reading them conduces to socially harmful sexual conduct on the part of normal human beings. . . . Macaulay, replying to demands for suppression of obscene books, said: 'We find it difficult to believe that in a world so full of temptations as this, any gentleman, whose life would have been virtuous if he had not read Aristophanes and Juvenal, will be made vicious by reading them.' "

If "obscenity" can be carved out of the First Amendment, what other like exceptions can be created? Is "sacrilege" also beyond the pale? Are utterances or publications made with "malice" unprotected? How about "seditious" speech or articles? False, scandalous, and malicious writings or utterances against the Congress or the President "with intent to defame" or to bring them "into contempt or disrepute" or to "excite" against them "the hatred of the good people" or "to stir up sedition," or to "excite" people to "resist, oppose, or defeat" any law were once made a crime. Now that the First Amendment applies to the States, *Stromberg* v. *California,* may the States embark on such totalitarian controls over thought or over the press? May Congress do so?

We forget today that under our constitutional system neither Congress nor the States have any power to pass on the value, the propriety, the Americanism, the soundness of any idea or expression. It is that insulation from party or majoritarian control provided by the First Amendment—not our gross national product or mass production or pesticides or space ships or nuclear arsenal—that distinguishes our society from the other planetary regimes.

Exercises

1. Read and analyze the language of both the First and Fourteenth Amendments. After your analysis, determine whether you agree with Justices Black and Douglas that the free expression clause of the First Amendment is "absolute" and that the Fourteenth Amendment extends this restriction to the states. Explain your view and how your interpretation of these amendments influences your evaluation of the opinions of Black and Douglas.

2. The Constitution and its amendments are a primary source for discussions of such controversial issues as freedom of speech and press, civil liberties, the right to choose an abortion. Choose one of these or some other constitutional issue and, using your library, determine what other primary and secondary sources you would need to write a paper on the issue you choose.

3. In the opinions we have just read, the problem of obscenity is treated within the framework of constitutionally protected speech. Using your library resources, such as guides to published articles or books, determine what other categories one might place obscenity within.

Writing Assignments

1. Using the preliminary research you did in response to Exercise number two above, write an argumentative essay on the issue you chose. Use the sources you decided upon for the exercises as a basis for your essay. Do not hesitate to use additional sources if you find them necessary.

2. Using the opinions of Black and Douglas as your primary sources, research the question of obscenity as both a constitutional and a moral issue, using secondary sources where necessary. Then write an essay—either expository or argumentative—discussing the opinions of Black and Douglas.

The uses of documentation in argument

The documented essay that follows brings this book to an end. In the uses it makes of documentation, we see once again how interdependent exposition and argument are. That interdependence has been a major concern of this book. We have seen that argument must use exposition for background information as well as in support of premises and conclusions. The inductive massing of evidence is another form of exposition that plays an important role in many arguments.

Following the essay, we have commented on features of the argument and the uses made of documentation in it. The essay is an excerpt from a book dealing with obscenity and the constitutional and other issues it raises. The chapter in which this excerpt appears opens with this statement of purpose:

> The libertarian position consists, essentially, of two propositions: (1) that the censorship of obscenity contravenes the First Amendment and the principles which lie behind it, (2) that obscenity is not harmful, or, at least, that the circulation of obscenity does not injure individuals or society to any significant degree. This chapter will be devoted primarily to examination of libertarian views of the First Amendment and the principles of a free society.

The author of the essay, Harry M. Clor, focuses here on the support two prominent spokesmen for the libertarian position, Justices Black and Douglas, find for their views in the writings of James Madison and Thomas Jefferson, the Founding Fathers most often cited in support of libertarian views.

Clor's critical essay shows how discussion of an important current issue can be grounded in a closely reasoned examination of prominent ideas, present and past. You are familiar with the current ideas on obscenity through the opinions of Black and Douglas in *Smith* v. *California* and *Roth* v. *United States,* reprinted earlier in this chapter. Much can also be learned from how Clor introduces the ideas of Madison and Jefferson, places them in their context, and examines assumptions and presuppositions. The footnotes to the essay illustrate one kind of documentation in essays of this type.

THE FIRST AMENDMENT AND THE FREE SOCIETY

by Harry M. Clor

1   Justices Black and Douglas find in the First Amendment an underlying principle—a principle which distinguishes absolutely between speech and action. According to Justice Douglas, what the First Amendment dictates is that "government should be concerned with anti-social conduct, not with utterances."[1] "Utterances" shall be absolutely free; conduct alone is sub-

[1] *Roth* v. *United States,* 354 U.S. 476 (1957) at 512–13. See p. 258.

ject to government regulation. This, again, is not quite the same thing as an assertion that anyone may say anything, anywhere, in any manner. But it is at least an assertion that government may never concern itself directly with speech. Government may not outlaw a certain kind or form of expression, because it must never concern itself with the *content* of expression—with what is said or written. No form of expression shall be subject to regulation on the grounds of its intrinsic evil or its tendency to promote harmful consequences. Expression is subject to regulation only when it is so closely related to illegal action as to be inseparable from it. Since it cannot be demonstrated that obscenity is thus related to conduct, the First Amendment prohibits any effort to control it.

2   While Justices Black and Douglas' interpretation of the First Amendment claims ample support in the constitutional text, it also claims to be supported by the views and intentions of the men who gave us the First Amendment. Indeed, it is often asserted that the views of these Justices *are* the views of those founding fathers who were most closely associated with the First Amendment. In the literature and judicial decisions opposing the control of obscenity, quotations from James Madison and Thomas Jefferson are frequently advanced as conclusive evidence that the First Amendment was designed to be absolute and to legislate that sharp distinction between expression and conduct insisted upon by today's absolutionists.[2] How are the doctrines of Madison and Jefferson related to those of Justices Black and Douglas and to the problem of obscenity control?

3   Madison's strongest and most explicit statements about the meaning of the First Amendment were made during the controversy over the Alien and Sedition Acts. In his *Report on the Virginia Resolution* of 1798, Madison said:

> Some degree of abuse is inseparable from the proper use of everything, and in no instance is this more true than in that of the press. It has accordingly been decided by the practice of the States, that it is better to leave a few of its noxious branches to their luxuriant growth than, by pruning them away, to injure the vigor of those yielding the proper fruits. And can the wisdom of this policy be doubted by any who reflect that to the press alone, checkered as it is with abuses, the world is indebted for all the triumphs which have been gained by reason and humanity over error and oppression; . . . the article of Amendment, instead of supposing in Congress a power that might be exercised over the press, provided its freedom was not abridged, was meant as a positive denial to Congress of any power whatever on the subject.
>
> . . . Is, then, the Federal Government, it will be asked, destitute of every authority for restraining the licentiousness of the press, and for shielding itself against the libellous attacks which may be made on those who administer it?

---

[2] See particularly Judge Curtis Bok's opinion in *Commonwealth* v. *Gordon,* 66 Pa. D. & C. 101 (Philadelphia County, 1949), and the concurring opinion of Judge Jerome Frank in *United States* v. *Roth,* 237 F. 2d 796 (2d Cir., 1956). While these judges offer a rigorous "clear and present danger" standard, it is evident that they regard even this concession to censorship as a deviation from the original intention of such men as Madison and Jefferson.

The Constitution alone can answer this question. If no such power can be expressly delegated, and if it be not both necessary and proper to carry into execution an express power—above all, if it be expressly forbidden by a declaratory amendment to the Constitution—the answer must be that the Federal Government is destitute of all such authority.[3]

4   These views are, substantially, those expressed by Jefferson in his *Kentucky Resolutions* and in various writings. Although Jefferson did not speak of the scope of the First Amendment free press provisions in words quite as strong or as precise as these of Madison, it would be difficult to make a case for any significant difference between them on this subject.

5   The passage quoted denies, in terms unequivocal, that Congress has any power to control the press or any authority to restrain its "licentiousness." Madison's language strongly implies that the First Amendment does not permit a distinction between restraints which do and restraints which do not abridge the genuine freedom of the press—a distinction between liberty and license. In 1799 Madison explicitly rejected such a distinction.[4] It would appear that for Madison the "proper fruits" of an unrestrained press much necessarily outweigh the evils which result from its "noxious branches."

6   But this statement of Madison's views does not conclusively settle all relevant questions. The specific context in which Madison speaks is political. The restraints with which he is specifically concerned are restraints upon political criticism—the criticism of the government, of public officials, or of public agencies. The "licentiousness" to which he refers is primarily, if it is not entirely, the licentiousness of vituperative and defamatory political speech. What would Madison have thought of restraints having nothing to do with politics, upon forms of speech having nothing to do with government?

7   Madison's language is unequivocal—Congress may not exercise any power over the press, But this would answer our question unequivocally only if we could know with certainty what Madison means by "the press"— what classes of written or printed materials he means to designate by the term. Does "the press" mean only newspapers and journals, or does it mean anything produced by a printing press? A logical reading of this and other Madisonian texts would indicate that he is not speaking only of newspapers. It seems unlikely that Madison would think that it is to the newspaper that "the world is indebted for all the triumphs gained by reason and humanity over error and oppression." Madison appears to have a rather broad conception of that press whose products must be unrestrained. But we cannot know with certainty whether his conception would be so broad as to include all which today can be produced by the art of printing.

8   Madison and Jefferson would deny to the federal government any power to restrain the licentiousness of the press, but they would not deny that power to the states. In 1799 Madison said that "every libellous writing or

[3]James Madison, *The Writings of James Madison*, ed. Gaillard Hunt (New York: G. P. Putnam's Sons, 1906) VI, 389–92.

[4]James Madison, *The Complete Madison*, ed. Saul K. Padover (New York: Harper & Brothers, 1953), p. 295.

expression can receive its punishment in the State Courts . . . whether it injured public officers or private citizens."[5] In his *Kentucky Resolutions* Jefferson asserted that the people of the states "retain to themselves the right of judging how far the licentiousness of speech and of the press may be abridged without lessening their useful freedom."[6] And in his famous letter to Abigail Adams, Jefferson wrote:

> Nor does the opinion of the unconstitutionality, and consequent nullity of that law [the Sedition Act], remove all restraint from the overwhelming torrent of slander which is confounding all vice and virtue, all truth and falsehood, in the United States. The power to do that is fully possessed by the several State Legislatures. . . . While we deny that Congess have a right to control the freedom of the press, we have ever asserted the right of the States and their exclusive right to do so.[7]

9   From these statements, and others from the same sources, it is evident that Madison's and Jefferson's opposition to the Sedition Act was not motivated solely by solicitude for freedom of speech and press. For Madison and Jefferson, the great evil of this act consisted in its infringement upon the inherent rights and powers of the states and in its tendency to promote a consolidated government. Their response to the Alien and Sedition Acts gave rise to their strongest statements about the scope of First Amendment rights. But in that response a concern for the prerogatives of the states blended with, if it did not take precedence over, a concern for free speech and press.

10   It is, then, of considerable significance that Madison and Jefferson held the capacity to impose some restraints upon speech and press to be among the inherent powers of the state governments and to belong to the reserved rights of the people of the states. Even though it be dangerous to endeavor to prune away the "noxious branches," Madison allows and Jefferson insists upon a power in the states to do so. They have not left us any comprehensive statement of the scope and limits of this power. It is clear that they would not look favorably upon frequent or severe state restraint of speech and press. But it is also clear that, in their view, the reserved rights of the states included at least the right to punish certain utterances of "seditious libel."[8]

11   It may be argued that these facts are not relevant to a discussion of the position taken today by Justices Black and Douglas, that these facts do not detract from the absolutism of the Madison-Jefferson view of the First Amendment, and that that amendment is now binding upon the states. That First Amendment which is binding on the states is, and ought to be, the real one—the one intended by the men who inspired and framed it. This argument, however, overlooks some important considerations. Even if it could

---

[5] Madison, *Writings of Madison*, VI, 334.

[6] Thomas Jefferson, *The Complete Jefferson*, ed. Saul K. Padover (New York: Duel, Sloan & Pierce, 1943), p. 129.

[7] Thomas Jefferson, *The Writings of Thomas Jefferson*, ed. Paul Leicester Ford (New York: G. P. Putnam's Sons, 1905), X, 89–90.

[8] See Leonard Levy, *Legacy of Suppression* (Cambridge, Mass.: Harvard University Press, 1960).

be shown that the Madison-Jefferson conception of the First Amendment is absolute in the same sense and to the same extent as is the Black-Douglas conception of it, it was not Madison and Jefferson who made the First Amendment binding upon the states. Madison and Jefferson did not assert an unqualified immunity for all speech and press anywhere in the United States. They asserted, at most, such an immunity as against the federal government. Those seeking the abolition of all state laws controlling obscenity cannot claim to be resting simply on the doctrines of Madison and Jefferson.

12   But there is a further consideration bearing more significantly on the relation between the old and the new absolutists. Madison and Jefferson thought censorship extremely dangerous, but they did not deny that a power to restrain some forms of expression must reside somewhere in government. For Jefferson, "the confounding [of] all vice and virtue, all truth and falsehood" is an evil which can conceivably come within the cognizance of government. And a distinction between "free speech" and "licentious speech" is one which, on occasion, government may have to make. Jefferson would have these powers lodged in the states, which in his view constituted the primary governing agencies of the country—those closest to the people and primarily responsible for their welfare.

13   These conclusions, however, seem to be at variance with the spirit of Jeffersonian thought as it appears in so many of his more philosophic pronouncements. The following oft-quoted statements appear to establish that fundamental principle which Justices Black and Douglas find at the heart of the First Amendment. In his *Bill for Establishing Religious Freedom,* Jefferson said:

> To suffer the civil magistrate to intrude his powers into the field of opinion and to restrain the profession or propagation of principles, on the supposition of their ill-tendency, is a dangerous fallacy which at once destroys all religious liberty, . . . it is time enough for the rightful purposes of civil government for its offices to interfere when principles break out into overt acts against peace and good order; and, finally, that truth is great and will prevail if left to herself, that she is the proper and sufficient antagonist to error, and has nothing to fear from the conflict, unless by human interposition disarmed of her natural weapons, free argument and debate[,] errors ceasing to be dangerous when it is permitted freely to contradict them.[9]

In 1814 Jefferson wrote in a letter:

> I am really mortified to be told that, in the United States of America, a fact like this [the sale of De Becourt's book *Sur La Création du Monde, un Système d'Organization Primitive*] can become the subject of inquiry, and of criminal inquiry too, as an offence against religion; that a question about the sale of a book can be brought before the civil magistrate. Is this, then, our freedom of religion? Are we to have a censor whose imprimatur shall say what books may be sold, and what we may buy? And who

[9] Thomas Jefferson, *The Living Thoughts of Thomas Jefferson,* ed. John Dewey (New York: Longmans, Green, 1940), p. 114.

is thus to dogmatize religious opinions for our citizens? Whose foot is to be the measure to which ours are all to be stretched?[10]

14   In these statements Jefferson does not speak only of the federal government, he speaks of the "civil magistrate." It is government as such which is forbidden to intrude "into the field of opinion" or to determine what books may be sold. It is government as such which is confined to measures dealing with overt acts. These passages reflect that attitude toward the sufficiency of truth and the efficacy of reasoning which is usually associated with Jeffersonian philosophy. On the basis of these views could not "an overwhelming torrent of slander" be adequately met by "free argument and debate"? and could it legitimately be met in any other way?

15   It is significant that both of these Jeffersonian statements are made in a context of religious considerations. In the *Bill for Establishing Religious Freedom* he is specifically concerned with religious doctrinal controversy and with allegedly unorthodox opinions. In his letter of 1814, the book at issue is a philosophic or scientific treatise which is under official inquiry because of its alleged effects upon religious opinion. I do not intend to suggest that the meaning of Jefferson's words must be rigidly confined to their exact contexts. But one should not forget the subject about which Jefferson is speaking—as is often done in literature supporting the absolutist position by means of quotations from Jefferson. To do so is to run the risk of misunderstanding him and, perhaps, to expose him to charges of blatant self-contradiction. It is quite possible that in the mind of Jefferson the propagation of religious beliefs, or of philosophic ideas impinging upon religion, stands on a different moral and intellectual plane from that of "an overwhelming torrent of slander." For Jefferson, the sanctity of religious belief absolutely precludes the intrusion of the magistrate. Religious doctrines are not civil business. It is evident (in the letter of 1814) that what mortifies Jefferson is the possibility that citizens of the United States could be subjected to an official religious dogma whose imprimatur shall govern their religious opinions and determine what they can read.

16   But Jefferson does speak in the language of general principle. Do his principles establish the proposition of Justice Douglas that in all areas and in all respects "government should be concerned with anti-social conduct, not with utterances"?[11] And how much support do they provide for the corollary of this proposition—that obscene publications are beyond the reach of government?

17   It should be noted that the distinction which Jefferson makes is not quite the same as that which Justice Douglas makes. Jefferson differentiates between the propagation of opinion or principles and overt acts against public order. His subject is doctrines, principles, and beliefs, and his argument is that these are none of the magistrate's concern until such time as they result in breaches of the peace. Thus, Jefferson has not quite said that all "utterances" and "expressions" are outside the magistrate's sphere. This difference may be negligible in some contexts, but it is not negligible in the context of obscenity control. If Jefferson regards *all*, not just religious or

---

[10] Jefferson, *The Complete Jefferson*, p. 889.
[11] *Roth* v. *United States*, p. 94.

philosophic, principles and opinions as beyond the scope of government, would he regard obscenity as embodying any principles and opinions? It would require some argument to show that materials now censored as obscenity involve the propagation of principles in the Jeffersonian sense of the term. Whenever Jefferson spoke of freedom of speech, press, and conscience he spoke in terms of truth and falsehood; that is, in terms of arguments addressed to the rational or spiritual faculties of man.[12] Would he think that suppression of obscene materials deprives citizens of any arguments or prevents the propagation of any opinions? We may speculate either that he would not think so, *or* that he would regard the censorship as more harmful than the obscenity. We cannot know the answer; we have no writings of Jefferson on the subject of salacious literature or, for that matter, on the subject of literature dealing with sex. This is another of those factors relevant to the intentions of the founders about which we cannot have certitude.

Documentation is an essential part of Clor's argument. Throughout the essay he presents evidence from various primary sources including public statements, philosophical writings, and personal letters. And this evidence is compared; no single piece of evidence carries the argument alone. And since the evidence is inductive, it is shown to have a degree of probability only. Clor's criticism of Black and Douglas, indeed, is that they have claimed certainty in the face of considerable evidence that puts their claim in doubt. Clor does not say that the authors of the Constitution put limits on freedom of speech and press, or that obscenity would have been excluded from any law against interference with this freedom; he says only that we cannot depend on these authors for conclusive support of an "absolute" interpretation of the First Amdndment. That support must come from elsewhere, if it can be found at all.

Clor's analysis shows us how careful we must be in selecting evidence from the past to support our positions. Central to his analysis is context—the context in which statements about freedom of speech and press were made. In the absence of direct statements of what these various contexts were, he must reconstruct them on the basis of indirect evidence. Thus, the concern of Madison and Jefferson over "infringement upon the inherent rights and powers of the states" considerably qualifies the view to be taken of their ideas—if the evidence Clor cites in paragraph 8 in fact has the weight he attributes to it. No idea in the essay, whether the ideas of Black and Douglas in the twentieth century or of Madison and Jefferson in the eighteenth century, is presented without attention to its context. The evidence is built carefully so that one piece of primary evidence is able to shed important light on another.

Though the discussion is highly focused on what may seem narrow matters of interpretation and historical background, the discussion has

[12] It is in a statement devoted to freedom of the press that Jefferson voices the expectation "that man may be governed by reason and truth." Jefferson, *Living Thoughts of Jefferson,* p. 120.

considerable importance for current issues like obscenity and censorship. Clor conscientiously provides the arguments most frequently cited
for and against freedom of speech and press. From so careful and technical an examination of the supporting evidence, we can proceed to a
broader discussion. Debates and arguments in this way are based on
probable evidence that is carefully gathered and compared.

Exercises and Writing Assignments

1. Determine what primary and secondary sources are available in your
   library for a study of the Kennedy assassination. Then locate reference books that list materials that you would need for a complete
   investigation and that are unavailable in your library.

2. Do the same for the issues related to the assassination of Martin
   Luther King, Jr. The *New York Times Index* will direct you to issues raised at various times about both assassinations, and examined in the report on the Kennedy and King assassinations of the
   1979 House Select Committee. You will find presentation of some
   of this material in *Time, Newsweek,* and other news magazines, as
   well as in the *Times.*

3. Examine the primary materials available in your library for a study
   of one of the following people, or another person of your choosing.
   These materials may include private papers, letters, diaries, autobiographical writings. Write an account of the usefulness of at least
   five pieces of evidence bearing on a personal trait, opinion, or action:
   a. Martin Luther King, Jr.
   b. Franklin Roosevelt
   c. George Washington
   d. Thomas Jefferson
   e. Abraham Lincoln
   f. Adolf Hitler
   g. Josef Stalin
   h. Albert Einstein
   i. Eleanor Roosevelt
   j. Emily Dickinson
   k. John F. Kennedy

4. Examine the speeches of a former president of the United States or
   government official, or the speeches of Winston Churchill and a
   comparable world leader, and look for evidence bearing on the following:

a. personality

b. political philosophy and concerns

c. attitude toward a specific event

Try to restrict your examination to speeches of a particular year, and possibly concerned with related issues. Much can be learned about Churchill from his speeches in the period following the Munich Conference in 1938 and, later, in the first months of the war with Germany. You will get from these speeches not just an impression of Churchill the man, but an understanding of how he viewed the issues of the war and the readiness of the British people for what was to come. Much can also be learned about President John Kennedy from his speeches during his first year in office.

5. Compare two documented discussions of a controversial historical issue, and state the similarities and differences in interpretation. Then compare the evidence given for each interpretation, noting what use is made of primary and secondary sources. Draw a conclusion from your findings about how each writer used these sources. Here are a few sample issues that might be studied:

   a. the meaning of the phrase "all men are created equal" in the Declaration of Independence

   b. the intent of the phrase "the right of the people to keep and bear arms" in the Bill of Rights

   c. the rights of States under the Constitution

   d. the "second assassin" theory of the Kennedy assassination

6. Using the library research techniques you have just studied and the methods of logical analysis you studied earlier, write an argumentative discussion of Clor's treatment of Madison and Jefferson in connection with Black and Douglas. Present your reasons for either agreeing or disagreeing with the author, and support your position with documented evidence.

Copyrights and Acknowledgments (continued)

Index